Praise for *Teaching the Whole Teen*
by Rachel Poliner and Jeffrey Benson

Teaching the Whole Teen is an insightful, hopeful, and very practical resource for teachers, parents and schools. The book stays rooted in the day-to-day practice of teaching the whole teen, and it articulates in very doable ways suggestions for how to better support teenagers in their development. It's accessible, inspiring, and a valuable read for all educators.

—Jennifer Abrams, Educational Consultant
Author of *Having Hard Conversations* and *The Multi-Generational Workplace*

This rich treasure trove of inventive, concrete, and well-grounded ideas offers a gift to our profession and to all who would strengthen the quality of life and learning for young people and adults under the roof of the schoolhouse.

—Roland S. Barth, Educator

An important contribution to the field of SEL [social-emotional learning] with a much-needed focus on teens in middle and high schools—this book highlights the importance of relationships to cognitive and social growth, explicitly teaching SEL skills, and the role of adults as models. Combining research and best practices from multiple disciplines, Poliner and Benson deliver accessible, hands-on tips and tools for educators and educational leaders. Through discussion of theory and helpful anecdotes from a wide range of school settings, this book provides an SEL guide that is culturally relevant for all teen and adult populations. Students and educators will benefit from the holistic approach and practical guidance presented in this book.

—Nova Biro, Co-Director, Open Circle

As a former elementary school principal first in a K–5 setting and then K–8, this book would have been an excellent and valuable resource for understanding teenagers and middle school students. I found so many practical strategies that I could have used with the students in the K–8 setting and shared with staff that had taught in a K–5 setting and also had to transition.

—Gustava Cooper-Baker, Principal
KCPS, UCM

I sincerely feel that new and veteran teachers will benefit from reading and discussing this book. Readers are guaranteed to reflect upon current practice and be introduced to countless teaching strategies that will improve the educational experience of their students.

—David G. Daniels, High School Principal
Susquehanna Valley Senior High School

Hallelujah! Benson and Poliner have written a book that many educators have been searching for—one that illuminates a pathway to develop important social and emotional skills that all adolescents need to master. There is much available in this domain that focuses on the needs of young children but fewer substantive resources for secondary educators (and parents!) interested in balancing academic accountability with vital skill development in self-efficacy, civic responsibility, and resiliency. These authors demonstrate a deep understanding of adolescent development and use that knowledge to illuminate pathways to strengthen important youth competencies. The authors frame their insights and practical strategies through a lens that is cognizant of the needs of the wide range of divers that populate our modern-day middle and high schools. The book is also filled with thoughtfi teaching lessons that can help educators infuse youth development into classroom work wi promising academic rigor. Additionally, there are pragmatic supports for principals who wa tate faculty discussions and parents who want to bring these lessons home. This book is ric insights and practical guidance for how we can help teens to become sharp thinkers anc contributing citizens.

—John D'Auria, President, Teachers21

(Continued)

Poliner and Benson empower our school communities to lay the foundations, practices, spaces, and rituals to educate the "whole child." They walk us through the various lenses students bring with them each day to school—the social, emotional, physical, cognitive, etcetera—and how those lenses interact with the cultures and practices in our communities. They provide us ways to foster the positive relationships that lead to students who are resilient and self-aware and ultimately better prepared to navigate the complexities before them. Understanding schools and their leaders, the authors offer practical and accessible tools that can really make a difference. This useful resource will quickly become a go-to guide for planning conversations, faculty meetings, parent education, and self-examining and rethinking our schools.

—Roberto D'erizans, Middle School Principal
Graded—The American School of São Paolo (Brazil)

Teaching the Whole Teen is a gem of a book, one that sparkles with brilliant insights, guidance, and invaluable practical resources to support "everyday practices that promote success and resilience in school and life." Poliner and Benson tap into evidence-based research within the fields of education, psychology (adolescent development), and social neuroscience to compellingly present why and how caring "whole school" environments, anchored by relational trust, can most optimally cultivate adolescents' positive learning and development in secondary schools. In paying attention to the vital importance of systematically supporting novice teachers' development of social-emotional skills and stress resilience, the authors attend to practice that is too often de-prioritized in schools. As they rightly assert, "how we support [novice teachers] to persevere and thrive will mirror our success, or failure, to do the same for whole teens." This book should be required reading for all involved in educator preparation and induction programs, including middle and high school leaders!

—Deborah Donahue-Keegan, EdD
Lecturer, Tufts University Department of
Education, and Co-Director, Massachusetts Consortium
for Social-Emotional Learning in Teacher Education

It is an honor to learn from the wonderful and important beliefs and strategies presented in this book. I will be incorporating many of the ideas in my teaching.

—Lyman Goding, Retired Principal
Plymouth Community Intermediate School, Bridgewater State College

At last we have a courageously written book that focuses on the needs of teens, versus the needs of the school systems. While this concept appears like revolutionary thinking, it is not. This is simply common sense whose time has come. The ideas and concepts advanced in this book promise to engage and motivate all students by strengthening their LOCUS of control, and quality of life.

—Jim Grant, Author and Consultant
Founder, Staff Development for Educators (SDE)

Teaching the Whole Teen provides educators and administrators a comprehensive resource for teaching our diverse student populations. The authors cohesively weave together the various principles of working with a myriad of diverse student populations including those that are often overlooked by other authors and educational researchers. Educators who are interested in elevating their practice and increasing authentic student engagement from theory into action should read this book.

—Lisa Graham, MA, NBCT, Director, Special Education
Berkeley Unified School District

If you think *Teaching the Whole Teen* is just another book about how to communicate with teenagers, then think again. Poliner and Benson have written a manual for how to provide social-emotional support in culturally responsive ways. It explicitly addresses the unique needs of students of color, students from poverty, and immigrant students in ways that other books don't. It is full of practice tools and clear guidance. This book should be read by every middle and high school educator.

—Zaretta Hammond, Educational Consultant

Finally, we have a book that applies the "whole child" concept to the turbulent teenage years. In *Teaching the Whole Teen,* Rachel Poliner and Jeffrey Benson provide high school principals and teachers with a hands-on guide that applies the lessons of neuroscience and social-emotional learning to support healthy adolescent development and maximize learning.

—James Harvey, Executive Director
National Superintendents Roundtable

Teaching and raising teens can be both fun and fiery! Poliner and Benson use the latest research to inform educators and parents about how to teach the teen, basing their work on the "whole person," and teens do change and become interesting people! This is the book to turn to when you are working with students during the teen years, when you desperately need help now, and when you are seeking solace.

—**John Hattie, Professor of Education**
Director of the Melbourne Education Research Institute
University of Melbourne

What a treat to read! Poliner and Benson have created a treasure trove of insights and strategies to improve teaching and leading. Their work is pragmatic and based on an appreciation and understanding of how teenagers learn and schools function. I was particularly struck by the specific strategies for principals. They are designed to facilitate both student and teacher growth. This book is interesting, informative, and insightful.

The authors recognize that successful change doesn't come from mandates. Rather, meaningful change is an organic process that is only effective when we approach problems through collaboration and with respect. Every principal, regardless of the kind of school that she leads or his years of experience, will benefit from reading it.

—**Thomas R. Hoerr, PhD, Emeritus Head**
New City School, St. Louis

In *Teaching the Whole Teen,* Rachel Poliner and Jeffrey Benson lay out a treasure trove of insights and reminders about what makes adolescents tick, and what that means for those who work with them each day. As our schools regain a sense of the primacy of social-emotional development, educators at any level will appreciate these tools, tips, and helpful prompts to bring out the best in relationships for learning for all students. There's plenty here as well for parents, counselors, and district leaders from two people with a deep sense of schools and the inextricable bond between growing and learning.

—**Larry Myatt, President, Education Resources Consortium**
Founding Principal, Fenway High School, Boston

In their book *Teaching the Whole Teen,* Poliner and Benson provide the reader with practical applications that support student success in and outside the classroom. Grounded in solid research and contemporary thinking, their book reminds us that we are not only responsible for educating the minds of students, but we also have the opportunity to establish the conditions necessary for them to reach their fullest social and personal potential. Let there be no doubt, we have the ability to make a real difference in the lives of young people and this book provides a solid framework to lead the way.

—**Russell J. Quaglia, President and Founder**
Quaglia Institute for Student Aspirations

Implementing SEL skills into the secondary grades can feel contrived and artificial, and many secondary teachers don't feel adequately trained or equipped to teach these skills. Finally the mountains of brain research that all teachers need to know and use have been put into a very useful and easy-to-read guide. *Teaching the Whole Teen* creates authentic ways to teach SEL skills that secondary curriculum almost always lacks. Rachel Poliner and Jeffrey Benson have put together the perfect guide to teach secondary students the skills they need for life!

—**Andrea Ramirez, School Improvement Facilitator**
James Bowie High School, Austin

It is deeply refreshing and reinvigorating to read Rachel Poliner and Jeffrey Benson's book, *Teaching the Whole Teen.* These are two experienced and skilled educators, but it is not in these characteristics, valuable as they are, that their greatest power lies. Poliner and Benson never, ever lose sight of the reasons for which those of us who became educators did so. They carry with great strength and constant clarity the focus on students, their needs, and their best interests. They remind us in every chapter, every concept, every focus and suggestion, that before standards, before testing, before government accountability, before politics, before all of the things that distract and pressure us every day, come the young people whose future we are shaping. Just as vital, they carry with deep assurance the reminder of the great joy and sense of fulfillment that springs inevitably, for both teacher and students, when this priority is maintained.

(Continued)

It is far too easy in the hectic day to day of unfunded mandates, changing curriculum, and increasing days spent on testing, to see the system and its needs instead of the students who are served by it. It is important to attend to and nurture the institution. If a school or district does not do well in the account-ability system, they find themselves unable to deliver those elements of education they know are so very important. Knowing as they do that the pressures of modern education will not go away, Rachel and Jeffrey only present techniques and scenarios that are entirely practical in that context. It is the gift of this book that they do so without compromising any elements of a complete education that we all strive to deliver.

Teaching the Whole Teen is full of the message we must never forget. Our students are precious individual people whose future has been entrusted to us. We must equip them with what they need to thrive in the world. These things include not only academic knowledge, and that is constantly changing, but an entire palette of skills, knowledge, and abilities. The authors know, with tremendous empathy, what the life of the typical teacher and administrator is like. It is because of this that they are able to craft suggestions and strategies that are sophisticated enough to be entirely workable in the real world.

This book is particularly timely because the discussion in educational circles has recently started to focus on aspects of teaching the whole child and social-emotional factors as they impact a student's ability to learn. While this conversation might make it appear that these issues have just been discovered, some educators, Poliner and Benson among the foremost, have always carried the importance of seeing the whole teen to all of their work. For those who are now looking for resources to enhance their knowledge and expertise in this area, this book will provide a wealth of highly usable information that they can implement immediately.

It is precisely because of the infinite number of interacting characteristics in and among human beings that education is so difficult to truly master and measure. Some disciplines, like mathematics and music, function within closed systems, where a complete understanding of the elements leads to success. Poliner and Benson have such an elegant way of holding and speaking about this complex dance that is teaching and learning. Without distilling it into one or two dimensions, which would misrepresent its essence, they work with specifics that school staff on all levels can instantly embrace and carry into their day. Each section of the book is grounded in research which is clearly referenced and synopsized. More importantly for the working educator in the field, there follows a series of suggestions and examples with specific emphasis on students of different backgrounds and needs. Included in these are sections with ideas on how to engage parents in the work with secondary children, an area where many educators are hungry for ideas.

—Marguerite C. Rizzi, EdD, Superintendent of Schools
Stoughton Public Schools

Those of us striving to help educators reenvision family engagement as a partnership between home and school have been given a powerful gift in *Teaching the Whole Teen.* The authors' suggestions of comple-mentary strategies for school and home speak to the importance of adults working together to support youth and provide tools for how to get there.

As both a parent of a teen and a school-family engagement professional, I was thrilled to find *Teaching the Whole Teen.* The roles that educators and families play in supporting the development of young people in every aspect of their lives can be either integrated and supportive or in conflict and disruptive. This book provides educators with strategies to ensure that students are encouraged to bring their cultures and communities into the classroom in order to be truly known and supported in school and to make the most of their educational experiences.

By providing strategies for all of the adults in a young person's life, both at home and at school, *Teaching the Whole Teen* makes it clear that we all have a role to play in supporting students' personal and academic growth. The examples and strategies in this book will transform classrooms and welcome families into schools to build cohesive communities with the shared goal of helping youth become their best selves—for life.

—Ann M. Walsh, Chief of Family Engagement, 1647

Teaching the Whole Teen is a wonderfully practical guide for educators who aspire to promote the social, emotional, and academic competence of middle and high school students. It offers compelling strategies for engaging, motivating, and inspiring young people (the "what" and "how") and rationales for applying them (the "why"). This important book should be used in preservice and inservice professional learning for teachers, administrators, and counselors. It will help them in their quest to educate knowledgeable, responsible, caring, and contributing young people.

—Roger P. Weissberg, PhD, Chief Knowledge Officer
Collaborative for Academic, Social, and Emotional Learning (CASEL)
Distinguished Professor of Psychology and Education, University of Illinois at Chicago

Cogent writing, smart content, practical insights, and not a word wasted: Reading Poliner and Benson's *Teaching the Whole Teen* is an unusually good use of an educator's time. Thankfully devoid of simplistic platitudes, the authors reflect real students and teachers and the challenges each group faces in their collective enterprise. Finally, we have a clear-minded, research-based education book written by veteran educators that annihilates the notion of "teen intellect" as oxymoronic and fully respects the complex realities of modern adolescent lives and brain power.

Poliner and Benson get it, and we are better for it: Here, they've captured middle and high school students' quest to mature and connect with both people and content beautifully, and they provide powerful tools to help students and the adults in their lives carve the path forward. The authors prove middle and high school students' innate resolve to become independent, resilient individuals, even as they stumble in the effort, and the authors demonstrate how mentors can help students accept their current selves while aspiring to be something more.

Teaching the Whole Teen manifests the best thinking in modern education, including actionable steps on developing students' self-agency and self-regulation, and how to develop communication and executive function skills so vital to school and life success. Their candid approach doesn't pull any punches: They speak honestly of the bigger issues at play in adolescents' education: developing a sense of purpose, autonomy, the influences of dominant cultures, dealing with academic and personal setbacks, restorative justice, and developing a healthy work ethic. Thankfully, too, they provide specific responses to the needs of English Language Learners, students in rural communities, students and families in LGBTQ communities, and communities struggling with racial conflicts.

Teaching the Whole Teen is the course all of us wanted to take as undergraduates in our schools of teacher education but was never offered. It answers the burning issues of student motivation, maturation, and how we can facilitate students' growth in school and at home. And hey, building leaders and novice teachers— There's specific material here for you!

From now on, when a middle or high school teacher asks me during an effective grading practices workshop how we can build responsibility, meaningful connection, personal fortitude, and healthy independence in today's students if we are no longer allowed to use grades to bribe them into compliance, I'm going to direct them to read *Teaching the Whole Teen*, then sit back and watch their faces light up in dawning realizations and teacher epiphanies. They'll finish the book, look up with conviction, and declare, "We can do this!"

—Rick Wormeli, Teacher, Writer, and Educational Consultant

The authors have painstakingly tackled a very pertinent issue for middle and high school personnel. They not only thoroughly examine the entire child but they also do so by leaving no stone unturned. The child is addressed, the culture is addressed, and the people who work with the children are addressed. This is a great resource for anyone working with adolescents.

—Janice Wyatt-Ross, Associate Principal
Bryan Station High School, Lexington, KY

Teaching the Whole Teen

For Lily, Elijah, Aubrey, and Ellery,
may your spirits shine far into the future.

Teaching the Whole Teen

*Everyday Practices
That Promote
Success and Resilience
in School and Life*

Rachel Poliner

Jeffrey Benson

CORWIN

A SAGE Publishing Company

FOR INFORMATION:

Corwin

A SAGE Company

2455 Teller Road

Thousand Oaks, California 91320

(800) 233-9936

www.corwin.com

SAGE Publications Ltd.

1 Oliver's Yard

55 City Road

London EC1Y 1SP

United Kingdom

SAGE Publications India Pvt. Ltd.

B 1/I 1 Mohan Cooperative Industrial Area

Mathura Road, New Delhi 110 044

India

SAGE Publications Asia-Pacific Pte. Ltd.

3 Church Street

#10-04 Samsung Hub

Singapore 049483

Program Director: Jessica Allan

Senior Associate Editor: Kimberly Greenberg

Editorial Assistant: Katie Crilley

Production Editor: Melanie Birdsall

Copy Editor: Diane DiMura

Typesetter: C&M Digitals (P) Ltd.

Proofreader: Laura Webb

Indexer: Sue Nedrow

Cover Designer: Gail Buschman

Marketing Manager: Jill Margulies

Library of Congress Cataloging-in-Publication Data

Names: Poliner, Rachel A. author. | Benson, Jeffrey, author.

Title: Teaching the whole teen : everyday practices that promote success and resilience in school and life / Rachel Poliner, Jeffrey Benson.

Description: Thousand Oaks, California : Corwin, a SAGE Company, [2017] | Includes bibliographical references and index.

Identifiers: LCCN 2016016168 | ISBN 9781506335889 (pbk. : acid-free paper)

Subjects: LCSH: Teenagers—Education. | Teenagers—Conduct of life. | Adolescence. | Holistic education.

Classification: LCC LB1607 .P59 2017 | DDC 373.18—dc23
LC record available at https://lccn.loc.gov/2016016168

This book is printed on acid-free paper.

SUSTAINABLE FORESTRY INITIATIVE
Certified Chain of Custody
Promoting Sustainable Forestry
www.sfiprogram.org
SFI-01268
SFI label applies to text stock

16 17 18 19 20 10 9 8 7 6 5 4 3 2 1

Contents

Acknowledgments

We are deeply indebted to the many dedicated and inspiring educators we've had the privilege of working with through the years. This book is an effort to synthesize and organize the endless lessons we have shared together. We hope that many of you will recognize your stories and your influence on our thinking and on the collective wisdom we offer throughout the book.

We are grateful for the support and guidance of Jessica Allan and the entire Corwin team.

We want to honor the memories of colleagues whose deep beliefs remain with us: Richmond Mayo-Smith, Steven Brion-Miesels, William J. Kreidler, Seth Kreisberg, and Charles Haynie. We thought of each of them many times as we were writing and were sustained by their visions of schools fostering a better world for all.

PUBLISHER'S ACKNOWLEDGMENTS

Corwin gratefully acknowledges the contributions of the following reviewers:

Jim Anderson
Principal
Andersen Jr. High School
Chandler, AZ

Gustava Cooper-Baker
Principal
KCPS, UCM
Kansas City, MO

Jason Cushner
Dorm Parent and School Reform Coach
Eagle Rock School and Professional
    Development Center/Rowland
Estes Park, CO

David G. Daniels
High School Principal
Susquehanna Valley Senior High School
Conklin, NY

Lyman Goding
Principal (retired)
Plymouth Community Intermediate
    School, Bridgewater State College
Plymouth, MA

Lisa Graham
Director, Special Education
Berkeley Unified School District
Berkeley, CA

Joy Rose
High School Principal (retired)
Westerville (OH) City Schools
Worthington, OH

Dr. Lisa Scherff
Teacher
Cypress Lake High School
Fort Myers, FL

Janice Wyatt-Ross
Associate Principal
Bryan Station High School
Lexington, KY

About the Authors

 **Rachel Poliner** is an educational consultant specializing in whole student approaches and change management. Her work has focused on school climate, instructional, and structural reforms: K–12 social and emotional learning, middle and high school advisory programs, high school redesign, and improving faculty climate. Her in-depth approach spans classroom and schoolwide structures, practices and programs, curriculum, staff development, district policies and systems, and coaching administrators, teams and teacher leaders. She is an author of *The Advisory Guide: Designing and Implementing Effective Advisory Programs in Secondary Schools* (Engaging Schools, 2004), and curricula, chapters, and articles on personalization, social-emotional learning, resiliency, dialogue, and conflict resolution. Poliner has consulted with public and independent schools in New England and across the United States; she has been a teacher, educational organization director, and a faculty member for master's degree candidates in conflict resolution education and peaceable schools.

Rachel Poliner can be contacted at RachelPoliner@LeadersAndLearners.org.

 **Jeffrey Benson** has worked in almost every school context in over forty years of experience in the field of education: as a teacher in elementary, middle, and high schools; as an instructor in undergraduate and graduate programs; as an administrator in day and residential schools. He has studied and worked side by side with national leaders in the fields of special education, learning theory, trauma and addiction, school reform, adult development, advisory programs, math reform, and conflict resolution. He has been a consultant to public and independent schools, mentored teachers and principals in varied school settings, and has written on many school-based issues. He is the author of *Hanging In: Strategies for Teaching the Students Who Challenge Us Most* (ASCD, 2014), and *10 Steps to Managing Change in Schools* (ASCD, 2015). The core of Jeffrey Benson's work is in understanding how people learn, the starting point for everything that schools should do.

Jeffrey Benson can be contacted at JeffreyBenson@LeadersAndLearners.org.

Introduction

Merging Two Missions

Teachers come to work each day with lesson plans designed to meet curriculum standards. Many of those teachers know that those standards alone do not address all the lessons they want their students to learn. There is a second part of their mission: for students to develop the skills to manage their adolescent years in preparation for adulthood. Most school mission statements include the goals of supporting young people to both achieve academically and contribute to their communities. Through every day lessons and expectations, in addition to academic mastery, middle and high schools aspire to help students develop social skills, problem solving, autonomy, civic responsibility, and goals for their learning and future.

Achieving both parts of the mission is very demanding. School days are brimming with requirements, structures, and routines—some new, some over a century old and clearly in need of reform—that make it difficult for educators to fulfill all the lofty ideals of their mission statements.

This book supports the fulfillment of the whole mission because middle and high school students come to school each day as whole teens. They have interests and questions, moods and needs, competencies and gaps, histories and dreams, relationships with others and awareness of themselves—in an infinite variation of degrees and combinations that resist any rigid definitions. When educators work with them as whole teens, they support their academic success and their personal development, which are interdependent and mutually reinforcing.

Innumerable educators have, through their practice or research, recognized the importance of seeing all students as whole people, wherever they are in their development. Many in the field, including our colleagues at ASCD's Whole Child Initiative, or The Stanford Center for Opportunity Policy in Education, emphasize serving the whole student. Those efforts have helped in our understanding. We chose not to create a specific program or to propose finite definitions. When we write about the whole teen, we ask the reader to join with us in maintaining a wide, deep, and complex understanding, which by necessity would burst through the boundaries of any explicit definition—as so many whole teens seem to do.

Who Is This Book For?

Teachers will find many classroom practices they can employ on their own to improve teaching, learning, and adolescent development. Collaborating with colleagues, they will find practices and structures that can be implemented in their middle school cluster, their high school department, their grade level, or their whole school.

School and district leaders will find practices for themselves as well as for teachers and students, and discussion prompts for faculty meetings. Whether your school is delving into social-emotional learning, character education, school climate efforts, or related approaches, the practices and structures offered will fit, deepen, and connect those efforts. Many district leaders implement programming at the elementary level to support both academic achievement and personal development, while struggling with how to serve both goals at their secondary schools. This book is full of strategies to develop school cultures and programs that work with adolescents.

This book includes practices for **teachers, counselors, and school leaders** for their own use, and language and ideas for connecting their practices across their roles, creating more unified approaches for working with teens. **Counselors and teachers** who are playing leadership roles on committees, research teams, and in professional development will find many options to support their efforts.

There are pages in each chapter in Part II so that **teachers, counselors, and administrators** can communicate and partner with **parents and guardians**, extending the concepts for use at home. While adolescent years can involve significant turmoil, it is too often the case—for many complex reasons—that families are less engaged with their teens' schooling than they were at the elementary level. We hope that the "Practices at Home" pages will support robust school-family engagement efforts. We encourage these pages to be shared in parent workshops and discussion groups, as part of staff professional development, when consulting with specific parents and guardians who turn to the school for support, and when seeking to expand the policies and resources that unite a community—to embrace the notion that all teens are "our kids" (Putnam, 2015). When adults are talking with each other, everyone—families, educators, students—benefit.

All adults who encounter students affect them. Numerous strategies in the book apply to the school's **secretaries, custodians, cafeteria workers,** and especially **professional aides**, who are often students' trusted allies. Sharing practices with them is impactful and a sign of respect.

Professors of education and candidates in teacher, school counselor, and school leadership programs often need a bridge from theory to practice. As much as we are active and enthusiastic consumers of research, we are practitioners. We anticipate that our applications of theory to practice will support their learning and effectiveness.

In addition to our focus on classrooms and schools, we make numerous connections to clubs, teams, and after-school settings. **Coaches, club advisors, tutors, mentors, internship organizers, and youth development agency staff** will find many relevant practices for their programs and efforts.

Finally, we hope **policymakers** will consider the information in this book. Education in the United States has gone through a few waves of accountability pressure in the last century (Mehta, 2015). Accountability alone does not foster effective teaching, learning, development, employability, or citizenship. Schools must have the robust support of policymakers in order to fulfill all the elements of their missions.

Overview of the Book

Part I, Seeing the Whole Teen, sorts through research on adolescent development, including what to call all those skills beyond the traditional 3Rs. We look at the many challenges and opportunities that are predictable parts of adolescence—and ones that are dependent on the specific young person. We consider teenagers who grow up in distinct communities, often coming to schools with distinct strengths, opportunities, and challenges. Part I offers insights from the study of neuroeducation, resilience, identity development, cultural competence, and several other fields. Educators' days are frenetic and packed; we hope that you find these chapters both valuable and succinct.

Part II, Everyday Practices, focuses on classroom strategies for Grades 6 through 12. We provide everyday practices to teach the whole teen, and to shape the classroom culture to model essential skills and values. Chapters include activities, routines and rituals, discussion formats and prompts, projects, teaching tools, and student handouts. Following those pages are discussion prompts for faculty to use in their individual and collaborative learning and planning processes.

Each chapter of Part II also includes "Practices at Home," approaches that parents and guardians can use with their adolescents, building many of the same skills being addressed in school. We hope that these shared and parallel practices offer a much-needed bridge between the often disconnected efforts of all the adults in the lives of teenagers.

Part III, The Whole School Surrounds the Whole Teen, looks at many ways leaders (we use that term to include many members of the school community) develop a schoolwide culture that supports the whole teen. We address the faculty culture, options for shifting school structures, the critical need to support novice teachers, and practices that sustain the leaders.

Helping teachers, counselors, parents, and administrators have a whole teen approach, teaching the skills *and* shaping the classroom and school cultures to model and reinforce those skills, is our goal for this book. Contributing to a thriving, healthy, and just society remains our larger mission.

Notes About Nomenclature

Grades 6 through 12 include a large developmental span, so we use varied terms to refer to the students: *teens, teenagers, adolescents, young people, students*, and occasionally *kids, preteens*, or *young adults*. Different terms fit the specifics of a given topic, or its spirit. Unless otherwise stated, we mean the terms to be as inclusive as possible. In your setting, students are also likely identified as advisees, daughters, sons, siblings, coworkers, team members, musicians, artists, athletes, employees, and much more—the range of roles they assume is vast, and every setting has opportunities to develop their skills and identities.

In parallel fashion, we know that many middle school and high school educators play several roles. Teachers and counselors serve as club advisors and athletic team coaches. Some administrators teach a course. Sports and arts staff typically work with students for multiple years, often serving as informal mentors. Any of these adults might run an advisory group. Though we refer most often to *teachers*, *faculty*, or *staff*, we encourage you to apply the concepts and practices in this book to all the ways you interact with the incredibly complex and fascinating people who attend middle schools and high schools.

Visit the companion website at
http://www.resources.corwin.com/PolinerBensonWholeTeen
for downloadable resources.

PART I

Seeing the Whole Teen

Everyone who teaches in middle school and high school was once a teenager—but not everyone experienced the "storm and stress" of those years in the same way. Not everyone hit the physiological and psychological markers of adolescence at the same time, and with the same impact. Not everyone began adolescence with the same context of family, neighborhood, culture, and history. Adolescence is an experience shared by all and experienced uniquely by all as well.

The lived experiences of having once been a teenager, and the experiences of working in schools filled with teenagers, often raises compelling questions:

- How are teenagers and their brains developing?

- What consistent developmental themes could guide our approaches, working from the youngest teens to the oldest teens?

- What lenses would focus our understanding for our work with teenagers who come from particular cultures? Who have unique identities? Who are consistently targets of prejudice and misunderstanding?

- What are the skills beyond standard academics that teenagers need?

- How is our school addressing the unique needs of teenagers through middle and high school? Do we have the frameworks and lenses that help us be coherent and consistent in addressing those needs?

- In what ways should secondary schools treat their students differently than elementary schools? And does my school do so?

- What frameworks and lenses might help all the school staff support teenagers?

- Can we lift up from the daily rush of responsibilities to focus on a long-term vision for our students—an optimistic vision for all our students?

Part I of this book opens and begins to answer these essential questions, and serves as a touch point as you explore classroom practices in Part II and schoolwide practices and structures in Part III.

1

The Whole Teen Comes Into the School

Every student in every class, every day, is a whole person—a physical being, a cognitive being, a social being, and an emotional being (at least!). It is not possible for students to leave any aspect of themselves at the classroom door. If you've got the physical kids in front of you, and are hoping for the cognitive kids, you'd better understand that they are bundled with the social kids and the emotional kids. Recent brain research gives ever more information and insight about the interconnection of those aspects. One part of the teenager cannot walk into the classroom without the others.

One of the struggles of teaching teens is that too many schools expect them to consistently isolate and repress most of who they are, so that educators access only a portion of their capabilities. The most effective educators treat middle school and high school students as whole teens, wherever they are in their development. A huge advantage of that approach is that all staff can help them build skills in every domain.

Skill building is crucial. Skills from communication to collaboration, from problem solving to persistence are teachable, coachable, and learnable. Those skills are always developed within context. Teens who are expected to treat others respectfully and fairly should be surrounded by an environment that models respect and fairness, or we should expect them to ask why it doesn't. Teens who are expected to develop listening skills should be surrounded by people who listen to them. Teens who are expected to persevere through school experiences ranging from inspiring to tedious need to be in a school with adults who are optimistic about students' futures and help them connect to their own optimism.

There is no consensus for what to call the approaches that develop whole teens. *Social-emotional learning*, *character education*, *noncognitive skills*, and *soft skills* are all terms in use. Those terms explicitly refer to what adults want students to learn, and are sometimes understood to refer to qualities in the environment as well.

Other terms refer more explicitly to the environments, such as *school climate*, *democratic schools*, or *peaceable schools*, though peel them back and you'll see that they certainly deal with skill building. Terms such as *personalized learning* or *student voice and ownership* are approaches that emphasize involving and supporting the students in each setting, and deal with some skills and structural aspects. Yet other terms, like *youth development*, deal with building many skills but are used more often in out-of-school settings.

Some of the terms have become associated mainly with elementary schools. Certain terms have more acceptance in some parts of the country, or in certain streams of research and advocacy. Some additional terms, such as *conflict resolution education* and *violence prevention education*, represent fields with similar approaches, and at times have held sway because of national issues and funding streams.

We appreciate and need the array of approaches represented by the various terms for working with adolescents. For example, the research on emotional intelligence and social-emotional learning offer innumerable important insights for educators as they consider instruction and classrooms practices. Focusing on character traits and personalized learning are helpful for identity development, which as we discuss below, is an especially significant task for evolving adolescents. Yet other terms seem to us to be more specialized or act as foundational concepts. *Grit*—having the passion and perseverance to strive and achieve—and *growth mindset*—knowing that you can affect your own development—make the other efforts more effective.

To have an impact on the lives of students, it is important to consider the structural differences between elementary and secondary schools. If one elementary teacher changes her classroom practices to emphasize community building and student voice, she has changed the environment for her twenty-five students for the year. If one secondary teacher makes a parallel set of changes, only a fraction of her students' day-to-day experiences are different. If the rest of the day, week, and year is alienating and passive, the overall message hasn't changed. The efforts on school climate, democratic schools, and student voice are all based in this crucial understanding—the whole school environment matters enormously for whole teen development. Recent efforts to understand social-emotional learning in secondary schools have also emphasized the need for a whole environment for whole teens (Cervone & Cushman, 2015; Hamedani & Darling-Hammond, 2015).

Aspects of all the above fields overlap and support the development of the whole teen. Emphases are somewhat different, skills and concepts are somewhat different, as are connotations and marketability to different audiences. Researchers and service providers can parse differentiations that do not provide any significant direction for teachers, principals, and school counselors. We will draw from many of the fields to craft a whole experience.

We will however, make no further reference to two terms: *noncognitive skills* and *soft skills*. Everything we learn and experience involves cognition; the brain processes all, even emotions. There are no noncognitive skills. Calling them noncognitive misrepresents and diminishes them. And although the business world has termed self-management and interpersonal skills as soft skills, we don't see what's so soft about them. They help people have a strong sense of identity and strong skills for tough situations. There's very little "soft" about being a competent learner, advocate, ally, or leader.

The approach we use in this book is grounded in our understanding of human development and the unique challenges and opportunities that teens face. We focus on teens, applying research to *their* needs, not trying to fit teens' needs into the research or any one framework. We invite you as well to keep your focus on the whole teen.

A Whole Teen Approach

The last two decades of research, including the new field of neuroeducation that draws from cognitive neuroscience, cognitive psychology, and education, has exponentially expanded our understanding of how the human brain works—and specifically, how teenage brains are developing. Teenage brains are different than those of elementary school students and have not yet developed into their more stable adult functioning. Veteran teachers in middle schools and high schools have always seen something developmentally unique about the ways their students think and feel and connect; the latest research gives a shape to all those observations and points to many best practices.

Evolving over eons, our brains learn by developing complex, interconnected neural networks. These networks are built of millions and millions of tiny connections that wind their way through innumerable paths in our brains. While there are areas of the brain that regulate certain capacities, such as vision, there is not any experience in our lives that resides in just one section. No facts or concepts exist in any single brain cell (Medina, 2014).

Facts are held by emotions and movement and meaning, as much as by other facts. We have whole brains, webs of understanding weaving in and around and through other webs of understanding. Our brains do not resemble malls of isolated stores or the hallways of a school. Significantly, our emotional networks are vast and strong, and our brains react to intense emotions before they retrieve previously learned information.

Our emotions drive attention and memory, therefore learning. Fearful and flooded emotions can distract attention and short-circuit memory, preventing learning, while anticipation, meaning, and trust enhance learning. Teens have an optimal emotional zone that motivates them (Hardiman, 2012; Immordino-Yang, 2016; Jensen, 2005). Teachers cannot impress upon students the themes of *Romeo and Juliet* without impressing upon their students the feelings they have toward them, and the goals they aspire them to reach. Knowledge is a twisting neural tapestry of feelings and ideas and relationships and hopes and beliefs.

Adolescents' brain connections grow into the frontal lobe, where long-term planning and balancing multiple priorities are ultimately managed—but for most teens not yet managed consistently. Approaches for understanding adolescents in schools must address their growing, and not fully developed, capacity for abstract problem solving, social connections, autonomy, and their sense of future selves.

Teens must be prompted to do different sorts of thinking than they did in elementary school. They have to be given abundant think time, challenges, and scaffolding to reflect, assess, synthesize, and construct meaning. Their developing metacognition—to think about their own thinking—requires structures and prompts from teachers that ask more than who, what, and where. They are constructing idiosyncratic, abstract, and emotionally relevant concepts.

Their concept formation comes from two brain systems. One system, comprised of multiple neural networks, is referred to as the "looking out" system, which pays attention to the immediate world around us. Other networks comprise the "looking in" system, which processes reflections, emotions, and longer-term abstract ideas (Immordino-Yang, 2016). Our brains toggle between the two systems; if one is on, the other is in stand-by mode. In order for students to process their thoughts, find compelling connections, and evaluate meanings for themselves, they need time to think—in discussions and all classroom experiences.

With their growing ability to think abstractly and conceptually, teenagers are having their first major experiences of seeing their own identities in formation, asking themselves "Who am I?" and making choices that are informed by their beliefs about themselves. "Identity is the embodiment of self-understanding. We are who we understand ourselves to be . . . " (Nakkula, 2008, p. 11). Teens build those understandings as they find out what they're interested in and what they're good at so far, as they try on or rub against adult beliefs and expectations, as they see how others perceive them. They need opportunities for that exploration, much of which can—and for many teens, must—happen in school. Since identity development " . . . is inordinately shaped by the contexts, relationships, and activities in which youth are most deeply invested, it is essential that our schools be environments in which young people choose to invest and through which their investment is adequately reciprocated" (p. 13). It is crucial that teens have "I am a learner" at the core of their identities and that everyone around them supports that belief.

Given the unique needs of adolescents, we will frame our practices within the well-researched field of resilience. The main skill areas of social competence, problem solving, skills for autonomy, and having a sense of purpose and future (Benard, 2004) are an aggregation that we find resonates with secondary educators. The research on resiliency, of which there's plenty, also stresses the contextual factors that foster resilience—attachment to caring adults, high expectations with high support to reach them, and opportunities for meaningful participation (Krovetz, 2008).

Like the other terms, resilience has some unhelpful connotations. The word is being used broadly in our culture to refer to everything from subways having to be resilient in the snow to investment portfolios needing to be resilient through stock market turmoil. We hear resilience reduced to overcoming a specific obstacle, persevering through anything, including school. We hear resilience applied only to at-risk students.

Resilience is an inborn human trait. Each of us, through our everyday efforts to be whole people, needs and develops resilience. This process includes our belief in what we can do with our lives, and how each one of us accesses our own capacity to embrace the opportunities—and not just solve the problems—we encounter every day. Resilience is thriving, not just surviving.

We explain the resiliency framework below to give a vision of positive development for whole teens. However, throughout the book, we will be more specific. Rather than writing that effective class discussions lead to resilience, we'll explain that they lead to more social competence. Rather than writing that involving students in classroom decisions leads to resilience, we'll explain more specifically that it leads to problem-solving skills and skills for autonomy. In turn, all of those skills do indeed lead to resilience, and to constructive character development, and to effective social-emotional learning, and to positive school climate and student voice. We're going with as plain a set of terms as possible.

By explaining the resiliency framework (or any framework), there's an opportunity and a challenge. The opportunity is to unpack the research and put forth a vision. The challenge is that when educators see lists of competencies or standards, it's too easy to lose sight of whole teens. They become deconstructed into lists of skills and scores. We encourage you to keep the vision of whole teens, who are learning to be socially competent, interdependent problem solvers, with aspirations for their futures.

Resilience Research Framework

In the following pages, we identify the skills of social competence, problem solving, autonomy, and a sense of purpose and future in the context of school and community. We describe various ways that teenagers utilize these skills. It may be helpful to periodically revisit these descriptions and lists. We offer them as a vision of teens in schools, not as a rigid list of behaviors to memorize.

We also identify a few difficulties students face who have not yet had the mentoring and experiences to build these skills. We delve into each area separately, but these areas should be understood as an integrated whole. A teen who is persistent but without empathy can bully others. A teen who is kind but not assertive can suffer in silence. A teen who is emotionally expressive but not aware of others' reactions can seem self-absorbed. No one skill works effectively alone. When students are struggling, it is important to see their struggles as skill deficits in their development, as schools do for students who may be strong in math and weak in writing.

Contemporary school structures and requirements do not make it easy to envision classrooms and schools where fostering resiliency would be the norm. Therefore, in each section below, there is an image of a classroom led by a secondary school teacher who has made social competence, problem solving, skills for autonomy, and having a sense of purpose and future an integrated part of the curriculum; they are images of well-established practices. Each image shows skill sets in action *and* key contextual factors:

- **caring adults**—A sense of connection to teachers matters; it conveys worth, prompts motivation, assures safety that increases academic engagement, and is a key factor in asking for and receiving support.

- **high expectations with high support to meet the expectations**—Low expectations are not motivating, and neither are unrealistic expectations that lead to quick failure; small successful steps toward something that feels significant build their own momentum and are often the prerequisite to leaps of understanding and concept formation.

- **opportunities for meaningful participation**—Teens need a voice and chances to contribute to their community. They need opportunities to practice self-efficacy. Participation prepares them to preserve democratic values and to embed their learning in a vision greater than themselves—which is a great motivator for academic achievement.

We believe that all the adults whom students encounter in schools are resources for developing the healthy whole teen. While the visions below are specifically classroom based—because the majority of their time is spent in classrooms—the skills and relationships described belong as well, and are often robustly fruitful, in advisories, after-school programs, and in the innumerable interactions students have with adults day to day.

Social Competence

A resilient person is much more than one who struggles alone, fixing his own problems, persevering through difficult circumstances, and "pulling himself up by his own bootstraps." Research shows quite the opposite—resilient people are far more often connected and communicative, not isolated (Benard, 2004). They needn't be extroverts, but do have effective social skills to attract friends and mentors, people who support them. They sustain those relationships with mutual interest and care. This reciprocity forms long-lasting relationships, through ups and downs, representing a sense of stability and a long-term perspective.

It takes a lot of skills to initiate and sustain that web of relationships. You can see students applying skills in many of the following activities that demonstrate social competence:

- developing long-lasting friendships
- identifying positive role models and attracting mentors, even when the students themselves may not be in the position to ask for the support they need
- reaching out to others for support, not necessarily to solve their challenges, sometimes for ideas or just to listen, and sometimes for serious help, such as dealing with an illness or trauma
- noticing others' emotions, when they need support, and offering it
- participating in groups, in roles ranging from leading to accommodating; noticing when they are contributing to or subtracting from the group's efforts; adjusting behavior
- appreciating others' styles, interests, and perspectives
- relating to a variety of people (adults, students, other genders, races, etc.)
- communicating with others to connect and to assert needs, whether in casual conversations, class discussions, or other situations—including listening, showing empathy, asking questions, asserting views
- behaving in trustworthy ways as part of building relationships and working in groups
- admitting mistakes, making amends, apologizing, forgiving
- displaying an interest in historical and societal contexts that impact relationships and checking assumptions held about others
- respecting others, acting as an ally, protecting others

And to be clear, while a manifestation of social competence is the ability to be polite to teachers, that is far from enough—there are too many stories in schools of the quiet and polite student who sneaks to the bathroom to cut her arms or contemplate suicide. Social competence is not necessarily loud, but it is robust.

To foster social competence, there are numerous opportunities to model and have students practice *inter*personal and *intra*personal skills (skills for interacting with others and skills for managing oneself) in the regular school day. Here's an image:

> As students come to the classroom, the teacher is at the door, greeting each one by name, and giving an extra word of encouragement to a few. She notices that a number of students look harried—perhaps they had just taken a test. She uses the opening minute to have everyone take some deep breaths, journal, make a task list, or use any other routine they've discussed to smooth out the transition to this class. The students' next task involves small group work, which they have practiced throughout the year; today, the teacher has assigned students to new groups, noting which students may need a trusted friend nearby, and which ones are ready to be stretched to work with students from other neighborhoods. Before they dive into the assignment, students review the directions the teacher has put on the board for getting started: "Discuss your individual strengths and the best ways each person can contribute to the group's success." During the collaborative work, one group needs to reassess the task and their roles; another has a difference of opinion and pauses to consider each other's perspectives more deeply; a third notices that a student has been out ill all week—one person volunteers to fill him in. The teacher sits to watch the class in action and catches the eye of a shy student; they smile at each other. She also takes notice of a small number of students who seems frustrated; she'll check in with them privately. Before the class period ends, the teacher prompts the students to begin the ritual of naming two ways the group worked well together and a way to improve next time.

Problem Solving

It is likely that problem solving is an integral part of being human, not just a skill we employ when things are going poorly. Part of the allure of game playing—whether board games, cards, or athletics—comes from the satisfaction we feel when we triumph against the dilemmas our opponents present to us. The creation of art involves a continual process of effort, assessment, and adjustment toward a final product. Cooking a meal engages us in working out a complex series of ingredients, tasks, and timing, so the satisfaction of serving the food comes with the knowledge that the experience of cooking was a worthwhile challenge.

This capacity to assess our conditions, develop and organize resources, craft primary and secondary plans, and adjust as we proceed with our plans are skills for daily life, as well as for students in middle school and high school. You can see students applying problem-solving skills in many of the following activities that demonstrate problem solving:

- planning for the short term and long term
- trying different strategies; self-assessing; being ready to adjust the plans or strategies
- developing and making use of resources; seeking outside resources when needed

- organizing materials and tasks

- thinking flexibly; identifying multiple options, multiple routes, multiple resources, with graceful ways of switching strategies; applying flexible thinking in different settings, such as classes, clubs, friendships

- prioritizing an array of responsibilities; managing increasing amounts of work

- managing time effectively—estimating tasks and time, scheduling themselves, meeting deadlines

- seeking to solve problems fairly

- understanding their role in producing conflicts; learning self-restraint to escalate as little as necessary; building skills to resolve conflicts

- learning to make decisions; internalizing criteria that are healthy and ethical

- expecting to make mistakes and learn from them

It is good that many schools give students an assignment notebook, a binder, or technology tools for organizing. So much more is needed. When we hear students say they are "stuck," "overwhelmed," "without any options," they are showing a need for problem solving skills. When students perceive that inevitable mistakes and misbehavior are not moments for reflecting and trying again, but for permanently losing opportunities, they are in environments that don't model problem solving.

Here are two images showing ways to have students practice problem solving in the regular school day:

It is a week before a big test. The teacher gives the class a self-assessment so they can prioritize their needs from among four areas: (1) to memorize key information; (2) to organize their notes, hand-outs, and quizzes; (3) to try practice test items to get a feel for how long it will take to do the various types; (4) to get a refresher lesson on certain key topics. Once they make a choice, the students are directed to one of four work areas. There are written suggestions in each area for how to proceed. The teacher pulls aside for one-to-one dialogues a small number of students who may have trouble with making a good decision, and these students develop a plan for the class period. After twenty minutes, the teacher gets all the students' attention and takes them through a brief discussion of how the work is going and any ideas for improvements to what has been happening so far. This is a ritual the students have done many times, and their responses are both humorous and insightful: some students make suggestions for the entire class; some share ways that they are working well as individuals; others admit that they are floundering and ask their peers for ideas. The teacher again keeps an eye on the handful of students who may not use this ritual effectively and coaches them through the reflection. At the end of class, the students fill out a self-assessment form, noting what they tried, how well they think it will help them on the test, and any recommendations for ways to use the time better. There is also an option to request a meeting with the teacher with a specific area of concern identified.

Meanwhile, advisory groups have been engaged in short-term goal setting, both individually and as a group, trying out routines to be more organized and successful. One group has a backpack clean-out each month with fun music in the background, another is rehearsing talking with teachers about making up missed work, and a third has created a calendar of due dates and deadlines to sign up for teams, auditions, and the financial aid workshop.

Autonomy

The journey of students through middle school and high school is an experience of increasing responsibilities. Teenagers navigate physically larger schools and community environments with diminishing adult oversight. They make very personal decisions about friendships, career interests, hobbies, belief systems, and risk-taking that will influence their success in school, and their pathway into adulthood. Secondary school provides a journey each student takes along the continuum from dependence toward independence, with many chances to experience the vital human ability to be interdependent. The teenage years are a chance to develop a strong sense of autonomy within the give-and-take of community.

Students who have the support to develop the skills of autonomy will more effectively make the most of their secondary school years. You can see students applying skills in many of the following activities that demonstrate autonomy and their developing self-identities:

- making better decisions, even when experiencing peer or community pressure
- managing responsibilities, following through, overcoming obstacles
- having more sense of control, leading to more commitment and persistence
- developing and expressing personal beliefs, goals, interests
- seeking to identify, manage, and enhance one's strengths and weaknesses; improving their skills and/or situations
- taking initiative; self-motivating; working towards personal level of mastery
- managing frustration, setbacks, rejection, indecision; demonstrating self-patience
- taking healthy risks
- setting effective boundaries for friendships, work, and other responsibilities; speaking up for themselves
- taking good care of health; using healthy coping strategies to manage stress
- managing emotions effectively
- controlling impulses, exercising self-discipline
- accepting responsibility and consequences for one's actions

If teachers (or parents) reading this book are thinking that building skills for autonomy starts in high school, please reconsider. Kids need opportunities throughout their lives, opportunities that fit their developmental levels, to make choices, manage themselves, and deal with consequences. It is crucial that students have practice at being independently responsible before they have lots of independence and responsibility.

Of all the attributes of resiliency, autonomy can be the most difficult for adults to support. Some adults see the risks and not the benefits. When teenagers assert their own ideas and decisions, some adults may take those actions as challenges to their authority. Teens need opportunities throughout middle school and high school to experience and demonstrate increased responsibilities. Twelfth graders should be expected to handle more autonomy than sixth graders because they have had the opportunities to be autonomous.

To foster resiliency, there are numerous opportunities to have students practice skills for autonomy in the regular school day. Here's an image:

> The students walk into a classroom where they've jointly made decisions with the teacher about how desks are arranged, how to access the teacher for extra help or requests, and about routines for today, the midway point on projects. They independently begin their tasks, which their teacher has worked with them to prioritize from a menu of options. Students seek out the teacher for advice, most often after they first tried a few ideas on their own, or consulted with their peers, as is the protocol the teacher has introduced, reinforced, and praised. They had a good deal of choice on their project topics, though all fit within the larger theme of the impact of science on society. Class discussions, which students have a role in facilitating, have raised important questions about issues the students themselves believe are critical: conducting research despite peers' skepticism, persevering through a lot of failures, issues of justice and unintended consequences, and the impacts when science challenges prior understandings. The projects include a self-assessment about students' work style and process, and new concepts they're grappling with. The projects are due any time within exam week; students have used planning forms to map out tests and assignments so they can manage their work load, and have committed to their own due date within the week. As they get closer to exam week, the teacher has worked with three students to lead one-minute calming rituals at the beginning of class. The teacher has also planned one-to-one meetings with a few struggling students who are not yet confident in making choices.

Sense of Purpose and Future

Why will students work hard day in and day out, especially through tedious tasks, if they don't have a goal, something to put the daily work into perspective? What keeps them going if they lack skills and optimism about reaching goals? There are indeed far too many students who face those questions, whether because they lack access to opportunities, or lack focus beyond the next high-pressure, high-stakes task.

Russell Quaglia and Michael Corso (2014) write about student aspirations: "Aspirations are both 'then' and 'now.' They involve both dreaming of the future and doing in the present. They are made up of a vision of where we want to get and, at a minimum, a willingness to do what is necessary to get there. When we genuinely aspire, we are facing our future *and* taking steps in the present toward it" (p. 14).

Schools support aspirations in many ways. Thousands of students every year discover what is important to them, and how to make choices and steps to advance goals, through classes, clubs, sports, the arts, after-school programs, and community service. Through these activities, students can see themselves and their futures as part of something greater and longer than their individual efforts. These bigger visions are a balance to teen daily drama, and place the responsibilities of the moment in a more compelling framework than merely getting through the day. As well, adults in these schools hold positive images of their students' futures, and convey that optimism.

To be clear, we are not saying that helping teens to have a sense of purpose and future allows our school systems to ignore the relevance, or irrelevance, of the academics they present on a daily basis. Quite the opposite—the research on resilience says that offering rich opportunities in which students can make their own connections to the work, find their own meaning, and apply their own unique ideas and interests to requirements is essential for developing a school culture that can be successful for the broadest range of learners (Benard, 2004).

Students who believe that the work they do in school contributes to the person they want to become, and the life they want to live, are strongly positioned for doing well in school. For some, their sense of the future may be focused on a professional goal; for others, it may involve their hopes for a family; some may find their inspiration in loving a subject or hobby; some may see their efforts tied to a community role or spiritual path that becomes a lifetime commitment. Any of these self-realized intentions, among so many, contribute to motivating teens. You can see students applying skills in many of the following activities that demonstrate sense of purpose and future:

- identifying personal aspirations and educational goals

- exerting effort to achieve

- seeking meaning in small and large opportunities to learn

- developing special interests and skills

- using creativity and imagination

- expressing hope and optimism

- acting on behalf of others driven by compassion

- accessing beliefs, faith, or spirituality to persevere

- using future goals to balance daily dramas and sustain perspective; delaying gratification for a larger, later goal

- connecting to larger missions and traditions

To foster resiliency, here's an image of connecting curricula to students' sense of purpose and future:

> It is the first day of a new long-term unit in class. The teacher shares the typical learning objectives with the students, then divides them into small working groups based on surveys and conversations they have had all year about students' interests and dreams of the future. The task for the students in their groups is to make as many connections as they can between mastering the given learning objectives and their own interests and dreams. They refer to posters on the wall: one poster lists the careers they have mentioned wanting to pursue; another lists the study skills they have said they want to master; a third lists the

personality traits they wish to develop; a fourth lists the places in the world they hope to live in; a fifth lists their positive visions of the community or world in the not too distant future. Throughout the year, the lists on these posters have been added to and amended as the students' vision of the world and their place in it expands. The small groups brainstorm how the new unit can match any of the collected aspirations on the posters. As is the class protocol, the students share with the other members of their groups what they find potentially relevant in the new unit. Then the students fill out a form identifying their own particular interests and concerns to be shared with the teacher. The teacher has been compiling these forms throughout the year, which allowed the teacher to identify a couple of students who have been struggling to make connections—those students will get some significant one-to-one time in the coming days. Once the students have finished with their sharing and forms, it is the teacher's turn to share his own sense of purpose and the future for the unit of work ahead. At first, the teacher found it challenging to clearly articulate to the students his own aspirations; now he sees this step as important for his own resilience as a teacher.

Shaping Your Own Whole Teen Classrooms and Schools

We hope you will craft your own combinations of the skills and images described above, and the practices detailed in Chapters 3 through 10, to advance your journey toward making your classes "havens of resiliency," in the words of Nan Henderson (2013). Call all of the above by any titles and any categories—perhaps your school or district already has phrases in use. More important than what you call the aggregation of visions, skills, and practices in this book is the determination to support every day, in every part of school, the whole teen.

2

The Whole Teen Comes Into a Dominant Culture

R ecently, a billboard went up on a busy highway in Massachusetts, featuring a picture of John Wayne, a movie star from many years ago. The billboard aimed to promote "grit," with John Wayne saying, "Don't much like quitters, son."

The designers of the billboard counted on the image of John Wayne to carry a lot of significance—the billboard did not explain who John Wayne was. The designers of the billboard also ignored the fact that half the people reading the message were female. The image of John Wayne alone was supposed to trigger a set of memories and beliefs about manhood and grit (which means way more than standing on your own, defeating enemies—it may not even mean that at all). You understood the billboard's message if you had a certain set of experiences and values.

Those experiences and values are part of the dominant culture that informs politics, movies, religions, myths, and innumerable aspects of daily life. It is a culture in flux. When John Wayne first made movies, there were no female or non-White judges on the United States Supreme Court, candidates for president did not consider the impact of Latino voters, and gay people were barred from marriage. Special education students had no legal protections. The culture was dominated in the courts, playing fields, mass media, and boardrooms by White men of European descent. For all the changes over the last decades, the designers of the John Wayne billboard could still rely on aspects of that culture to convey their message.

The implicit messages of that culture continue to influence the development of the whole teen—and the ways schools are structured to convey those messages. What does that powerful culture ask of our teachers and students? Madeline Levine studied the children most immersed in, and expected to succeed in, our schools: the children of affluence, who have the most direct route to prestigious colleges and influential careers—the offspring of the dominant culture. She writes, "Affluent communities excessively emphasize individualism, perfectionism, accomplishment, competition, and materialism, while giving short shrift to more prosocial values such as cooperation, altruism, and philanthropy" (Levine, 2006, p. 178). Even the whole teen of affluence is squeezed into a partial model of success, and that model dominates American education.

"School culture is relatively consistent across the United States and reflects the individualistic values of the dominant, European American culture" (Rothstein-Fisch & Trumbull, 2008, p. xiii). That school culture, both toxic and beneficial to affluent teens, impacts educational policy, funding, structures, and rules for all children, most of whom grow up outside of the context of affluence. Individualized report cards, honor rolls, tracked classes, high-stakes testing, and a focus on lucrative careers and well-known colleges are dominant features found in secondary schools in most every community. Your school may not have an abundance of "rich kids" but you likely are engaged in procedures and expectations that mirror the high-pressured communities those kids live in. Most school communities have roots deep in the dominant culture that has never reflected the whole nation, or the whole teen—the whole teen comes into a *limited* dominant culture.

What is the experience of school for teens who do not come from, or identify with, the dominant culture? They may be like people speeding past the John Wayne billboard, unaware of his cultural significance. In the case of the billboard, their lives will probably not be impacted by what they could not make sense of in the few seconds the billboard was in view. For students, often with only a few seconds to make sense of their teacher's messages, the impact has much greater significance.

Consider a moment the way people learn (see Chapter 1, pages 9–11). Facts connect to previously known facts, skills link to previously known skills, and knowledge builds upon previous knowledge, growing neural networks of understanding. School department curricula depend on students in every room having a predictable neural network of shared understanding; for example, if you know who John Wayne is when your teacher references him as an example of grit, you are more likely to understand the next part of the lesson.

Conversely, a reason many students do not remember facts and skills is because those abilities never gained membership in a previously held neural network of understanding. The lessons the teachers share float away like helium balloons, unsecured to what is already known. Students from outside of the dominant culture are just as capable as any other students—but their neural networks are often constructed with experiences that are not leveraged for understanding. For instance, if a teacher wants to offer a model of grit, for some students a reference to the lifetime struggles and triumphs of Nelson Mandela, whose picture is tacked to their bedroom door, will trigger an understanding of grit in ways that a reference to the actor John Wayne can never match. Sharing a fund of facts and references with the teacher is one aspect of a student's chance for a successful learning experience.

The curriculum is not only facts; it includes the expectations for children to sit, to talk or not talk, share or not share, and compete or collaborate. Many students' strengths are marginalized when academics, codified by standardized curriculum, is seen as the "exclusive domain of the school" (Valenzuela, 1999, p. 73). Schools that impose a limited, monolithic culture of learning on a diverse population of students are less effective, and always have been.

It is helpful to remember that all students have strengths. The skills that comprise social competence, problem solving, autonomy, and a sense of the future are not all or nothing. These skills are in all of us, from "a process of human adaptation, encoded in the human species and applicable to development in both favorable and unfavorable environments" (Benard, 2004, p. 10). Some environments evoke previously held ideas and skills; other environments make no use of them.

One environmental factor that is essential to all whole teens is a safe, supportive classroom and school, filled with caring and trustworthy adults. "Authentic engagement begins with remembering that we are wired to connect with one another" (Hammond, 2014, p. 50). The human brain has evolved to learn best when not under threat, when it can marshal all of its neural networks and processes for concentration, reflection, and synthesis. We see this when students take their time on tasks, ask for support as they need it, and intentionally aim for mastery. That situation is first and foremost mediated by adults who explicitly care—who consistently reach out to students by doing more than presenting lessons and getting everyone to class on time. Adults make the school culture a safe place to learn through positive relationships.

When under threat, our brains are dominated by survival strategies; its other functions are temporarily suspended (Rosen & Hull, 2013). Putting that situation into the context of school, Zaretta Hammond (2014) notes, "When we look at the stress some students experience in the classroom because they belong to marginalized communities because of race, class, language, or gender, we have to understand their safety-threat detection system is already cued to be on the alert for social and psychological threats based on past experience" (p. 45). The "relaxed alertness" that is best for learning happens when who you are is affirmed, and when your concerns are at the center of the curriculum—when the schools' and teachers' expectations, and frames of reference, align with your personal and community understanding. Relaxed alertness is far less likely when your beliefs, experiences, and connections to the curriculum are marginalized.

There are a handful of ways students behave when they are at the margins of the school culture from the moment they come into the building. In classic psychological terms, people will fight, flee, or freeze. Schools have their own ways of provoking such short-term survival strategies. Some teens rebel, rather than abandon integral parts of their self-identity, as Angela Valenzuela notes in her study of Latino students. Some shut down, scared to take risks when they do not know who has their back, a reaction most apparent in the thousands of students who come to school with trauma histories (Cole et al., 2013). Some drop out; the dropout rates of students of color have always been higher than those of White students (National Center for Educational Statistics, 2015).

No single teacher or school can shift decades' long, institutional and intentional negligence, marginalization, and racism—but individual teachers, teams of teachers, and school communities can make a huge impact on the safety of all the teens who enter their building. Knowing students both as members of their self-identified cultures, and as individuals within that culture, creates bonds of trust that allow students to learn. Students' development of autonomy and sense of the future, traits that compel them to invest in their schoolwork and life work, is intrinsically linked to how they see their identities growing into young adulthood. Starting with an acknowledgement and affirmation of their identities—their individuality and their group membership—is an integral part of supporting whole teens.

Alfred W. Tatum (2005), as a young Black male, found hope through reading. He reminds us that adolescents need at least one institution that brings them hope—and that institution can be school. He is emphatic that Black students do not need Black teachers to succeed; they need teachers who can help them articulate their hopes and who respond to their needs. This is not true just for Black students sitting with White teachers; it is true for gay students with straight guidance counselors, for Native American teens with Jewish advisors, for rural and poor high school seniors asking their affluent principal for a meeting.

We encourage adults to identify their own cultures, a step that is essential in knowing how you may be connecting, or disconnecting, from your students. No single strategy speaks to every teen. Edward Fergus, Pedro Noguera, and Margary Martin (2015) found that a focus on African American history was not by itself enough to promote consistent engagement with Black teens.

While student engagement in academics is highly dependent on the trust and caring from reflective adults, that emotional foundation piece is not enough. As Tatum, Hammond, and Eric Jensen all point out, teachers need to know the vocabulary, skills, and knowledge their students have—all highly determined by a student's background—and not assume at any time that the biological arc of teenage development alone provides students with equal academic preparation.

There is one theme that emerges consistently as a link to relationships with struggling teens and their autonomy, problem solving, social competence, and sense of the future: acknowledging the historical and political conditions within which they are challenged to succeed. Teens have a growing capacity to analyze the impact of history and society's structures on their lives—they won't be shocked when schools acknowledge the challenges to our democracy that they have experienced in their communities. As Martin Haberman (1991) states, "Whenever students are involved with applying ideals such as fairness, equity, or justice to the world, it is likely that good teaching is going on" (p. 293).

Mary Helen Immordino-Yang (2016) writes of teaching her seventh-grade science class about the evolution of different skin colors—not knowing how powerfully this explanation of natural selection would subsequently influence her students' relationships and ethnic identities. Perhaps rhetorically she asks, "Why . . . did so many of my students suddenly seem to take a new interest in science?" (p. 8). She gave them information, and a safe place, to discuss an issue—understanding of race—that all of them needed a chance to discuss and understand.

The forces of history and society—the building blocks of the dominant culture—will look very different in the many contexts where teenagers are growing up. From his work supporting reading programs for Black adolescent males, Tatum (2005) urges teachers to craft lessons that address the turmoil in the lives of students; those lessons are catalysts for engagement and relationship building. When choosing text for reading, he urges schools to ask, "Will it move them to examine their in-school and out-of-school lives?" (p. 116).

This is not a special intervention for Black adolescent males; it is a critical concern when making choices in all curricula for all students whose lives are tumultuous. For instance, as far removed as they can be from the day-to-day oppression many other teens face, the tumult in the lives of affluent youth, who often struggle to meet the demands of their community, is appropriate and meaningful content for them—and may help them develop empathy for the intensity of other people's struggles. Teens from every community benefit from curriculum that brings their whole selves into school and helps them make sense of aspects of their identities. As Michael Sadowski (2008) writes, "if adolescents view themselves through societal prejudices about what it means to be African American or poor or gay or an immigrant, they may have difficulty realizing their full potential as learners" (p. 5).

That curriculum has another tremendous motivator—the potential for teenagers to take action. Students learn essential parts of autonomy-mastering institutions and systems, the contexts of the adult world. Fergus et al. (2015) note that leadership programs for teens predict academic success. They also write that students gave positive reports about teachers "who helped them develop their own sense of resiliency by supporting them in finding and shaping their voice as a member of society" (p. 126). Action, engagement, service to others, and a sense of purpose—integral traits of the whole teen.

Examine Your School's Culture

There are many ways to measure the effectiveness of a school. One way is how the students perform on standardized tests. By looking at how those test scores break down within subgroups of the student population, various stories emerge. For instance, the difference between how Black, Latino, and White children score on tests of basic skills nationwide has been a call to arms to close the "achievement gap." Important differences in the effectiveness of schools for vast numbers of children had for decades been obscured by noting only gross averages. Without data and disaggregating the data, it was possible to overlook significant institutional shortcomings.

Understanding how effective your school context is in supporting the whole student requires both data and identifying the ways subgroups of students emerge from the data. Regulations may require that you separate data by gender and race. What other subgroups exist in your school? You can start by looking at how all the subgroups measure in standardized test scores, graduation rates, dropout rates, discipline and suspension rates, and percentages of students in special education—all data that is generally made available to the public. That step begins the conversations about how well the school serves various subgroups.

You may also be well served by going beyond traditional measures of school effectiveness. Data are much more than standardized test scores. Jeffrey Benson (2015) says, "Schools are overflowing with information that can be creatively gathered and used to improve conditions. By gathering and analyzing data for themselves, school staff can cultivate a renewed sense of purpose, highlight meaningful accomplishments, and identify benchmarks around which to rally" (p. 16).

Many organizations, internet websites, and publications provide instruments called *school climate surveys*. These surveys can provide data about the experiences and perceptions of students, teachers, and parents through a variety of lenses: relationships, discipline procedures, access to resources, safety, personalization, mental health, and effectiveness of teaching styles. This is a huge swath of the whole teen's daily landscape.

Perceptions are data. That data too are then disaggregated. Wouldn't it be useful to know how different groups of students rate the fairness of the discipline procedures? Are there different perceptions about feeling safe or welcome? Do the options for school clubs and teams interest all groups equally? Does the school support with equal weight how all students connect the curriculum to their futures? The whole teen, as an individual and as a member of significant subgroups, exists in a school culture that can be analyzed. In Chapter 12, there is further discussion of such school climate surveys.

An entire school system can administer a climate survey, as can one school, grade level, or even a single teacher or advisor. As another source of information, many secondary school teachers start their year by asking students to fill out an informal survey, requesting information about how students learn best, and about what helps them feel safe in class. As you read through this book, you may find many elements of social competence, problem solving, autonomy, and a sense of future that compel you to collect data through your own classroom climate survey. You will discover many layers of experience within any dominant culture.

The Whole Teen Comes Out of a Context and Into Your School's Culture

The integral traits of the whole teen are part of the developmental characteristics of humans, in whatever context they grow up; evolution has wired us to experience predictable phases of development. But nobody experiences adolescence in exactly the same fashion, due to the variations in our packets of DNA and the ways each community and family provide experiences for their children. Teens are both unique and similar; our shared evolution as a species allows for variation within a set of genetic boundaries.

Preparing for the similarities and differences of whole teens can be daunting for those who work in secondary schools. Skillful teachers know that even their most effective approaches only apply to *most* teens in *most* settings *most* of the time.

The rest of this chapter explains particular contexts within the dominant culture, contexts that influence how many teens come into school. Those contexts require adults to keep in mind a handful of lenses on best practices. Those contexts are not absolute and unwavering; the practices are not absolute either. For instance, while all the children growing up in poverty do not exhibit the same challenges and opportunities for learning, they are *more likely* than other students to benefit from the best practices. Collectively, those practices would be beneficial for all teens; they may be critical for some.

We cannot address the needs of the innumerable diverse contexts within which children grow; we chose ones that reflect a significant population in terms of numbers, not importance—all students are important and must be understood to be taught. We urge you to look at your school's population of subgroups and contexts, disaggregate some data, and expand your repertoire. Work with more than the dominant culture's set of approaches; it will help you teach all kids better.

A note on trauma: Students with trauma histories come from every community. Bessel van der Kolk (2014) notes that children who are "oppositional, defensive, numbed out, or enraged" (p. 86)—behaviors that may lead to a variety of labels and diagnoses—are often victims of trauma. These students have diminished capacity for agency and self-regulation—not no capacity, but a diminished capacity that is often dependent on the stress in the current environment. As many have noted, the human brain cannot effectively learn when it is primarily focused on establishing safety, a primary need of traumatized students.

A lens on trauma should inform our understanding of all students who come from communities with extreme needs and pressures. However, it would be a disservice to label all of the experiences of students from outside the dominant culture as trauma—that would promote a deficit narrative of our nation's subgroups, overlooking the unique strengths and capacities in every community. All students who enter a school need to feel safe and supported in order to grow into their best possible selves. That is especially true for the students in the subgroups below.

Teens of Poverty

Poverty's impact on students is that they often grow up with an inordinate amount of chaos and uncertainty, to an even more extreme degree for students who are transient and homeless. The problem-solving strengths they have developed from their experiences of surviving on the economic margins are not the foundation of typical school functioning. Their sense of future and options may be very limited. Teens of poverty are at risk of being less prepared for the expectations of day-to-day school than economically stable teens.

Lens on Best Practices: **They come into school needing stability and opportunity.**

Structure long-term relationships:

- Loop grades
- Schedule year-long courses
- Maintain the same advisory group for more than a year
- Break large schools into houses with fewer administrators who get to know students better
- Ease access to health care professionals (nurse, counselors)

Maintain routines and traditions (and make sure the teens know their role in them):

- Say hello to every student every morning
- Classes, groups, advisories, teams, and clubs have rituals at the beginnings and ends
- Announce and practice ahead of time changes in schedules and routines

Provide explicit support to access school and community-based resources:

- Take field explorations—with abundant preparation and without fees; if an activity is part of the curriculum, all students need to be able to participate
- Schedule extra time with guidance staff
- Connect with internships, mentors, employment programs, community agencies
- If there are participation fees for clubs and athletic teams, have a fund so that all students can participate

Teens of Affluence

In a dominant culture often driven by materialism and celebrating the life of the rich, one might wonder how the whole affluent teen could have any developmental struggles worthy of our consideration. Levine (2006) even provocatively asks, "Don't kids from affluent families get all the help they need?" (p. 26). The answer is no. They often deal with continuous and extreme expectations for success, and are micromanaged to that end, diminishing their autonomy in crafting their own sense of self. With an emphasis on materialism, they can be pressured for outcomes, rather than effort, losing sight of the intrinsic value and engagement of learning. They can be overly sheltered from personal responsibility or awareness of and empathy for others. They may suffer in silence, as asking for help can be seen as shameful versus a social competence, until they suffer many mental health disorders and addictions well above the national averages.

Lens on Best Practices: **They come into school needing a stronger sense of self in relation to others.**

Support setting realistic standards of competence and excellence:

- Collaborate on developing rubrics of quality for their work
- Provide guidance on prioritizing their expectations
- Provide opportunities to assess strengths and needs without shame
- Encourage autonomy to choose available resources for support
- Include them in parent conferences
- Support them to manage their own schedules, assert their own needs, identify options, craft plans
- Encourage them to have intrinsic goals—their own aspirations; parents' aspirations might add more pressure than inspiration

Support a broad array of social competencies:

- Encourage identification of feelings—their own and others
- Give them practice asking for support; explore what they mean when they say, "I'm okay"
- Use such phrases as "Make space and take space" in groups for both saying their opinions and leaving room for others to do the same

- Diminish peer pressure to conform, using strategies such as the opinion continuum (explained in the Appendix)

- Emphasize qualities of character, and service to others, in history, science, arts, math, historical biographies and fiction, and in debriefing group work

- Incorporate service projects, alone or in groups, which include preparation and reflection

Teens of Color

The impact of racism is often amplified by multigenerational poverty. The historic and contemporary forces of racism are most easily identified by those who suffer from their impact—and can go unobserved by those who are not directly impacted. Some school staff may view many teens of color, who have diverse self-identities and cultures, as being the same, merely because they are not White. Lisa Delpit (1988), in her provocative and landmark work, "The Silenced Dialogue," points out the many implicit rules and expectations that are encoded in how White teachers talk to their students, often leaving Black children confused or underserved. Valenzuela writes that the dominant school curricula for Latino students "dismisses or derogates their language, culture, and community" (p. 62). The conditions of racism and poverty are often magnified for Native American students. They encounter their identities in the dominant school culture as idealized myths, or as a historical footnote to American progress, with few contemporary role models, and few who have walked in their shoes successfully in both the dominant and Native American cultures. Many children of color grow up in highly oral, traditional cultures where social competence is emphasized through collective effort; they may feel their strengths marginalized in classes that emphasize a lot of student silence and individualized success.

Lens on Best Practices: **They come into the school needing to see their identity as an essential part of the culture.**

Don't assume preexisting knowledge and acceptance of your social competence norms:

- Explain and practice following the implicit rules; for example, when a teacher's permission is needed or what hallway behavior is expected

- Develop class and group contracts

- Employ restorative justice options that address an array of cultures

- Given the current culture of high-stakes standardized testing, review the formats and strategies in the days leading up to the tests

- Support students, both formally and informally, to discuss and share their ideas and work

Explore and expand a sense of future:

- Make connections between the curriculum and their lives with project-based learning, trips, and class discussions

- Bring in potential role models and mentors

- Provide clearly defined steps to accessing guidance and community supports

Include issues of justice, equity, and racism into the curriculum:

- Reference the history of all the groups that comprised eras and movements, including in the sciences—no single story or perspective is adequate
- Use local and current issues that have meaning to students as content for all subjects
- Invite family members and community leaders to share their experiences and offer suggestions for making connections

Teens Who Are English Language Learners (ELLs)

Close to 10 percent of children in the United States are ELLs; in major cities they represent upward of 15 percent of the population. They encounter schools that support them in very different fashions, from mandatory full inclusion to newly established bilingual programs. Their classmates are rarely given directions on how to support them when they encounter language difficulties. The majority of their teachers speak only English, while many of their parents still struggle to understand that language. They may be expected to function independently when they cannot, and to negotiate the complex world of adolescent socializing that is bound up in the subtle meanings of words and phrases. They may come from countries where the facilities, rules, roles, and expectations for students are extremely different.

Lens on Best Practices: **They come into the school needing to feel robustly welcomed and supported.**

Promote autonomy for non-English speakers:

- Post welcome signs in multiple languages in the entrance hall
- Make copies of all school documents available in multiple languages in the main office
- Create a list of translators for all to access
- Allow ELL peers with more English proficiency to coach ELLs in both languages
- Don't interfere with ELLs using their primary language with siblings and peers
- Post the lunch menu in multiple languages

Promote social competence across language and culture:

- Learn to pronounce non-English names correctly
- Provide instruction in school procedures, such as filling in a schedule change request, getting the teacher's attention, or trying out for teams and plays
- Provide instruction and support for understanding the social expectations: how to get a teacher's attention in class, lunch time routines, accessing personal belongings, sharing homework
- Walk through the steps of how to get support for any needs that arise
- Explicitly invite more family members than just parents to school events, including "parent" conferences
- Survey ELLs to expand options for curriculum, celebrations, clubs, and other aspects of the school culture

Teens in Special Education

More than 10 percent of students have identified special needs, often impacting every developmental aspect of the evolving whole teen. The focus on identifying and measuring their disabilities in order to access services can eclipse the recognition of their many strengths. By the time they get to middle school and high school, many teens with special needs have experienced much failure; they may not see their own potential. Two very common impacts at the intersection of our dominant school culture and disabilities are disorganization and slow processing, undermining problem solving and autonomy.

Lens on Best Practices: **They come into school needing support to utilize their strengths.**

Provide tools and time to problem solve:

- Provide "think time" for every question and request to be processed and responded to

- Collaborate on planners that work for their idiosyncratic ways

- Provide direct guidance on keeping their materials organized and tools to self-assess how they are managing

- Carefully place them in pairs and groups so that their strengths are in play

Emphasize their autonomy:

- Don't rescue them quickly and don't let them drown—negotiate helping them with the next step, which students then explain in their own words

- Let them finish their own sentences

- Reference lists of emotions to support them identifying how they feel

- Support setting short-term goals, helping them have evidence of their own mastery and areas where they can choose to seek assistance

Teens in Rural Settings

Eleven million children attend rural schools in the United States. The strengths of rural life cannot always overcome the challenges. Rural teens have a higher rate of poverty than the rest of the nation, and only 27 percent of them go to college. To save money as populations have plateaued or declined, some rural districts consolidate, requiring students to ride buses great distances every day. Teacher retention is a problem, decreasing the school functioning as a stable community with a sense of purpose and undermining the long-term relationships with students that foster social competencies. The distance students must travel can decrease the options they have for after-school programs and expanding their career aspirations—a critical concern, as many of the jobs that provided their parents and grandparents with employment are no longer available. The isolation from a large community has a significant impact on atypical youth, who often do not have a cohort for safety and support. This can be especially critical for rural LGBTQ teens.

Lens on Best Practices: **They come into school needing connections to maintain motivation and expand possibilities.**

Focus on aspirations and career development:

- Discuss all the careers and jobs that impact the functioning of the school

- Invite alumni to discuss their career paths and struggles

- Provide internet programs to explore careers

- Provide information about geographically accessible government and training programs

- Assign career exploration projects within the standard curriculum

- Make connections with local businesses and the nearest colleges

- Develop pen pal relationships with teens from diverse communities

Maximize relationships with peers and adults:

- Loop with teachers for more than a year

- Keep advisories intact multiple years

- Provide core curriculum courses and electives that last the full year

- Structure and encourage the use of technology for school staff to have contact with families

- Build rituals and celebrations into the school day and schedule

- Provide supports and social connections for atypical teens struggling with isolation

Teens Who Identify as LGBTQ

Healthy whole teens develop a strong sense of self. That's a difficult task for students who do not align their sexual preference or gender identification within the norms of the dominant culture. LGBTQ students are often a targeted minority. As a group, they are subject to higher rates than their peers of being bullied, depression, and suicide. The threat of violence and isolation disrupts how brains function and develop, potentially minimizing the capacity to connect, problem solve, and to have a positive sense of the future. Not surprisingly, LGBTQ student absentee rates are high, diminishing the impact of all of their strengths and skills toward school success.

Lens on Best Practices: **They come into school needing to be safe.**

Incorporate the safety of LGBTQ students as an explicit part of the school structure:

- Provide full support for in-school groups such as a Gay-Straight Alliance

- Allow access to a single user bathroom, often found in the health office

- Interrupt joking, teasing, and bullying of LGBTQ youth in all aspects of the school

- Administrators and staff attend events that support LGBTQ students
- Protect privacy by not talking about the personal decisions of LGBTQ students
- Encourage the use of school counselors who are trained to support LGBTQ students
- Teach all students about LGBTQ issues; establish norms for asking and talking about LGBTQ issues; make clear what information is—and is not—for public discussion
- Talk directly and supportively with students who express discomfort with LGBTQ peers

Support autonomy and a positive sense of future:

- Include and identify prominent LGBTQ people in the curriculum
- Invite social justice organizations to make schoolwide and class presentations
- Provide information through advisories, the health office, and announcements of local social service providers focused on LGBTQ youth
- Encourage LGBTQ students to be part of school leadership groups

PART II

Everyday Practices

Learning a Skill Through Everyday Practices

What are the experiences that helped you learn to read, play basketball, or play a musical instrument? Most complex skills require exposure, introduction, demonstrations, practice, coaching, more practice, chances to apply the skill, more coaching, and yet more practice. Even then you're not done. There is no "done." The same is true for any self-management skill and interpersonal skill, skills that help the whole teen develop. If you really want to listen patiently, understand perspectives, collaborate on projects, and motivate yourself toward a goal you care about, you'll be practicing all your life. On the up side, every interaction and event is an opportunity for that practice.

Consider what it takes to learn to communicate effectively as a teenager in varied school settings. Students need to be introduced to each other, and specific lessons are important. The communication skills become internalized and effective, however, through exposure to people around them using good communication skills, coaching from caring adults, application to different settings and subject areas, and everyday practice.

By *everyday practices*, we are especially focused on teacher language, routines, rituals, and instructional moments. Everything that you say, your *teacher language*, is part of your teaching practice: how you greet students; how you ask about their thinking; how you give instructions, explanations, and feedback; how you talk with colleagues and parents. Your practices also include your regular *routines* for the classroom: how you develop class norms, how you run discussions, how you set up groups for collaborative work, how you assess students, how you ask them to self-assess, how you make decisions, how you arrange the room. Group *rituals* can include how your class opens and closes each day or week, how you introduce and conclude an academic unit, how students celebrate each other's accomplishments and cultures, how they remain sane during exam week. And, by *instructional moments* we mean all those opportunities to teach and reinforce, whether to individual students or the whole class, taught directly or infused into subject matter, the skills identified in Chapters 3 through 10.

The examples above of teacher language, routines, rituals, and instructional moments are partial to be sure. These and other practices are opportunities to help students learn to manage themselves and their academic studies, interact well with others, solve problems, and develop a sense of who they are. In the process, they'll be more prepared to learn the subject material you're responsible for, and the classroom will a better environment for students and for you.

You'll see brain research in Chapter 7 showing that it takes time to rewire the brain to establish new habits—this applies to students and to you. Therefore, we encourage you to focus on only a few new habits at a time. We've put a box (☐) next to each practice header so you can mark the ones that are priorities for you and your students. Score the practice on a 0–5 scale, or check (✓) the practices you already use and star (✱) the ones you need to try.

Also, talk with colleagues about which practices should be adopted, adapted, or reinforced in multiple classrooms, as well as with families who may want to establish practices at home.

Everyday Practices Are Part of the Fractal Nature of Schools

Organizational development expert Margaret Wheatley (1992) has applied the concept of fractals from geometry and nature to human organizations. "The very best organizations have a fractal quality to them. An observer of such an organization can tell what the organization's values and ways of doing business are by watching anyone, whether it be a production floor employee or a senior manager. There is a consistency and predictability to the quality of behavior. No matter where we look in these organizations, self-similarity is found in its people, in spite of the complex range of roles and levels" (p. 132).

In a fractal, the shape or values seen at one level of magnification are consistent at all levels. Consider a circle—every part of a given circle has the same curvature. Every piece of that particular circle—even the smallest microscopic section—has to curve in the same way to join all the others and form the circle.

Fractal organizations, more specifically, fractal schools, have core values and organizing principles demonstrated in all the ways that students experience that school. Let's say that collaboration and communication are among the school's core principles. Students should witness adults modeling those skills, and students should have many opportunities to practice them in class routines and analyze them in subject-area content. They should experience collaboration and communication in student–administrator committees and in student activities.

When school leaders intentionally shape their school culture and practices in a fractal-like way, the impact on students is multiplied, since they'll have recurring experiences of different applications and styles. With aspects of the school consistently representing the same characteristic, they reinforce each other; they're more sustainable. Leaders don't need to micromanage people about their actions because the path is clear; the whole community can creatively implement the same values in varied settings and varied ways. In those ways, fractal qualities, as core organizing principles, spread and permeate the school.

Fractal qualities are not necessarily positive. If your school has a pattern of isolation or blame, those might be the qualities that are expressed in self-similar ways throughout the school.

The emphases of this book, as you learned in Chapter 1, are experiences that support whole teens—fostering social competence, problem solving, opportunities for autonomy, and developing aspirations, best done within a context of caring adults, high expectations with high support, and meaningful participation. Chapters 3 through 10 offer innumerable everyday practices to make supporting the whole teen fractal qualities in your interactions with students. Part III, Chapters 11 to 14, extends the fractal metaphor to the larger school (and district) environment.

Putting Part II to Work

The practices in Part II are for classrooms, advisory groups, athletic teams, clubs, bands, and any other groups that students participate in. We most often use the words *teacher* and *class*. At times, we specifically mention advisory groups and advisors because those groups are often well suited for the practices needed to develop whole teens. In all cases, the purpose of the practices apply to all the ways the school staff interact with students, including secretaries, custodians, and cafeteria workers.

All chapters in Part II include readings to share with parents and guardians; most chapters include handouts and templates for students, and planning templates and other tools for teachers. For simplicity of numbering, we refer to all of these items as *Tools*. All of the tools are available at http://www.resources.corwin.com/PolinerBensonWholeTeen for easy printing and for adapting for students. Some students will write more, and more clearly, on lines, others without lines. You may have a particular question you want to add or delete for your class. The online student and teacher tools are modifiable.

We know that some teachers will read this book chapter by-chapter; others will identify an area of need or interest and go straight there. We put research where it is most relevant, close to its application, rather than in one research chapter.

The skills involved with social competence, problem solving, autonomy, and having a positive sense of the future are reinforced in large groups, small groups, and in one-to-one interactions. Some chapters, such as Chapters 3 and 4, are geared primarily to working with those skills in groups and classes, while other chapters, such as Chapters 9 and 10, are geared primarily toward supporting the growth of individuals. It is important that the culture of teaching the whole teen in school infuses all settings. For instance, socials skills need to be attuned to both private and public conversations, and a positive sense of the future is both a personal and a societal vision. Achievement is more than an individual's score on a test; it is measured in our collective enterprise of justice, equity, and safe communities. The group and individual practices in the book endlessly reinforce each other.

For those of you looking for skills to support executive functioning, they permeate Part II, such as Chapter 4's emphasis on decision making, Chapter 7's emphasis on learning to manage work, Chapters 8's emphasis on emotional self-regulation, and Chapter 10's emphasis on applying lessons in school to life. The capacity for executive functioning is shifting and expanding throughout adolescence and must be nurtured everywhere at every age.

Adolescents' shifting and expanding capacities are one of the biggest challenges their teachers face. Because students in Grade 6 and those in Grade 12 are very different from each other, we offer adaptations for different grade levels in key practices. We trust that teachers, forever creatively meeting the needs of their particular students, will adapt them further.

3

Connecting to
Adults and Peers,
Not Just to Academics

There *will* be a peer culture in class, in advisory, in clubs and teams, in the cafeteria, and across school. It might be a culture that demonstrates optimism or pessimism about the future, that offers a sense of community or feels alienating, that honors only academics or that recognizes many aspects of young people's lives. Having a culture is not an option. The options are: will you and other adults proactively and intentionally help to shape that culture, and if so, how? This chapter offers ways to start that process.

Another question to consider: why is having a culture that includes a sense of community and attachment so important?

Quite simply, students learn best when they are in a supportive community, whether it's their family, religious organization, sports team, or school. There are now many avenues of research pointing to the dramatic impact of one's sense of connection to school and sense of comfort in school on academic achievement. Some of this research comes from social neuroscience, a new field that has demonstrated the role of emotional states on learning states that are heavily impacted by relationships. "The brain is a social organ . . . the modern brain's primary environment is our matrix of social relationships. As a result, close supportive relationships stimulate positive emotions, neuroplasticity, and learning" (Cozolino, 2013). When we like and feel supported by the people we're with, we're more likely to show up to class, participate, take risks to learn, and be in a mental state that allows our brains to take in and remember new information.

Further, having a sense of attachment to adults and peers at school is a primary protective factor in the research on resiliency and in prevention of self-harm and violence

(Benard, 2004). A connection to our community (even to a single adult) can protect vulnerable students from their worst impulses—conversely, the lack of a connection to community can be debilitating to an individual and tragic for a school community. Too many of the school shootings in the last two decades underscore the risks we all take when teenagers feel isolated and alienated. Adolescence and anonymity are a dangerous combination.

Having a sense of community also supports adolescents' healthy identity development. Teens are looking outside their families for role models, ideas, and social connections—a natural developmental step. We can foster teenagers' sense of their place in the world through the act of having conversations with them, because even when we disagree with their perspectives, someone is paying attention to who they are right now, taking them seriously, hearing their views, asking questions, and offering other views. Being in conversation with students is not at all the same thing as endorsing their opinions or habits, but it does endorse that they are valued as whole people. As their views change over time, we bear witness to that growth and value their process of developing who they are.

Yet another avenue of research is listening to students themselves. Russell Quaglia crafted a survey, *My Voice*, to study students' perceptions of school. It is given nationwide, to over 50,000 students annually. Though results vary from school to school, he has found correlations that are very consistent. For example, regarding students' perception of whether teachers care about them, he finds "students who felt cared for as individuals by their teachers are . . . more likely to engage in pro-academic behaviors. Such students are three times more likely to report putting forth their best effort, working hard to reach their goals, and pushing themselves to do better academically than are peers who do not report believing teachers care" (Quaglia & Corso, 2014, p. 67).

Quaglia and Michael Corso (2014) dug beneath those data points: "On *My Voice* surveys, we have found a fairly big gap in perception when just 55% of students believe teachers care about them as individuals, while nearly all teachers say they care about students. When we discuss this gap with teachers, they relate how hard they work, how carefully they plan lessons, and how they correct tests and papers in a timely fashion. When we bring these efforts to the attention of students, they say that is a teacher's job, it's what they get paid to do, and that it doesn't mean teachers care" (p. 41).

Their research extends to peer relationships as well. Students who agree with the statement "I feel accepted for who I am at school" are "8 times more likely to believe they can be successful, . . . 4 times more likely to agree they enjoy participating in class, 4 times more likely to report they feel comfortable asking questions in class, . . . 3 times more likely to say they put forth their best effort," among other beneficial correlations (p. 59).

So, how can you show you care, and connect with students? How can you encourage them to connect with each other? And, what are ways to establish supportive practices and a sense of community? Here are some starting points with students; see Chapter 13 for building community and shaping the culture among the adults.

Practices That Build Sense of Connection

Connect first.

When some of us became teachers we were told, "Don't smile till December." The notion was that students wouldn't respect us (translaton: obey us), or take our subject and us seriously, if we were friendly. We had to be firm and stern to set the "right" tone. What awful advice that was! It's now common sense, backed up with social neuroscience and education research, that a bond with you, the teacher, matters enormously. Students who develop a sense of connection with the teacher are more likely to participate, ask questions, and accept feedback. Two stories of teachers demonstrate simple yet significant ways to initiate connecting with students.

- A high school English teacher used to have her students introduce themselves during the first class and name a summer activity. Since students' interests vary, as do their opportunities, needs, and family resources, the summer stories varied, sometimes highlighting social divisions. She tried a new approach: she introduced herself and described a summer experience that changed her perspective, then asked students to do the same—share their names and a summer experience that changed their perspective about something. She reported that the sharing was richer and that the class gelled as a group faster than in prior years. Her opening question was both safe and meaningful, especially to teens whose perspectives are indeed changing. They discovered they were all having perspective-stretching experiences—a common connection across the class and with the teacher on day one.

- A middle school social studies teacher offers another story, which involved changing the sequence in his opening days. In the past, he had his students take the U.S. citizenship test on the first day of school, when students got very few questions right, and take it again near the end of the year, when students got almost all the questions right, showing them how much they'd learned. He had done community-building activities and discussed class expectations on the second and third days of school. His new approach was to switch the sequence of days to focus on connecting first, and using the citizenship test to launch the academic focus on day three.

On the first day, thinking about how important it is for students to find a connection with teachers, he showed slides about himself. He mentioned every odd little bit about himself he could think of—places he'd lived or traveled to, his hobbies, his favorite color, music, movies, and other interests and experiences. He reported that many students soon found moments to tell him what they had in common with him, what connection they'd found. To discuss the expectations for the class on the second day, he asked students what they were looking forward to and what they were nervous about. He shared his hopes and concerns. He then shared letters from last year's students to his new students about the class. Finally, connected to his cluster's practice of having parents write information they want teachers to know—an experience he knew makes eighth graders antsy—he read a letter to students from his mother about what she thought students should know about their new teacher. Besides being funny, a good quality for day two, he made himself vulnerable, just as students would feel with parents writing about them. He had the best return rate on those letters from parents that he'd ever had.

Help teenagers learn names
(as you learn them as fast as possible too!).

Most of us behave differently, usually better, when we feel known instead of anonymous. We are more likely to be present, more likely to feel supported, and more likely to participate—all contributing to building a sense of community. These connections apply to the adult knowing students' names and students knowing each other's names.

Making the effort to learn names, and pronounce them correctly, welcomes and shows respect for everyone. It can be hard to learn students' names quickly in middle and high school, and hard for preteens and teens who are self-conscious or socially awkward, to ask for others' names. The first few days offer the least awkward opportunities since there's no expectation that anybody could possibly know everyone else's name already. A few name games can help enormously.

No matter what name game you use, emphasize that students are introducing themselves to the whole group, not just to you. One (perhaps surprising) tip is to *not* thank students for introducing themselves. If you thank students, you will likely see each subsequent student's eyes turn to you, not to the whole group. Thanking them reframes the task as accommodating your request, rather than learning to be a member of a group.

Note that one name exercise on the first day alone is not sufficient. Though almost everyone needs more than one chance to learn names, many people feel embarrassed that they didn't learn them all. As the teacher, advisor, coach, or band leader, you can break that ice with name games on the first two days and again a week later. Framing the exercise as "I'm still learning names; I'm sure I'm not the only one," diffuses self-consciousness and lets you share your thinking transparently, modeling your own attention to community building. Check again a couple weeks later, or on the first day of the next month. Here are three name games for classes, advisories, or other groups that support the whole teen.

- **Summer memory.** If you ask students to say their name and something they did over the summer, besides surfacing unequal family resources (not a community builder), you will often hear a blunt "nothing" because the question is vague. Instead, you can suggest three adjectives, such as tasty, healthy, or helpful; ask students to choose one of the adjectives, and say their name and what they did over the summer having to do with that adjective. Everyone has a choice; there's no wrong or shaming answer. Teachers or advisors can also add parameters, such as "occurring within 50 miles" or "involving no cost."

  Variations of this activity can foreshadow academics; for example, in science class, students can share a summer memory about an aspect of the natural world they noticed, or the tiniest object they held. Since not everyone will have read a book or watched the news, pick summer experiences that are the most inclusive of diverse teenagers' lives. Middle school teachers, who usually share the same group of students across a team or cluster, can plan together which summer memories they'll use so that students aren't repeating the same information in each class. The ritual for the students will become predictable, while the content of their answers will be unique each time.

  It's even better if you suggest three adjectives or topics and then ask students for other ideas, deciding together on which three to use—you've included them in designing their own get-to-know-you exercise. Fostering engagement starts with such tiny steps. Some interesting and occasionally funny descriptors have been: "sweaty," "involving water," "accomplished by myself," and "a new first." In all cases, you're the adult with the responsibility to coach and the power to veto terms that are unhelpful to group bonding. "Hmmm, since the point of a name game is to get to know each other in a constructive and inclusive way, what are descriptors we could use that are constructive and include everyone?" In this process, you've worked on social competence (learning names), problem solving (making a group decision that meets the group's needs), and autonomy (increasing sense of ownership and positive identity).

We sometimes bring three objects as options for a talking totem, an object we'll pass around the group as we introduce ourselves, such as a magic wand, a squishy foam brain, and a wooden fish, letting the group choose which one they'll use. In that case, they've contributed to two low-stress decisions before participating in even the first name game. Though it's a short and easy addition to the exercise, students who have a chance to shape an experience, even in these tiny ways, usually participate more actively and feel more ownership.

While you're working on learning names, listen for other information that tells you something about individuals or the group. You might hear about a summer experience that prompts you to ask a follow-up question in a quick chat or check-in (more on check-ins below), skills or experiences that connect to class material, or learn something about the group's sense of humor.

- **Name, sound, and motion.** A common name game is to introduce yourself with a descriptor that relates to you and starts with the same sound (even if it's a different letter) as your first name, as in "creative Carlos" or "swimming Cindy." Each person starts at the beginning of the circle and then adds themselves. "She is reading Renee, he's helpful Jose, and I'm biking Brian." The alliteration and repetition helps everyone learn names surprisingly quickly. You can ask everyone to add a motion that demonstrates the descriptor as well, with each person repeating the descriptor, motion, and name. In that case, lots of neural networks are involved—verbal, visual, and kinesthetic—engaging more parts of the brain and helping the new information (names) stick.

A few additional instructions are important for a whole teen approach:

- o Give a minute for pairs to help each other choose a descriptor; they'll learn about each other in the process.

- o Set this important rule: Everyone must pick a positive descriptor; these terms become lasting labels, so nobody is allowed to choose "stupid Sami," "nasty Nicole," or other negative descriptor.

- o Mention ahead of time that the point is to learn names and have fun, not to embarrass anybody. So, if someone hasn't remembered a name when it's their turn, anyone can give hints by acting out the descriptor, saying the first sound, or whispering the name.

- o Everyone will remember more names if they demonstrate the motions silently every round. Repetition supports remembering (for academic material too). And, when lots of people are doing the motions, the atmosphere is playful, and the speaker can feel less self-conscious.

Two weeks later, you can use the same name game, going backwards, or having everyone sit in a different order.

- **Yesterday's review.** A common practice is for a teacher to ask the class, "Who can tell us what we did yesterday?" The question is often answered by a few predictable students. Instead say, "Everyone, think for thirty seconds of something we did or said in class yesterday, and to practice names, say what happened and who did it. For example, 'I remember that Marie answered the question about Abraham Lincoln.'" This more inclusive practice allows the names to be reinforced, the class content to be reviewed, integrates many students into developing the class' shared memory, and underscores that the class community is built on students' attention to each other.

Build a ritual of saying "Hello."

We accomplish a lot when we say "hello." We are acknowledging another person's existence and individuality. We are welcoming them into our environment. We are conveying that we notice them and, if we smile, are glad they are present. For teens who feel anonymous and alienated, a simple greeting offers a connection. For students who feel herded from class to class, hearing lots of "Okay, move along!" and "Everybody, get to class, get to class!" a daily greeting can make the whole school culture feel more personal. A direct and personal hello from the teacher also activates the regions of the brain that are associated with that teacher, which includes academics—the greeting sparks the memories of the work you do together.

We have three stories to share. The first is from a very large high school with warm climate architecture—several buildings on a sprawling campus. When tardiness to class became a problem, the first impulse was to assume it related to distance between classes, which was indeed significant in many cases. But analyzing the data showed otherwise—distance was not a consistent factor. Administrators interviewed students, an important data-gathering tool. The responses included a consistent theme: "I get to Ms. Smith's class on time because she says hi every day. She'll notice if I'm not there." "Why bother rushing to Mr. Jones' class? He doesn't care; he doesn't even know who I am." Being known matters. This school initiated a practice of saying hello at the classroom door to every student, every class, every day. Tardiness declined dramatically. The staff could have imposed a new rule or more severe consequences for tardiness; they could have spent many days trying to adjust the schedule. None of those steps would have significantly impacted the problem and none had the extra benefits of involving student voice and improving school culture.

We told that story at a different high school at a Social-Emotional Learning (SEL) Committee meeting. A curious social studies teacher decided to see what difference saying hello might make in his suburban, high-achieving setting, even if only he were implementing it. He stood outside his door to say hello to his students, as well as any student who passed by, and to be a presence in the hallway, an environment students in many schools find hostile and chaotic. At the next SEL Committee meeting, he reported on his experiment. "After two weeks, students who had never been enrolled in my classes were stopping by to check in with me. A few even started visiting occasionally to talk. How hungry for connection are our students when all it takes to find a few new mentees is saying hello in the hall?!"

Our third story offers an adaptation. A teacher in an urban school stands in her doorway, able to see the hallway activity as well as monitor her class. As the students enter her room, they have the option to say hello, or hello with a high five, a fist bump, or a handshake. In that interaction, she is connecting with and taking a quick mood check of each of her students. Her ritual takes two seconds per student, but the value in each student getting a chance to say what they need, and having that need met immediately, is a powerful entry into her class. Through this social connection, they are more attuned to her academic agenda than had they simply trooped in on their own while she was erasing the board.

Have a regular practice of one-minute and two-minute check-ins with students.

In our work helping school staff develop their cultures of connection, we do an experiment. We ask them to post a list of all of their students on the wall if the enrollment is small, or a random 20 to 30 percent of students in each grade if enrollment is large. We give each teacher ten sticker dots to post next to the names of up to ten students they've spoken with over the last week. By "spoken with," we don't mean to ask or answer a question in class, or discuss an assignment, or even to say hello, but a real conversation. It doesn't have to have been a long conversation, maybe checking on their new after school job, or the club they joined, or their latest game or performance. It doesn't have to have been unrelated to academics. The conversation could be about the college they visited or the new homework habits they're trying to establish. How widely and equally spread out do you imagine those sticker dots would be in your school?

We've seen many schools, especially those without advisory groups, where the dots are not widely or evenly spread at all. You can establish a regular practice of short check-in conversations with students. In middle schools, where a team of teachers work together with a discrete number of students and have joint planning sessions, they can quickly identify which students need more connecting. High school teachers can make a chart to track their connections and conversations, intentionally chatting with each student at least monthly.

After asking the usual "How are you?" which too often is (or assumed to be) perfunctory, you might be surprised to hear how they respond to follow-up questions—as long as you're showing that you really want to hear what they have to say. "How is the fall going so far for you?" "What's something new for you lately?" "What was your most interesting class this week?" "What are you proud of this week?" Sometimes the quiet students are slipping under the radar, or the most challenging students are spoken to only for disciplinary reasons. Being aware of your own patterns of connection can have a profound impact on what is achieved in your classes.

As a reminder that all adults in school can check in with students, we share a story from a middle school assistant principal who on the first day of school, peeked into a class that was just getting settled and asked students to show a thumbs-up, thumbs-sideways, or thumbs-down about how their day was going so far. He saw lots of thumbs pointed up and sideways, but one was pointed down. He took note of the student and chatted with him later in the cafeteria. The student quickly opened up; he was having regular first day issues and didn't know anybody. The next day they chatted again. By October, the student had found friends and had become the assistant principal's loyal helper.

Celebrate accomplishments and each other.

Students are having birthdays, making teams, getting jobs and drivers' licenses, trying out new hairstyles and colors. What do they want to celebrate, and how should those celebrations happen? For example, in some of the schools we've worked with, advisory groups celebrate birthdays. They use one of their early fall advisory meetings to organize a calendar and decide how to deal with summer, weekend, and holiday birthdays. We've encouraged a couple of limiting parameters for the celebrations—"no cost, no calories"—which prompts a creative conversation about songs, games, poems, handmade cards, having special privileges, all sorts of ideas that vary group to group and across grades. Without the parameters, the conversation would likely have been much less resourceful or inspired, focusing on cakes, cupcakes, and flavors. Celebrations that are crafted by your students will feel more sincere and do more for developing the group's identity and sense of community. (Don't be surprised if students try bending rules—what about sugar-free soda or homemade cupcakes? It's an adolescent development task to test the rules, but you'll prompt more creative thinking and more understanding of rules in general by sticking to the *spirit* of the parameters, even if someone can identify a tricky loophole. The goal is community, not legalistic maneuvers.)

Build a sense of teamwork and teamwork skills.

Team-building activities give lots of opportunities to learn about each other's work styles, communication habits, participation and leadership preferences. They also give chances to build skills in all those areas. (See Chapter 5 for more tools and tips for getting into groups and debriefing teamwork.) There are many resources available with challenge activities, group problems, and trust-building exercises. (Try *Great Group Games* by Susan Ragsdale and Ann Saylor.) Consider these key practices:

- **Build activities incrementally from low challenge to greater challenge, from short and puzzling to longer and complicated.** Set the group up for success in their first experience, not with an activity that's so easy it's silly, but with one that takes a short time, is fun, with only a few group decisions involved.

- **Observe carefully** as groups work on their tasks. You'll see actions and interactions to ask about during the debriefing time. "Gina's group, you looked like you had different ideas about how to get started; how did you resolve that?" You might also see behavior that prompts you to have some private conversations, for example, with a student who didn't figure out how to have his idea heard or a student who took over her group.

- **Be sure to save time to debrief** to foster reflection and learning, and to help the group grow as a group. A minimalist debriefing is to ask for two ways the group worked well together and one suggestion for working more effectively next time. Such a routine helps to build the habit and skill for reflecting on and adjusting behavior. These questions will prepare the group for when they are involved in traditional academic tasks. If you've observed the groups closely, you'll have more questions to ask. Note that sometimes debriefing is needed to diffuse challenging emotions or resolve tension.

- **Different kinds of team-building activities will bring out different skills**— verbal, spatial, artistic, musical, analytical—so use varied activities. Include questions in the debriefing that prompt some insights. "Which activities were inside/outside your comfort zone?" "Does working on a task outside your comfort zone change how you participate in the group—for better or worse?" "How did you act when you were out of your comfort zone and feeling confused or not confident?" "When you were in your comfort zone working on a problem that's fun and easy for you, but not for your partners, what was hard or fun or interesting about the experience together?"

- **Encourage students to play different roles**—organizer, encourager, facilitator, notetaker, whatever roles are needed for different tasks.

Build community with your students and advisees through group rituals.

Rituals bring communities together; rituals bring families together; rituals bring whole cultures together, helping them to have an identity and to endure over time. Rituals build community in classes and advisories as well. They are shared and predictable experiences because everyone knows what to expect and how to participate. Since they are recurring experiences, with support, you can involve your students in shaping and running the rituals.

- **Classes can create a ritual for the beginning and end of a unit.** Mariale Hardiman (2012) suggests starting a unit with a map of major concepts, activities and assessments, which is filled in over the course of the unit. Hardiman emphasizes the importance of mapping to help students' brains connect new information with concepts learned already. Such a practice builds cohesion in the classroom community as well.

  Besides the formal assessments at the end of a unit, a class can have their own closure process—naming the most important new understandings, their favorite character or aspect of the unit, the most interesting assignment, and the skills they think will be useful in the future.

- **Classes can have their own soundtracks.** Students can create playlists of music for when they enter class (which will encourage prompt attendance), for recurring activities (instrumental music for writing), and for the end of the lesson. Soundtracks can help students introduce each other to songs from various cultures, and in that way introduce themselves to each other.

- **Classes can have a quick go-round check-in every Monday.** "Name one thing you did this weekend that was new"—or healthy, or something you read, or something you listened to. The question can connect to academic content, sharing in the go-round interesting data they heard in the news, or an event, invention, or story. In a world language class, ask students to respond in another language. Besides building community, this practice can help young people learn about the larger world and even possible careers. If you have concerns about time for this task, have a few students share each Monday, so everyone has a turn at least once a month, and no single class session bears the impact of everyone needing time to share. What is important is the consistency of the ritual. Teachers who have begun Monday go-rounds have told us they knew this year's students better by October than they knew last year's students by June.

- **In advisory, you can have a jar, hat, basket, or book of questions** that advisees have written and/or questions from various publishers. (We like Mary Alice Ackerman's *Conversations on the Go* and the "In a Jar" questions from Free Spirit Publishing.) The advisor can choose a question and choose a format, such as talking in pairs for two minutes. At the end, ask advisees how the two-minute length worked for them, and if they want to use pairs again next time, or maybe a go-round or an opinion continuum (both formats are explained in the Appendix).

The next time, perhaps hold five question cards and have someone pick one. After two or three experiences, ask if advisees are ready to be in charge of this ritual (maybe in pairs) and sign them up on a calendar. Discuss carefully what steps are involved—choosing a question ahead of time with the group's readiness and interest in mind, choosing a format, facilitating. Support advisees to make sure they're ready their first time they facilitate.

- **Use one-minute appreciation rituals** to end class, or after a meaningful discussion or presentation: "The floor is open to thank anyone who helped you have a good class—maybe someone added an idea to our discussion that sparked your thinking, gave you a good suggestion, role-modeled doing hard work, made us laugh, or who made you smile and feel more comfortable being here."

- **Establish community rituals.** Once advisory groups have built familiarity, established rituals for birthdays, learned to participate effectively in conversations (sharing time, listening openly, offering nonjudgmental feedback), a number of groups use a regular ritual of asking "What's a high or a low in your life lately?" The highs and lows can be academic, cocurricular, or out of school. The groups celebrate the highs and problem-solve the lows, offering encouragement, suggestions, a study buddy, or other support. The advisor is always present, listening for opportunities to coach and for referral needs, but the ritual becomes so well established that advisees can facilitate. This practice is especially suited for schools with mixed-grade advisories, since most of the group can model the ritual for the few new members, and older students often have more experiences and resources to share. It's also well suited to schools in which the advisor loops with the group multiple years, since the longevity of the relationship builds trust and real understanding. (Note that these groups start with lots of low-stress conversations about interesting and useful topics to launch their culture of conversation and build up to more challenging topics and meaningful rituals.)

Create peer support routines and rituals.

Building community doesn't end in September. Learning names and getting to know each other is just the beginning of a strong support system. The early activities establish the platform so that everyone in the community feels like they belong and wants to support each other through whatever comes up. There are a lot of benchmarks on the way to finishing middle school or high school that students can commit to and support each other through—service projects, tests, the transition from eighth to ninth grade, tenth-grade portfolios, science exhibitions, standardized tests, college application season. Prior to the events or projects, teachers can scaffold students to do any of the following:

- **Study sessions**, comparing notes, identifying main ideas and supporting evidence

- **Presentation rehearsals** with one peer, then a larger group, each time hearing three things that worked well in the presentation and two suggestions for improvement (Tool 6-2)

- **Feedback trios** with regular routines, such as self-assessment first, then positive comments about what worked well as well as suggestions from one's feedback partners, ending with identifying the two most important things to add, change, edit, or polish (Tool 6-3)

- **Committing to graduating together far in advance:** We worked with a large urban school with single-grade advisory groups that stay together all four years, with the same advisor throughout. After a few months of settling-in tasks with her ninth graders (learning their way around the building, learning to keep track of homework, etc.), an advisor had them look up their future graduation date. She then had them make their invitation lists—who did they want witnessing their graduation? Who would be impressed and excited for them? They designed the invitation, and talked and wrote about what they wanted to be known for at graduation. They even planned their group's graduation party, what food they would serve, what clothes they would wear. Additionally, they talked about getting there together and supporting each other along the way. The advisor referred to that commitment when the group had a good term, when someone needed academic encouragement, and when someone felt like quitting. Whether through advisory or other means, building community is especially powerful when students and a teacher or advisor stay together multiple years, rather than the traditional ten months (see Chapter 12 for more on how schools can structure longer relationships).

Throughout the year, welcome new students and advisory group members.

Some schools enroll only a few new students during the year; others see new students arriving most weeks. Either way, it's important to help new students feel welcome and acclimated. Minimally, most teachers will announce the new student's name to the class. However, this doesn't help the new student learn others' names, or in any significant way be brought into the culture of the community. Instead, after introducing the new student, use a new name game, maybe one that involves learning just a few names per day. For example, have everyone line up by their birthdays and meet their birthday-month mates. Or, group by favorite pizza toppings and meet classmates with similar tastes. Also, use small groups during class, reminding everyone to introduce themselves before plunging into their tasks.

You can use classes, advisory groups, student government, or school spirit clubs to make plans for new students so that young people take responsibility for the community and practice social skills and leadership skills. What does a new student need to know? What would help them feel welcome, not only in class or advisory, but in the cafeteria, at games, or other parts of school life? Students can brainstorm, create a plan, and gather materials.

The absence of an established community welcoming ritual is a bitter memory to this day for one of the authors, who moved in tenth grade from a large urban school system to a small suburban town, one in which all the students had been together for their entire school careers. Without anyone offering a welcome and orientation, *every* experience, from eating lunch to finding classes and materials to signing up for teams, required initiating a conversation with a stranger, and then piecing together random bits of information about how the school operated. Meeting peers took yet more initiative. The energy and attention needed to adjust and fit in was energy and attention that could have gone to academics.

Encourage participation in clubs, sports, and the arts, and encourage appreciation of varied activities and accomplishments.

The development of interests, risk-taking, commitment, and confidence are all part of promoting grit, persistence, and optimism for academics, friendships, and life goals.

These attributes are enhanced exponentially by participation in school groups and subcultures. Students deepen their sense of who they are as they choose activities that are not required; practice social skills in managing relationships that are not bounded by classroom requirements; engage problem-solving skills through working on projects and teams; and establish their sense of purpose and future by identifying and developing their passions.

Some students will find their way to clubs, teams, and performing arts without your help. Others may not. We have worked with schools with varied approaches to encourage participation in cocurricular activities:

- Having team, club, and band members make two-minute videos to show to the youngest grade, or for the high school to show to the rising eighth graders

- Having team, club, and band members rotate through advisories and homerooms to encourage participation and answer questions

- Organizing an activities fair so all students can see what's happening

- Making surveys to get student input on teams and clubs, or listening for students' interests and requests, and supporting students to create new activities

- Having an advisory group, school club, or class attend a game or performance together to support a group member

- Mentioning in class that you're going to the game or play, and invite students to attend and sit with you.

In any of these experiences, ask students to answer such questions as

? Which activity do you already know how to do or play?

? Which activity have you never tried?

? Which activity has the toughest schedule? The easiest schedule?

? Which activity has the most complicated equipment? The equipment you like the best?

? Which activity connects to something you might want to do after high school?

In whatever ways activities are publicized, chat with students about their choices. For example, it can help to encourage students to take a risk and try something new for a few months, or try it with a friend. For students who seem to try everything and stick with nothing, help them find the best fit, then over time check in with them to help them problem-solve and sustain participation. For students who are involved in numerous activities to pad their college applications, dissuade them of that notion. Colleges are more interested in people with activities that show passion, skill, and perseverance than widespread dabbling. When students engage deeply in activities, they develop important attributes.

Discussion Options for Faculty

- Which practices in this chapter seem especially important for your students?

- What insights do Quaglia and Corso's data points (on page 38) offer you?

- How do your opening days support the goal of connecting with students? What could be added or prioritized to foster a sense of connection?

- What name games do you use? Make a collection; teachers are bound to know many. Use one or more with faculty and staff.

- What other kinds of techniques do you use to remember names quickly?

- What do your hallways sound like and feel like to students? Observe for a few days or interview students to learn about the community culture.

- In a faculty meeting or a cluster/team meeting, do the exercise with lists of students' names on the walls. Give each teacher and administrator ten sticker dots to place next to the names of students they've had a conversation with that wasn't specifically about classwork or discipline. What are the patterns of sticker dots showing? What can you do about any gaps?

- What teamwork activities are you using? What community-building rituals are already established? What can you add?

- In order for students to support each other academically, do they know what rituals and practices they can implement? Do they know *how* to implement them? Who in the faculty has a practice for students to support each other? What else can you do to help students launch supportive routines and groups?

- What are the current ways you support students who enroll throughout the year? What can you do to bolster that process?

- How do students learn about cocurricular activities? Think about students who span the spectrum from involved in none to involved in everything. Where are the opportunities to coach these students?

Practices at Home

Routines and rituals are important, perhaps more so for teenagers in the family. So much is changing for teens, from interests to friendships to career goals to their understanding of the world of politics and power. Some predictable routines can help them have a stable base through all of these changes, and keep all of you talking with each other. Think of rituals as involving relationships and emotions—morning greetings and evening check-ins, holiday and birthday celebrations, Sunday pancakes, Friday movie and popcorn—and routines as helping to sustain a regular and healthy rhythm—where to keep things or do homework, having chores to do; even hygiene practices are important routines.

Teens often ask to be given significant freedom, to be released from family rituals. Consider this research from behavioral scientist Michael Norton, who has focused on rituals and their impact on grief, the experience of consuming food, their use in the workplace, and their role in families. In an interview, he explained that having holiday rituals is a predictor of families getting together for holidays and for enjoying the day—even for family members who don't like the ritual (Boston Public Radio, 2015). While you can offer freedom around the edges, rituals will likely help teens to stay involved in the core of family. Their friendship circles offer them many benefits, but kids are not best at raising kids—families are.

"For all health-risk behaviors across all socioeconomic levels, family structures, and races and ethnicities, when teens feel connected to their families," they have lower rates of substance abuse, violence, pregnancy, and suicide (Benard & Marshall, 2001, p. 2). All of our recommendations rest on the foundation of maintaining a dialogue—some predictable rituals and routines will help.

We offer an inspiring example:

> A mom we know had the ritual of saying, "Good night. I love you," to her daughter from the time her daughter was able to speak, and her daughter said the same words back to her. But when her daughter became thirteen, she stopped consistently saying her part of the ritual; she might say just, "Good night" or "Thanks, mom" or "Okay, you too" or even just "Okay." The mom never stopped saying her own part of the ritual. When her daughter became sixteen, she started again to repeat back to her mom the entire phrase.

Keep a ritual of eating meals together, or at least some predictable meals every week—weekend breakfasts, Monday and Friday dinners—even if your teens try to skip dinner, or to be on the phone or online when the family is eating. As teens join teams or get jobs, it can be difficult to find timing that works; it is important nonetheless. Safeguard these rituals as places and times for talking to and looking at each other—electronic devices are not on or near the table and are not competing for your attention, or their attention.

If teens push against participating in family rituals, use the opportunity to get their input. Teenagers' need for autonomy means they will benefit from, and might welcome, being involved in decision-making and designing family rituals. They can be important contributors to holding the family together if they know their suggestions will be considered and integrated into the existing rituals and traditions.

Celebrate accomplishments and milestones. Even teens who insist they're too old for a birthday party at home need to feel attention.

Give them a little time to settle into the home before talking. Teenage moodiness is a struggle for them as well as for you; many teenagers manage their way through the innumerable social interactions of the school day and are exhausted when they get home. We are not saying to tip-toe around them; only to be patient.

Use routines and rituals to engage your teens in conversation. It can be a more comfortable and less self-conscious experience for teens to talk with you while taking a walk, watching a game, while shuttling them to school or an activity, or while raking leaves or chopping vegetables. It's less intense than a face-to-face discussion.

Have a regular routine of talking about school. It may be part of your dinner ritual, with you sharing something about your day too. You may give your teenagers the option to pick a time later in the evening. They may choose to talk immediately one day, and the next day completely forget that there was a plan. Your interest and the expectation to communicate is never in question; negotiating the time and place to do so is often what the teenager needs in order to feel respected and willing to share.

Ask questions that can't be answered "yes" or "no" and that find a balance between being too vague and too picky or prying. The question, "How was school today?" is often too vague—and the teenage brain is often far too disorganized—to prompt a rich response. Try these questions about the school day, or parallel questions about non-academic parts of their lives.

- What's one good thing that happened today?
- What's your favorite class? What's good about it?
- What's a problem you solved on your own lately?
- Is there a teacher who really seems to get who you are? Tell me more about him or her.
- What is happening in school that might really help you when you are older?

Earlier in this chapter, we mentioned the small book of questions, *Conversations on the Go*, for use in schools. The questions could prompt conversations in families as well. Here are a few examples:

- What is one of the best talks you remember having with a family member?
- What makes a parent "cool"?
- If you could take lessons in anything, what would you learn?
- If there was one school year you would *never* do again, which one would it be? Why?
- Have you changed as a person during this past year? How and why?

One last note: your desire to maintain family traditions and rituals, and the teenage desire to find their own, merely makes all of you fairly typical, and we hope you find comfort in that fact.

4

Creating a Culture
of Shared Responsibility,
Not Just Obeying

Middle and high school students can develop responsibility by consistently being given support and practice to help shape the culture of their classes and schools. Giving teens responsibility and a voice in schools is not all or nothing; there are innumerable opportunities in the everyday practices of teaching and learning that allow students to grow into responsible young adults. Robert Brooks and Sam Goldstein (2001) say it well: we minimize power struggles with students when they feel a sense of empowerment. When we don't channel their responsibility, we marginalize many students into passivity, or into unproductive rebellion. Fortunately, the opportunities to scaffold student responsibilities are as rich, deep, and unfolding as the curriculum in any subject area.

Consistently giving teens well-structured responsibilities teaches them to work with others: they solve problems, accept differences, learn their own strengths and beliefs, manage conflicts, and build relationships that can sustain them for years to come. Bonnie Benard's (2004) summary of research in this area is clear: "Students who experienced autonomy-supportive school environments are more likely to be curious, mastery-oriented, problem solvers, intrinsically motivated, and committed to democratic values" (p. 79).

Unfortunately, what students commonly experience as their role in helping the school run smoothly is a passive one—skimming through the student handbook, and then obeying a set of rules and accepting consequences. Of course, the adults must be clear about absolutes that concern safety and legal responsibilities—expectations that the vast majority of students have no trouble accepting. But what other opportunities are there for students to share in building the culture of responsibility? How can the culture of responsibility in schools and classrooms prepare teenagers for life in a democracy that asks so much more than obedience to laws?

We have seen teenagers develop shared responsibilities for the everyday practices that make their school and classes function. Throughout this book, almost all the practices have as a foundation the belief that a teenager can work with peers and adults to problem-solve the concerns that arise in schools, and that those teens find deep personal meaning in their efforts. Schoolwork of this nature actively shapes a teen's brain toward social responsibility and social connections, foundation stones for almost all applications of academic skills.

When Hudson, Massachusetts, students were systemically given support to become responsible for their learning, Douglas Reeves (2008) wrote: "Hudson has made significant gains in every area of achievement in the past seven years. In my interviews with students, teachers, and leaders, the level of commitment, engagement, and passion was among the highest I have seen" (p. 84).

The focus of this chapter is less on the *individual* teen developing skills; instead the attention is focused on the general structures, routines, practices, and norms that students can help shape to make a predictable culture for everyone. For instance, in Chapter 5 you will read about ways students can give each other feedback when they are on collaborative work teams; this chapter discusses how the class as a whole speaks with each other, so when students work within peer groups, there is already a norm of giving feedback. In Chapter 10, individual students are supported in accessing their own community-based resources; this chapter discusses how to work with students to make their classroom resources accessible to all.

When teenagers have a voice in setting expectations, the entire school thrives. This chapter offers practices so that more students participate through their voices and actions in building and sustaining a culture of shared responsibility.

Practices That Launch the Culture of Shared Responsibility

Teach and use decision-making and problem-solving processes.

Teachers make dozens of decisions in every class, every day. What should be on the walls? Will a discussion be in pairs or the whole class? Will a presentation require the seats to be in a circle or rows? Some of those decisions need to be made by the teacher, based on her experience, awareness of meeting different students' needs, and knowledge of the standards to be met. Any other decisions that teachers can share with teenagers enhances their capacity to choose wisely, not impulsively. Not only do the students get more practice at problem solving, they develop more of a sense of ownership of the class and interdependence with the teacher and peers.

- **Identify opportunities for students to share in decision making.** One way to give voice to teenagers' growing capacity to take responsibility is for the adults to choose from a continuum of options (Senge, 1994) explained below. This is a wonderful tool for letting teenagers know that there are very often clear avenues for them to exert their increasing ability to influence their environment. It is not all or nothing when it comes to adult authority and expectations. Fully explain these options to the students. Once they are familiar with the options, start discussions by informing the teenagers what level of their input is requested, such as, "Students, I am in *consult* mode right now." With support to effectively provide their ideas, teenagers can channel their input into useful responses.

You will see this continuum in Chapter 13 applied to faculty culture.

Tell-to-Collaborate Continuum

Tell

The teacher makes the decision and tells the teenagers, which sometimes is, or at least sounds like, a command. A *tell* type of decision is often uncomplicated, requiring only compliance. The teacher seeks no input, and teenagers who raise concerns are at risk of being seen as disrespectful, irresponsible, or reflexively uncooperative.

Examples: The fire drill protocol allows for no discussion of alternative routes; standardized test protocols must be followed exactly as written.

Sell

The teacher makes a decision and is selling, hoping the teenagers will buy in. The *sell* includes how the decision fits with the goals and values of the school or how it will affect the students. It is a preemptive action to the customary, "Why are we doing this?" The teacher presents the benefits of the decision. When using *sell* mode, the teacher continues to own the entire process and is counting on students' understanding of the situation, or their trust in the teacher as an effective leader, to support their acceptance and follow through.

Examples: The teacher enthusiastically predicts how much can be learned from reading Shakespeare, given many students' fears of that challenge; the teacher schedules a review session before a big exam and explains how useful it will be.

Test

The teacher assumes that he knows enough to put a plan into action—to give it a test run. The teacher also knows that getting feedback from the teens as the plan proceeds will support its effectiveness. In *test* mode, the teacher communicates, "I've made this plan for us to use for one month (or some other time frame). I need your feedback along the way to see if it is a good plan." The teacher continues to own the process, while providing a way for the teenagers to exert their influence.

Examples: The teacher develops a new way for students to share their essays; students are given the option of annotating a single math problem to demonstrate understanding instead of completing five similar problems; the class tries a new routine of taking a one-minute break midway through the class to stretch and revive energy.

Consult

Teenagers don't always want to be in charge; they do want to know that their feelings and ideas are respected. In *consult* mode, the teacher communicates, "I have to make a decision about *X*. To make a good decision, I need and want your input." This is one of the most powerful opportunities on a day-to-day basis for teenagers to learn how to contribute to their community. They can brainstorm ideas and take the risk of suggesting an atypical point of view, knowing that the teacher will ultimately be responsible for sifting through their input before making the final decision. When the teacher presents her plan, she can say, "Thanks for all the input yesterday. A handful of you will definitely see how your ideas helped to shape this plan." Even when the teacher hears an idea that simply cannot be part of the final plan, she can say to that student, "There was no way this time to incorporate your input, but it was really interesting. Keep up your contributions."

Examples: The teacher wants to decide whether the students listen to each other best with their chairs in a circle or in rows, and asks for their opinions; the teacher is putting together a final test and seeks ideas about the types of challenges the students would want to tackle on the exam; the teacher wants input on how the order of events in the coming week's plans will make most sense to the students.

Collaborate

The teacher is no longer the final decision maker; instead he supports the students in owning the process and the outcomes. The teacher works with the group to gather input, plan, make the decision, and implement the plan. The teacher may offer this option to a self-selecting group of students, allowing those who have the most investment to be empowered to lead the process. This option builds decisions that are implemented with creativity, complexity, and subtlety by each person. The teacher may need to take a very active role in organizing the conversation and in supporting the students to listen to each other.

Examples: The teacher is helping the students develop and publish a yearbook; the class is responsible for the schedule of events on the day of a field exploration; the students arrange the room and the presentations for parent night; the students and teacher codevelop norms for discussions, for collaborative work, or for presentation feedback.

- **Teach students to know their *interests*, and not get stuck in *positions*.** Your interests are what you really need taken care of by rules, procedures, and decisions; identify your interests before brainstorming actions. For instance, in one of the activities below, we recommend that students be part of setting up the classroom furniture. Start the class decision making with the question, "What are our most important interests?" List them on the board. The students may realize many of the following interests or needs: ease of movement through the room, both independent and collaborative work, increased eye contact during interactions, surfaces needed for materials, access to class resources, maximizing light, minimizing noise. Once the students have articulated all the interests, decisions become a collaborative effort, sifting through all their suggestions to meet their interests.

What often gets in the way of making decisions based on shared interests is when people cling to a position, which is a single strategy or unilateral solution. Many times, we've heard classes become dominated by two students arguing for their own solutions. For instance, if the class as a whole has not yet identified all their interests in setting up the desks, one student might suggest desks in rows, and another might immediately counter with desks in clusters. The two argue back and forth, without the class knowing exactly what they want to accomplish with their decisions, or how to find common ground or alternatives. The interests become secondary to whose position would win. Good decision-making is grounded in meeting interests, not positions.

The notion of positions and interests can become a daily part of adult relationships with students, helping them grow into young adulthood. A teacher we've worked with in a middle school had taught his students about positions and interests. One day, as his students were filing into class, he was very busy organizing materials. A student asked him to write a pass so she could go to the nurse for a scheduled medication. Without looking up, he said, "I can't do anything for you now. You have to wait." His student, in her most wise teenage voice said, "I see you have an interest to be ready for class. Would it meet your interest if I wrote out the entire pass and you just had to sign it?" "Yes!" he said, "that will work." And he had his first good laugh of the day.

Knowing the difference between a position and an interest can allow students to generate multiple solutions for a shared problem. As you go through all the opportunities for students to take on responsibilities in this chapter and the entire book, ask them, "What are our most important interests?"

Here are two examples of schools we've worked with where an interest-based conversation supported everyone's efforts:

o Rules are positions; why the rules are in place are interests. When we want adolescents (who developmentally need to be increasingly in charge of themselves) to follow rules, we should share the interests. Staff in a high school were unhappy with the amount of time they were spending struggling with students as they enforced a dress code, a series of specific rules about lengths of skirts and pants, and depths of neck lines. From a conversation in a staff meeting, the adult interest in a dress code emerged: to have a calm learning environment in which they did not get into struggles about clothing—quite the opposite of what their rule provoked! The staff brought their interests to the school's student council, which not surprisingly shared the same interest. The students also added their interest of not being publicly shamed. The school developed, instead of a rigid code (they did retain non-negotiable dress rules about safety), a protocol of having counselors talk one-to-one with students whose way of dressing was interfering with their learning. This outcome supported the interest of student reflection, problem solving, and connecting to future goals.

o "Do your homework" is a position. What are the interests? We worked with a school where math homework completion was far too rare. We interviewed teachers and students about what they thought the interest of homework was. Some teachers said they assigned homework to introduce a concept; others said it was for practice; others said it was diagnostic so they could see who was struggling with which skills. Students, in contrast, were certain homework was either busy work or punishment, since they often felt unprepared to do it successfully, or because they didn't get prompt feedback. The faculty realized they needed to explain their interests ("The work you do tonight will help me know what to do to get you ready for the exam"; "This task is simply to give you more repetition so you can do this work automatically.") Instead of guessing what the teachers were hoping to see, the students could focus on the important interests that the teachers hoped the task would realize. And, after thinking about interests, the teachers altered some of their assignments; for example, if assessing progress and giving feedback to all was an interest on a specific day, they needed to assign five problems, not twenty.

Communicating about interests rather than positions is a key interpersonal skill, in addition to helping groups function well. See Chapter 5, page 75, for an application to collaborative working groups and Chapter 8, page 148, for an application to sharing perspectives. See more on this topic in Chapter 11 for school leaders and in Chapter 13 for faculty culture. We are indebted to, and highly recommend, the seminal work on this topic, *Getting to Yes* by Roger Fischer, William Ury, and Bruce Patton (1991).

- **Recognize and leverage class and group assets.** Before jumping into problem solving and decision making, start with an appreciation of the group's strengths and past successes. This approach is similar to how teachers begin a new unit of study: they review the skills students have previously demonstrated, activating the parts of their brains that have competency and motivation to achieve—as opposed to deflating their spirits by reminding them of what they can't do and what they have failed to do. When you start with an appreciation of abilities, you access those abilities for the task at hand.

Unfortunately, people often start problem solving by focusing on a problem. While that approach seems logical, it is often deflating to start with what's *wrong,* and can lead to unproductive accusations and an erosion of group cohesion when it is most needed. Instead of "I'm hearing complaints about working in lab groups—people not pulling their weight, having arguments. It sounds like you have trouble collaborating with each other," you could say, "Your lab groups worked well last week. What helped last week go well?"

With this approach, students recognize that if they've done something before, they can do it again. At the core of this approach is a simple idea: all groups have had moments of functioning well, and all its members have at some point contributed to a group running well. Appreciative questions are an excellent way for a group to begin its work and to remember its promise and potential when it hits a snag. Using an appreciative approach to solve a problem reduces the risk that problems escalate into blaming and disillusion, which often happens when students are focused on what isn't working. Examples of appreciative questions are

- ❓ When have you successfully dealt with a situation like this before?

- ❓ When you've worked well with other students, what has it looked and sounded like?

- ❓ In what ways have you been able to give and get support in groups?

- ❓ What are the most important rules and procedures we already use that can help us now?

- ❓ What is something you've been able to contribute to a group's success?

See Chapter 7, pages 128–129, for an explanation of the appreciative approach, and a way to use it with individual students around learning habits.

Build mutual accountability by setting class and advisory group agreements together.

There are some aspects of school and classroom culture that are not up for discussion, nor should they be. Rules related to physical violence, verbal abuse, and illegal activity are non-negotiables. A civil society, and a civil classroom, must have unshakable boundaries in those areas so that there is safety to learn.

Safety to learn includes more than prohibiting egregious acts of harm. Learning in a group is a social activity. Knowing that you will be treated respectfully when you share an idea—and knowing how and when to share your idea—creates a safe space to learn from each other. As well, trusting the group to support you when you are confused, or have a burning question of personal interest, requires developing explicit expectations for all.

Many schools—elementary through secondary—involve students in contributing to agreements about the workings of the class. Over the course of their middle and high school years, students are more able and more in need of this opportunity—it contributes to being respected and sharing ownership for the culture of the class, club, team, or advisory. Each school setting may require unique agreements regarding how to gain the floor to speak, where to keep supplies, how to access supplies, guidelines for moving safely, and expectations for collaborating effectively. Teens should be increasingly expected to share in developing all such aspects of the culture.

The following protocols and activities can be used throughout the school to write shared agreements:

- Use positive, strength-based wording that identifies the behaviors students have been able to do when they've been at their best; for example, "We take the time to listen to people who have different opinions."

- Remember that you, the adult, are also a member of the group. Your input and non-negotiables can be a valuable part of the discussion if students haven't raised certain topics.

- Specific goals of shared responsibility should be embedded in the questions you ask: "What agreements do we need so that everyone feels comfortable and participates?" will prompt more purposeful ideas than a vague "What agreements do you want?" To such an open question, they could honestly answer everything from, "Let's read comic books," to "Not being given much homework." Consider the following questions to start the process:

  ? What are the ways you can treat each other in class that make learning go well?

  ? How can you help each other when the work is particularly challenging?

  ? What are ways we can give each other useful feedback? (See Chapter 6, pages 102–104, for feedback formats.)

  ? How can we know when you want to be left alone for a while so you can refocus?

  ? When three people need me at once, what can we do so everyone's needs can be taken care of?

- Get down to specifics. When students say they should "respect each other," ask what behaviors are most important for the group to function well. "How would I see and hear that you are being respectful?" Some of the specifics might be worth adding to the agreements, as in, "respect each other's space and things," if that's what students clarify. Without the extra discussion and wording, it would be hard to know what behavior had been asked for and agreed to.

- Keep the list short enough so that the agreements are about important ways of relating and are easily referenced.

- After the students make the agreements, put them in writing and have a signing ceremony. This does not guarantee that students will abide completely by their agreements, only that they acknowledge their best intentions. We worked with one struggling student who would not sign his class agreements. He said, "All of that stuff is hard for me. I know I'll mess up." His peers respectfully considered his reluctance and came up with the idea that he could put the words, "I'll try" next to his signature. In some ways, that intention is true for everyone. To underscore that group agreements can be ambitious intentions for all, ask students to journal, pair-share, or talk in the group to consider the following:

  - ❓ Which agreement(s) am I confident I can follow?
  - ❓ Which one(s) might be difficult for me to do every day?
  - ❓ Which ones could help me outside of class?

- Part of making agreements is a shared responsibility in upholding them. Ask the students, "What can you do when you feel the agreements are not being followed?"

- Agreements work well when they are referenced and reviewed. Teachers can take the lead by saying, "I'm glad to see how we held to our agreements in class today when..." or "Going into this activity, let's remember the agreement about...." Upholding an agreement is a learned skill; prompting their memories and best intentions is similar to how to we remind students to cross-multiply, use quotation marks, or check their notes.

- Once agreements are made, post the shared agreements where they can be referenced, reviewed, and updated. When students occasionally, and inevitably, do not adhere to the details of the agreement in their uneven development of responsible behavior, adults can frame the students' struggles as a conflict between them and the agreements they helped write, rather than framed as a power struggle between the teacher and student; for example, "We usually do well with our listening agreement. What do we need to do today to make it work?" That approach builds personal responsibility, social competence, and autonomy.

- Circle a few days on the calendar when you will all review the agreements. We recommend doing a review at the end of the first few days, which gives you a chance to praise commitments while they are still in their early stages of being enacted, and to edit some wording as needed. As part of the review, consider asking the following:

  - ❓ Which of our agreements have we kept almost all the time?
  - ❓ Which agreements have we done more often than not, even though they were hard to do?
  - ❓ Which of our agreements are we struggling with often? What can we do about that?

❓ Should we edit any of the agreements?

❓ Are there any additional ones we should add?

Engage the disengaged.   ⬜

Leadership is not all or nothing. Believing in one's capacity to lead can be developed in all students—even small opportunities to experience leadership can build that strength. Unfortunately, schools often require academic success as a prerequisite for leadership opportunities. Since traditional success for many students is not imminent, those students spend too long on the margins of involvement, reinforcing their disengagement. Reach out to them. Ask them to be on a classroom committee, to give you input for a class initiative, to help you set up the materials for a project, and ask them to support other students.

Develop student agreements for
when there is a substitute teacher or advisor.   ⬜

In addition to lesson plans and the usual safety and procedural information that are standard for a substitute, brainstorm with the students the roles they can assume on those days. Most substitutes will welcome the support, and you will be giving the students a chance to display their commitments to the classroom culture you have jointly created. Which routines can your students run without help? What additional group agreements are needed to make days with substitutes go smoothly and demonstrate the ways the group is capable of managing itself?

The students will benefit from a chance to rehearse their substitute routines—rehearsing can take just a few minutes, and result in hours of more effective classes and advisories for the rest of the year. For some fun, teachers and advisors can role-play being a bumbling substitute in need of much guidance, or ask a student to play that role.

Work with students to set short-term group goals.   ⬜

In addition to the group agreements above, students can be motivated by working on short-term group goals. Working on group goals will also help them learn about setting goals for themselves, which is described in detail in Chapter 7, pages 123–124. Periodically a short-term goal can help the group recommit to an aspect of their larger agreements. Critically, the goals are not about things that are being done for the students, but instead are markers of collective effort. For instance, "Take us on a class trip each term!" is not a goal they accomplish through their actions; however it may be reward for achieving a class goal. Offer the following statements as examples that students might write for work effort goals, social goals, and procedural goals.

Work effort: By Friday, we'll help everybody find a reading book that they really want to read. This week we help each other get all our homework done.

Social: We'll have a good laugh once a day. We'll go the full week without anyone being interrupted when speaking.

Procedural: This week, we'll be consistent about plugging the laptops in to be recharged. All week, we'll use our procedures for putting away supplies at the end of our class so we can leave on time.

The rewards for achieving their goals depend on the age and the characteristics of the group, everything from time to chat on their own or play a game, to an increase in independence, a letter to parents, a schoolwide announcement, or a visit from the principal to provide direct praise.

Support everyone in contributing to a culture of conversation.

Students enter schools with extremely different personal, family, and community experiences about the expectation to speak up. Some have been told not to say anything until they are called on. Some have learned that silence is safer than taking the risks of being wrong. Some have been told never to contradict an adult, while others have learned that standing up for themselves is a sign of intelligence. Some have been raised in communities where the adults have praised them for asking questions and developing their own opinions. Many have also seen and heard the ways issues are discussed in the news and social media, which run the gamut from respectful exchanges to disrespectful insults.

In addition to those diverse backgrounds that impact involvement, many teenagers need more time than they are given to fully consider what is being said in class. They'll need time to search through their memories for confirmations or questions, and then to frame a response. A common effect of learning disabilities, a history of trauma, executive functioning weaknesses, medical disabilities, or attention disorders is that students process slowly. While they may ultimately have very worthwhile contributions to make to a class discussion, they are rarely afforded the time (even just ten seconds of silence) to collect their thoughts.

Many of the established practices of school minimize student voice, such as, when classroom "discussion" is a single exchange between a teacher and student, in which the teacher asks a question that requires no more than one correct response. The teacher knows what she wants to hear and seeks a student who can say it, or drops the question once her answer has been offered. Student voice is minimal when the predictable few teenagers who always offer to speak keep speaking, while others who are quieter, or slower processers, or more hesitant to participate, stay quiet. Some teachers will then cold-call on students to startle them into attention, a move that isn't likely to result in students developing the will to jump into conversations or the skills to do so.

Ease students into a culture of conversation and teach students about different techniques for discussion. Over time, you can decide together what format and tools would be helpful for the topic at hand. The following ways of fostering a culture of conversations will benefit all teenagers:

- **Use go-rounds with short, nonthreatening, prompts or questions.** This practice is particularly significant at the beginning of the year to build a culture of conversation, and good for reviving participation whenever the group needs a lift. If some students don't talk comfortably and voluntarily in the first few days of class, they may stay in that pattern for the year. The point is to help students get used to talking—safely. Ask questions that can be playful and that don't ask for a single right answer—students need the chance to be funny, or thoughtful, or personal in their answers. For instance, in a language arts class, you could say, "We're working with metaphors this week. What's a metaphor for how you felt about the storm yesterday?" In a science class, you could ask "What's your favorite element and why?" See the section on group rituals in Chapter 3, pages 45–46, for more ideas.

- **Use nonverbal ways of getting into a discussion.** Showing a thumbs-up, thumbs-down, or thumbs-sideways is a way to communicate an opinion. So is using a "fist-to-five": holding up a fist means "no" or "strongly disagree" and holding up five fingers means "I agree completely" or "absolutely, I got it." Students can hold up any number of fingers to indicate the strength of their opinion. You can ask for volunteers who show different thumb positions or different numbers of fingers to say a few words about the reasons for their choice. If you use these formats consistently, students will know how to participate, and increasingly may choose to talk.

- **Start with pairs.** Turn-and-talks, or moving around the room to find pair-share partners, give the maximum number of people the opportunity to communicate their thinking—literally half the class at a given time. Most students find it less threatening to talk to one person than the entire class, or they don't have enough confidence in their ideas to offer them to the group. As well, airing one's ideas to the entire class with the teacher listening often means students will be steadily checking out the teacher's approval or disapproval, rather than freely sharing what they are right then thinking. (See the Appendix for instructions on both formats.)

After a turn-and-talk, teachers often want to hear from the pairs. Rather than asking students to repeat what they said to their partner, teachers can solicit different responses by saying, "Let's hear from a few people what they heard their *partner* say." Fulfilling this request encourages good listening and the skill of summarizing. Teachers should always give as much attention to the directions for the listeners as they do for speakers. For instance: "Identify one idea from what you heard that you might be able to use in your report"; "Listen for the vocabulary words and be ready to share a phrase your partner said that might help you remember the word."

- **Build up from pairs.** After students are comfortable with speaking and listening in pairs, combine the pairs into quartets, and then groups of six, or eight. The interest of developing students' autonomy and self-advocacy, and confidence to speak to a group, can be developed steadily through the year.

- **Use timers to equalize speaking time.** At times everyone will benefit from being given a definitive amount of time to speak. The fastest and loudest students may still go first, but the more reflective students will get their chance as well.

- **Use "listening labs."** This protocol of very specific steps assures that every student gets a chance to speak, and have structured practice in patient listening to their peers. The steps of a listening lab are found in the Appendix on pages 248–249.

- **Use techniques that support all students thinking about questions.** The following techniques greatly increase the likelihood that students will think about and be prepared to answer every question you ask the class. In all cases, teachers *do not call on the first person to raise a hand*, which is both very common to do and consigns far too many willing students into being observers.

The techniques below also support students to listen fully to the ideas of the previous speaker—instead of focusing only on the breathing and speech pattern of the speaker to know when to jump in. Speed of response is not equal to thoughtfulness, wisdom, or consideration of alternatives. Make time for pondering. Make time for summarizing, synthesizing, and richly evaluating what other students have to contribute. Make time for higher-order thinking in response to questions.

- **Start with think time.** "Everyone, take two minutes to develop an answer to this question. You may write down some ideas in a list, in sentences, in images. I want you to go beyond the first ideas in your head. I will then call on you, one at a time."

- **Incorporate turn-and-talks into group question sessions.** "This is a great question for everyone to consider. I think you need about thirty-seven seconds for silent thinking on this one. I will tell you when that time is up, and then you should share your answer with the person sitting next to you. Then I am going to go around the room—this time, let's start with Andrew and go counterclockwise—and you have to tell us what your partner gave for an answer. So listen carefully."

- **Give the order of speakers ahead of time.** "Everyone will have twenty seconds of silence to consider this question. Then I am going to ask Enrique and Liz their ideas. Then I will ask Davis and Clarice to say if they agree or disagree with Enrique and Liz. Then I will ask Jenny and Roseanne to add any ideas or reactions."

- **Support each person to contribute one piece of the answer to a complex question.** "Everyone, I am not asking you "Why did Juliet stab herself?" but instead, "What are some of the reasons she stabbed herself?" I will then go around the room, starting this time with Danielle, and have her say one reason. We'll keep going around the room, collecting ideas, until we have heard all the ideas you have. Say "Pass" if all your ideas have been said. When we collect all the ideas, then I am going to have you work on your own to organize them into...."

- **Use a talking list, visible to all, when many want to jump in.** "I see lots of people want to speak. Raise your hand when you feel like speaking, I'll add you to the talking list, and you can put your hand down and focus on listening. You can see when your turn is coming. So far we've got Jenny, Eric, Danielle, and Liz. Okay, you can start Jenny." A student who knows everyone's name can also manage the list. (See more details in the Appendix.)

- **Expect everyone to retrieve a lower-order memory question.** "Class, this is a question that actually has just one right answer. I want you to go into your memory and see if you can retrieve this fact. I'll give you five seconds of silence to explore your memory, and then I'll call on someone who raises a hand. If you agree with the answer you hear, you can give a thumbs up."

Also see the sections in Chapter 6 on "Practice and model asking open-ended questions" (page 101) and "Encourage multidirectional discussions" (page 102).

Establish formats for in-depth discussions.

For in-depth discussions, often about controversial topics, teachers need to provide strong leadership to help students write a specific set of agreements or to use established protocols. In the absence of the students agreeing on how to proceed, those who are loudest, or in the moment most passionate, dominate conversations when the issue may be critically important to everyone. With solid agreements or protocols in place, teachers will be able to praise their class after a discussion of a controversial subject by saying, "You all handled that well, sharing what you know, and listening to others share what they know. We stuck to our agreements," rather than the discouraging, "Well, if that's how poorly you handle a conversation, don't expect me to do that again." The time it takes to prepare discussion protocols with students yields significant behavioral and cognitive outcomes.

The following protocols allow students to engage in sustained and in-depth conversation:

- **Classroom debates** can build the skills of organizing ideas and producing well-articulated arguments. The benefits of debates are most robust when teachers provide abundant preparation time, including rehearsal sessions. Equally important for skill development will be the rubric for assessing student work. Craft assessments that focus on the efforts to prepare, clarity of presentations, patient listening, respectful questioning, demonstrations of mutual support, and appreciation of good ideas. Such a skills-based rubric will undermine the tendency to assess a debate simply as a winning or losing activity.

- **Dialogues** offer an alternative to the win-lose culture of debates. While offering similar opportunities as a debate for preparation and participation, a dialogue can robustly develop the skills of exploring new options, synthesizing diverse and complex perspectives, asking questions that seek shared wisdom, helping others understand, developing compassion, engaging in collaborative problem solving, and grappling with how one's ideas and beliefs fit into a diverse community. For more information on holding a classroom dialogue, see *Dialogue: Skills for Classroom and Community* (Benson & Poliner, 2012).

- **Socratic dialogues** have been in use for thousands of years. There are many online resources for holding a Socratic dialogue. At its best, this method honors each student's experience of a subject, supports each student in sharing that experience, and encourages consensus building. Socratic dialogue is as much about the process as it will be about any result.

Arrange the furniture and classroom resources to support student interaction and responsibility.

Photos from classrooms a century ago show students sitting in rows, their chairs literally screwed into the floor. The message of such a set up is clear: students are to focus solely on the teacher, and the teacher is the only one who can speak directly to the group. There are no expectations to build skills beyond simple compliance. Educators had not yet developed the understanding, or the mission, to develop in their students' interactive, higher-order brain development. It was "old school" in the most restrictive fashion.

In some schools, desks in rows remain the default method for setting up a room. Classrooms with desks in rows symbolize the value of individual work. This set up may be useful for administering silent standardized tests, and for quiet writing time, when we want to minimize visual distractions. Rows certainly make conversations difficult: students have to talk to the back of someone's head, twist their necks to see how other are reacting to what they are saying, and miss completely many people's facial reactions. It is hard to listen carefully when you can't see a speaker; you miss their body language, which communicates a significant portion of what a speaker is conveying. Form follows function; desks in rows suit certain tasks but should not be the default arrangement in the 21st century.

Every student has an equal right to see everything clearly. Move the furniture to maximize the academic and social competency goals of the lesson. Chairs and desks in a circle, U-shape, arc, square, three sides of a square, or concentric circles and squares, symbolize the value of connection and communication. When students face each other during a conversation, they are more likely to capture the whole meaning of what someone is saying, and are more likely to pay attention to how their own comments impact others. If the furniture is movable into small clusters when needed for collaborative work and small group conversations, all the better.

Moving the furniture may not be sufficient to break the students' habit of talking only to the teacher, or the teachers' habit of speaking after each student. Adult restraint, use of think time, discussion protocols listed in the section above, hand motions showing the topic is still open, and explicit instruction and encouragement ("This is a group discussion, not just with me)" are going to be needed. Teenagers will require repeated reminders and lots of time to break an old habit and build a new one.

Students can also be asked to make recommendations for the best places in the room to keep supplies and resources. An aspect of autonomy and problem solving includes learning to organize one's workspace to be most efficient. The vast majority of teens are ready to participate in this responsibility. These decisions are excellent opportunities to choose a *test, consult,* or *collaborate* mode from the options at the beginning of this chapter.

Take a restorative justice approach to classroom discipline challenges.

Everything teachers do is a curriculum and a choice: whether your feedback will be asset based, whether students will be given preparation to really collaborate, whether your practice of discipline will teach responsibility and accountability to the class community. How you manage discipline in your classroom is a practice, just as how you give feedback and how you conduct collaborative learning are practices. It is all curriculum for the developing whole teen.

Many classrooms and schools (and our larger society) have a punishment-focused discipline system. The key questions are

- What rule was broken?
- Who broke it?
- What's the punishment for breaking that rule?

Schools with zero-tolerance policies are extreme examples. In contrast, restorative justice is based on different sets of key questions:

- What harm was done? How can that harm be repaired? Who's responsible for that repair?
- What's the disagreement? How do we address the conflict and meet the needs of individuals and the community?

Restorative justice systems prioritize reestablishing a shared sense of community and safety, with everyone in the class developing the empathy and skills to participate in that safe community. For those who may fear that nonpunitive practices such as restorative justice do not send a strong enough message to those who break rules, a wide-scale study shows that "behavioral control is a significant predictor of negative classroom misbehavior" (Tokuhama-Espinosa, 2014, p. 72) compared to less punitive approaches.

There will inevitably be students who need a lot of feedback, intervention, and lessons to learn a new skill set to replace their disruptive actions. Restorative justice can deliver all those community expectations. Rick Wormeli (2015) writes, "When a student is disrespectful to us, instead of taking it personally, we realize that he's 14 and has only an occasional filter on impulse control. We focus on the positive young adult he's becoming and help him see how his words and actions have consequences, guiding him in making amends and restoring trust, with tomorrow as a fresh start" (p. 12).

In Chapter 12, we discuss schoolwide and districtwide restorative justice programs. We offer it here as a practice that fosters self-discipline and mutual responsibility within the classroom. We also offer in Chapter 6, pages 107–108, the steps of a good apology, which can be incorporated into restorative justice protocols. For some situations, a good apology with amends may be the best way to resolve a discipline issue.

Restorative justice doesn't happen in an unfriendly chaotic environment however. To implement restorative justice practices, be sure you've built familiarity and community (Chapter 3), developed and used group agreements (Chapter 4), and practiced effective communication strategies in established routines for inclusive, respectful conversation (Chapters 4 and 6).

Restorative justice formats vary; three to consider are

- problem-solving meetings involving the whole class
- smaller restorative circles to work out specific conflicts, including the person harmed, the person who caused the harm, some peers, and the teacher or advisor
- reentry circles for students returning after a disciplinary action

Common to all the formats are sitting in a circle, making or reaffirming the group agreements, stating the issue, listening to the impacts (harm done), ideas for repairing the harm, and agreeing on next steps.

Discipline is such an important part of managing groups of diverse students within the often stressful environment of a busy school day. Doing discipline well, as a curriculum that fosters the whole teen, is an opportunity to be embraced. Students learn more when they feel safe and curious, and less when they feel intimidated and afraid. They need environments that encourage making commitments via group agreement processes, sustaining those agreements over time, and restoring a sense of community when it's been damaged. See the References for more information on restorative justice, including middle and high school stories.

Develop with your students the rituals, roles, and responsibilities for day-to-day functioning.

In Chapter 3's practice, "Build community with your students and advisees through group rituals," we discuss many ways for students to build rituals, traditions, and celebrations for classes and advisories. Here we consider the day-to-day business that teachers and students rely on for a sense of calm predictability. Sharing these tasks teaches the students how a community functions. Taking on these tasks is not a reward granted to the best students as a privilege—everyone gets a chance to contribute to the best of their abilities and potentials. One way to gain a connection with resistant students is by offering them an appropriate role in the business of running the class, a responsibility usually reserved for only the most compliant teenagers. Offering these opportunities to show that they are capable of being responsible may be for some teens a first chance to be trusted.

Either on a voluntary or revolving basis, consider how your students can take on the following responsibilities:

- caring for class plants
- serving as the class DJ, providing a soundtrack for specific activities, such as coming into class
- writing with a peer group the first draft of a quiz or test
- serving as in-class "experts" during independent work time
- posting class notes online
- operating the timer for activities
- setting up rituals for entering and leaving class
- chairing the classroom discussion or managing the talking list
- organizing and maintaining the classroom "chill out zone"
- writing the first draft of a classroom newsletter for parents
- contributing to parent feedback night
- brainstorming a variety of homework options
- developing timelines for required tasks
- maintaining bulletin boards
- collecting information for announcements
- telling a "joke of the day"
- managing recycling

Discussion Options for Faculty

- Which practices in this chapter seem especially important for your students?

- Which skills mentioned in this chapter are especially important for you to practice?

- How can your high school students be expected to take on more collaborative responsibility than when they were middle school students? How can your middle school students get a good start on sharing school-wide responsibilities?

- Referring to the tell-to-collaborate continuum, who has asked students to consult with you on a topic of concern to the class? What opportunities do you have coming up where you can ask students for their concerns and ideas prior to your decision making?

- Who has written class agreements? What processes have you used? What have you learned from that process?

- What effective planning have you done with students so that days with substitute teachers go more smoothly?

- What unique short-term class goals have any of you found successful to establish with your classes?

- Besides cold-calling, what ways have you used to get the majority of your students to share aloud their ideas and thinking?

- What are the benefits and drawbacks of having desks in rows? In pairs? In clusters? In a horseshoe or circle? Who has tried different formations, and how did it go? Whose room has difficult constraints? What creative solutions might help?

- In either formal or informal fashions, who can speak to the outcomes of a restorative justice approach to discipline? What small steps can you take to experiment with such an approach?

- In what ways are you now prompting students to handle responsibilities in class?

- In what ways are you now asking students to reflect on their efforts to be responsible? How can you ask that of them frequently?

Practices at Home

In ways that are sometimes very obvious, and at other times very subtle, children figure out from their elders what they are supposed to be responsible for in the family. For instance, some children take care of their siblings or grandparents. Others have to keep their rooms cleaned in a certain way. Some must earn money. Others are expected to simply cause no trouble. Children learn what they are responsible for by what they see, hear, and are explicitly told to do, or not do.

The teenage years can alter everyone's expectations of responsibilities. Teens are developing the thinking skills that allow them to ask "why" more than they ever have before, in some families appearing as constant critics. Through their friends, school curricula, and the media, they are seeing various ways that families operate. Inevitably, they will be comparing and contrasting all that worldly information—and feeling it as well.

Teens can interpret how much you care about them by how much you ask of them. They can feel everything from being burdened with too much, to being abandoned because no one asks them to do anything. They will see families that make no acknowledgement of the ways teenagers change from children, and they'll see other families that seem to be giving up all their rules and letting the teenagers do whatever they please—or it may look that way to them. They will also see families in which teens are assigned chores without any chance to contribute their ideas, and families where parents do the tasks that the teens themselves could surely do. Hopefully they will see families in which there is an ongoing conversation between the adults and teens about what needs to get done, and how each member of the family can best do their parts.

The practices below provide you with ways to allow your teens, as they each develop their skills, to share responsibilities with the rest of the family. Two large concepts from earlier in this chapter can provide much benefit at home:

- **Tell-to-collaborate continuum:** Teens have very different abilities to be responsible. Some parents decide it is simply easier to *tell* their kids what to do, with no questions to be asked. That approach can be a problem for teens who have developed some abilities to contribute to planning. Some parents expect their kids to be full participants, to *collaborate* in every decision. That approach can overwhelm kids who need some very clear directions and expectations. The tell-to-collaborate continuum is a great tool for adults to choose how much responsibility they want to give to their particular teens. As kids get older and gain more skills, look to move them along the continuum toward more full participation in getting tasks done.

- **Share with teens your interests, not only the rules.** Interests are what you really need the rules to accomplish. Teens can contribute more than just obeying. Two examples are

  o The adult says, "You must be home by 10 p.m." The kids have no chance to make the plan better because they don't know your interests. Your interests might be that you want them to be safe. Start with the interest: "I need to know that you will get home safely." The kids might know that it would be safer for them to get home at 10:15 because they could take the bus rather than walk.

  o The adults say, "You have to finish your homework before you listen to music." The teen thinks she may be able to work better with music on, or may do well with a short break to listen to music between tasks. If the adults said, "My interest is that you finish your homework and it is well done. How can that happen?" the teen can present her plan to meet that interest.

Review and adjust teenagers' specific chores. You can ask them directly, "What do you think someone your age can be responsible for around the house?" Be clear about what is non-negotiable. Be supportive: "Do you need any help doing these chores?" How they do the chore can be up to them—encouraging creativity and ownership. For instance, "When you are buying vegetables, you choose what we'll make when Grandma comes to dinner tomorrow."

Encourage their observations and ideas about how the home is arranged. We know a teenager who was responsible for folding the towels and putting them in a particular drawer. One day she said, "Wouldn't it be better to keep the towels in this other drawer where everyone can reach them?" As teenagers' brains develop, they become more able to see what could be, compared to what is. Make use of that new ability. Share your interests so they can contribute to such decisions as how to set up the seating for holiday meals (interest: Grandma needs to be closest to the kitchen), where emergency keys can be hidden (interest: out of sight of one particular neighbor), and how to make a good place to do homework (interest: the couch has to be available to everyone).

Find opportunities to set short-term family goals with kids. Goals depend completely on what a family as a whole would like to do better and then reward itself for the efforts: at dinner this week no one interrupts; by Saturday night, all the rooms are clean; holiday cards are in the mail by Tuesday. Goals can also be personalized for teens' motivation: "I will finish washing the pots and have my homework done so I can be online for an hour tonight."

Make respectfully speaking and listening a top priority. Listening to teenagers does not mean you agree with them. Listening teaches them to listen. Their responsibility to speak clearly and respectfully is grown every day, in every interaction they have with every adult in their lives. Listen during the week to the tone of people's voices when they see each other in the morning, or the ways the family discusses sports or politics during dinner. How can respectful speaking and listening be more a part of your family culture? What lessons are the teens learning when they hear how the adults speak and listen? In Chapter 6 and earlier in this chapter, you can read more about developing a culture of conversation.

Practice restorative discipline at home. Teenagers can be expected to clean up their messes and make any amends necessary to build trust. This is different than punishment, and completely different than hitting kids to make them fear you, in the hope they will behave well when you are not around. Geoffrey Canada, the originator of the Harlem Children's Zone, said to parents who were using corporal punishment, "You are spending all of your time trying to beat this child into submission" (Weir & Marx, 2009). Restorative justice is an alternative to more than corporal punishment. Teens have to hear how their actions impact the people they live with. This teaches self-discipline, not just obedience when someone is watching.

Plan for when the teens bring friends home or are home alone. In the absence of very clear and shared understandings about the expectations for friends, teens can get in trouble. Teens are often torn between what they believe is right, what their parents have told them to do, and what their peers are encouraging them to do. Teens can also feel very anxious when home alone—being anxious often leads to mistakes in judgement. Reference the tell-to-collaborate continuum so that you are clear about the absolute rules, clear about what can be tested to see if it works, and clear about what is in the teens' need and right to decide. When you want to collaborate on planning, be sure to share your interests; for example, "I don't want to hear from the neighbors that they were disturbed. How will you make sure that interest is met?"

5

Learning Collaboratively, Not Just Nearby

Humans differ from other animals in many ways, and perhaps one of the most significant ways is our ability to learn with and from each other. When a groundhog dies, for instance, any specific knowledge of the world that the groundhog has picked up dies with it—but humans pass along knowledge and wisdom through our ability to tell stories, to point, write, read, draw, make videos, graphs, charts, and sing. Human civilizations and all of our progress have depended on this shared social construction of the world.

Reading and writing, videos, and electronic media are relatively new inventions, compared to how long humans have roamed the earth; learning as a social skill in families, small groups, clans, tribes, and villages is an evolutionary accomplishment built into each of us. Lev Vygotsky (1978) put it this way: "Every function in the child's cultural development appears twice: first, on the social level, and later, on the individual level; first, between people (interpsychological) and then inside the child (intrapsychological). This applies equally to voluntary attention, to logical memory, and to the formation of concepts. All the higher functions originate as actual relationships between individuals" (p. 57). From our earliest lessons as children into the most modern high-tech industry, humans function as interactive and interdependent beings. Schools have a huge part to play in how well teenagers will manage that essential skill of civilization.

Discussing her research into the effectiveness of teams, Anita Woolley, Thomas Malone, and Christopher Chabris (2015) concluded, "Though we may still idolize the charismatic leader or creative genius, almost every decision of consequence is made by a group." They found that the most effective teams featured members who communicated a lot, participated equally, and possessed good emotion-reading skills. What Vygotsky knew about how humans learn as social creatures remains the foundation for whole teens to thrive in the 21st century.

When students are consistently scaffolded to develop their abilities to learn with others, they grow a broad and deep set of skills. They listen, compare perspectives, weigh options, incorporate values, take stands, adjust their stands as they learn, develop action plans, follow through on commitments, and support others in their efforts to reach common goals. This high-level, student-to-student learning happens whenever they are encouraged to share ideas, find a peer to be a partner, work in formal groups and teams, and observe how others do their work.

Learning in groups has huge implications beyond the walls of the school. Students learn that social competence demands a more complex set of skills than hanging out with their childhood friends. Knowing that they can successfully collaborate with others opens a vast array of possibilities for family, community, and careers.

Collaboration is enhanced by self-assessment, which is found in several places in this chapter. These opportunities can allow students to see both individual and group responsibilities. The timing of the self-assessments also allow for formative considerations and for summative conclusions. Because collaborative learning allows students to develop complex social skills that enhance the standard academic expectations, student self-assessment of processes and outcomes is critical to their learning.

Some teachers doubt the benefits for their strongest students of learning with those who are less skilled or have disabilities. The research in this area is clear, though counterintuitive to some: "Inclusion education results in greater numbers of typical students making reading and math progress compared to non-inclusive general education classes" (Eredics, 2015).

Our century old model of fixed rows of desks, individual worksheets and the predominance of teacher talk is useful in certain ways—but is now as disconnected to Woolley and colleagues' analysis of the skills needed for success in the modern world as would be a classroom without electricity. To support the development of social learning skills, we need teaching tools and a belief that the effort to learn in groups will bear academic fruit, breaking the mold of students compliantly working solo at their own desks. The practices below will support teens to develop a more complete set of skills as young adults, learning with each other.

 ## Practices That Develop the Skills of Working Collaboratively

Before: Prepare students and advisees for collaborative work.

The middle and high school curriculum involves increasing levels of complexity—preparing students to move from fractions to algebra, from plot summaries to analyses of themes, from mixing paint colors to mixing reactive chemicals. We know that teenage cognitive development demands lessons that match their growing capacities, and schools build academic curricula that leverage teen development. The same is not usually true for learning with others. Many teens have no more than their elementary-school-level social experiences of sharing and taking turns, even as we expect them to work with a more diverse peer group and interact with far more interpersonal nuance.

Our efforts to develop group skills with teens reflect the common observation among adults that it is sometimes hard even for us to work with each other. Without preparation, assigning students to sit together and handing them a task is as likely to result in conflict as it will in achievement. Those who assign students to a group without preparation will eventually hear, among others, these two common complaints: (1) "I need a new partner." and (2) "I'm doing all the work." Without preparation to fall back on, there are no simple solutions to such statements. They could be coming from the most dedicated or the least motivated student.

Given the risk-benefit possibilities of assigning group work without teachers confidently preparing their students, many schools emphasize individual skill building, as limited as that mode can be. It is also no surprise, in these circumstances, when students say they prefer to work alone. At least there will be less conflict, even at the cost of learning.

Throughout this book, we have integrated many skills that can help avoid conflict, or manage the inevitable conflicts that arise, so students can learn with and from each other. Those skills have been framed in the context of a whole class led by the teacher (Chapter 4), or for person-to-person communication (Chapter 6). In this chapter, we focus on the many skills that are developed in small-group and paired learning. The upfront time teachers and advisors can devote to preparing teenagers for learning together will pay big dividends in academic, vocational, and social success; you can help teens to truly be prepared to be part of, and contribute to, their communities. The following activities prepare students in the initial stages of working with peers.

Make agreements for working together.

Help students envision a well-functioning group before they plunge into the academic expectations. This activity is similar to the one in Chapter 4, pages 61–62, on setting group agreements for the entire class. If you have done that task with the students, this activity and the ones that follow should be familiar to them. With the entire class, or in their groups, ask students to recall when they have been in a group that worked well, whether in school, on teams, community settings, or their homes. Then ask them to identify what made that group work well. If necessary, scaffold their thinking with the following questions:

- In what ways did the task or goal of the group keep everyone together?
- How was leadership determined?
- How were different roles determined?
- In what ways did people give each other feedback and support to do well?
- How did the group handle differences in work styles, learning styles, or individual needs?

With those experiences and insights fresh in everyone's minds, have the students brainstorm work guidelines and agreements. Remind the students that these are guidelines and can be revisited at any time during the tenure of the group.

Learn to understand and appreciate how different styles are inherent in learning and working together.

Students can explore their preferred styles for learning and working before they begin to work with their group on the given academic task. Enlarge or copy Tool 5-1 onto signs in the four corners of the room. Ask students to think about how they work on projects, what they focus on first, and what they tend to be motivated by most as they work through the steps. Then ask them to go to the corner with the sign that has words that best describe them. They will now be in a group of students who have similar styles.

Have them talk with the other students in their corner about the following:

- ⑦ What are five more words we could agree on to describe our style?

- ⑦ What's great about our style? How does our style contribute to a project group?

- ⑦ What can be challenging about our style? What are the possible weaknesses of our style? It might help to imagine using the style in an exaggerated way.

- ⑦ What specific roles and tasks could we propose that we do in the coming project to contribute effectively?

- ⑦ What's important about having project partners with different styles?

Next, have them sit with their project partner or group, to share their insights from being with their like-styled peers, and to craft any agreements that would be conducive to integrating varied styles.

As an ongoing practice whenever you use collaborative learning, use these questions to continue the discussion with the whole group, with specific groups, or when coaching students individually.

- ⑦ In what ways are you are using your style well or too rigidly?

- ⑦ How are you appreciating and effectively utilizing others' styles?

- ⑦ Is there a style missing from your group? How did all of you compensate?

- ⑦ How are you expanding your skill set to try other styles? After all, having more skills and the ability to adopt styles helps you deal with more challenges and different situations.

Use hypothetical scenarios to prepare students for inevitable conflicts.

Even the best preparation cannot prevent all conflicts, especially when students feel pressured, confused, or left out. Tool 5-2 contains three short scenarios to read and explore with the class. Students can identify what prompted and escalated the conflict, and what could have been done differently or less dramatically.

If you've used the hypothetical scenarios in your preparation for group work, when students are having a conflict, you can say to students, "You're having a conflict. That's okay. Is there anything we learned in those scenarios that can help you now?"

For additional scenarios, you can also ask students about their own stories of conflicts when collaborating. You might develop a growing repertoire of scenarios to use over the years.

1.   Read the scenario.

2.   Ask the students to identify in each scenario the specific words and actions that contributed to the escalation of the conflict.

3.   Ask them to identify which of those actions or statements might also prompt them to be more upset or react badly. Making commitments to avoid such words and actions with each other can be woven into group agreements.

4.   Next, ask the students to brainstorm possible solutions for the characters in the scenarios—and then to choose the solutions that might best satisfy every character's interests. This is a good time to introduce, or review, the positions and interests concept in Chapter 4 on pages 56–58.

Among a number of things we want students to learn from this activity is that there are three steps they can take when a conflict arises (at first it may be necessary for you to lead them through the steps):

1.   Allow all people involved to identify what upset them. This is not a sequential blow-by-blow account of who did what to whom first, which is rarely useful and tends to seek out whom to blame. Instead, allow each person to say what upset him or her.

2.   Brainstorm solutions.

3.   From the array of possible solutions, choose their ways to get back on track as a group, ways that permit each person to feel satisfied.

Consider roles to play in groups and learn to play varied roles.

Students can become accustomed to playing a certain role in groups even at a young age and not develop the flexibility and added skills for other roles. We are not advocating forcing teens to take on roles or responsibilities that would overwhelm them if they lack the skills or are too anxious to perform well. The following questions will help them and you find the opportunities to offer new learning experiences:

❓ Some of you take on leadership roles in groups. Some of you are good at carrying out a given plan. Some of you keep an eye out for how everyone is feeling. Some of you are great at getting and organizing materials and resources, including technology. Some of you bring humor or a sense of adventure into a project. Some of you keep a close eye on clocks and calendars and schedules. What roles do you most often find yourself taking on in a group?

❓ What roles would you like to try in this task?

❓ What questions might you have if you take on a new role?

As projects move along, monitor who is playing what role. Discuss roles and taking risks with the whole class, specific groups, or when coaching students individually.

Discuss varied ways to demonstrate leadership.

Many students may be ready to be leaders as they develop their skills for problem solving and autonomy, but associate leaders with only a bossy forceful personality. Write (or project) the statements on Tool 5-3 on the board and read them with students. Ask them the following:

? In which ways does your group need people to be these kinds of leaders?

? Are other forms of leadership needed for your project?

? In which of those ways might each of you be willing to be a leader?

These or additional statements about leadership can be useful when reflecting after collaborating or when shifting to a new group or task.

Practice planning group work.

Use Tool 5-4 after students settle into groups and look over the scope and expectations of their assignment. This task will help them develop the problem-solving skills of planning and resource management, and the autonomy skills of taking initiative, following through on commitments, and setting personal mastery goals.

Utilize a range of methods for setting up groups and work partners.

Students come to class with a range of strengths, interests, and learning styles. Some students are extremely flexible, working well with almost anybody, serving as reliable anchors through the process of learning. Some students' needs and concerns require a more thoughtful placement because the task at hand and the available peers suggest a particular grouping. These students, who are sometimes seen as difficult, can actually flourish and make uniquely important contributions when their teachers make very deliberate groupings with them in mind. Groupings must go beyond keeping the most skilled students together simply because they have the most skills.

From the styles activity above, you can put together learning groups that have representatives from each corner. However you choose to make groups, we do not endorse as a regular practice forming groups of students who all share the same style. Homogeneous groups will often lack the diversity of different perspectives and skills, limiting learning, and will not prepare students for other settings.

It is also an option to let students choose their work partners, which has some pros and cons. We interviewed a group of high school students about the different ways their science teachers were assigning partners. Some of them admitted that when given the choice, they felt social pressure to pick their friends, even when they knew they'd get less work done. Those students preferred having the teachers make the groupings, balancing skills across the class. As much as teachers might and should seek opportunities to give students voice, some students may be burdened by too many social concerns: How will my best friend feel if I don't choose her? What if the person I'd like to ask to be my partner rejects me? What is the teacher going to think about me if I choose that person? What if no one chooses me?

Consider these methods for grouping:

- **Random assignments:** There are tasks that may be well done with students randomly assigned to groups. Random assignments demonstrate the values that everyone is to be respected as a learner, and that one needn't be close friends to work together. They also give the opportunity to learn social competencies for working with others, very useful for the varied settings students will encounter in life. If putting students into random groups, we recommend taking the time to do the preparatory activities above, because random groups may contain students who initially find their differences to be problems rather than benefits.

- **Teacher-selected assignments:** In almost every class there are students who do not yet hold as a goal to get along with everyone, or the social competencies to do so. Tool 5-5 is a teacher tool for developing grouping options for students who require from teachers a bit of behind-the-scenes planning, scaffolding them toward effective group membership. The handout focuses on the strengths of struggling students: their readiness to take on a new task based on their skills and knowledge, their unique interests and motivations, their particular learning style.

- **Student choice:** We have worked with a teacher who periodically gives students opportunities to choose their learning partner, and reinforces their developing skills of autonomy and problem solving by always saying, "You have to pick a smart seat, not a social seat." When a pair of students is struggling to stay on task, she asks them very kindly, "Can you two be smart together? If not, let's call this a social seat and save it for a different time." What has surprised us in our observations is the frequency with which the students take this gentle cue as a motivation to focus, or actually decide that the choice of partners was not a "smart seat" and give up their pairing. Only rarely has the teacher needed to insist that the pair separate. By then the evidence was clear that the students had indeed picked a "social seat" and they accepted a new spot to work in class.

- **Limited student voice:** If you'd like an alternative to totally controlling partnerships or totally leaving it to student choice, ask the students for a list of three to four people who would be good partners for them and use that input to build the assignments.

Use long-term groups and short-term groups.

The variety of groups in a class can mirror the variety of groups and committees in a school community. Some groups need to be together for a sustained period of time in order to complete complex tasks; school sports team are examples of the importance of group cohesion and shared learning through a long season of practices and games. Some groups sustain through an entire school year, or through multiple years, for example, the drama club and the Gay-Straight Alliance. Other groups pull together to tackle a single concern and then dissolve, such as the group who will decorate the school cafeteria for a dance. In a class we might have groups that separate after a single activity, others that sustain through a unit, and still others that continue through the year, becoming a durable source of support. When putting together collaborative learning groups, consider the following:

- Do the goals include building social competencies as well as standard academic skills? Those two goals may not always require the same amount of learning time.

- Is there a single product to produce, or is the group responsible for an on-going function?

- Do the benefits of long-term learning with the same peers outweigh the benefits of maximizing diversity through regrouping?

During: Support students through the many steps of the group project.

One of the most common concerns that adults have for teens is that they may not have the skills to work through difficulties, preventing the benefits of long-term commitments from being realized. Without those skills, teens will settle for less than they might accomplish academically, diminishing their development, and the contributions their work will make to their communities. Angela Duckworth's notion of "grit" includes perseverance and passion for long term goals—both of which can often benefit from some support. The following activities will help students maintain their efforts through the work needed to achieve their goals.

Revisit their Group Work Plan.

Remind students to periodically revisit their Group Work Plan, Tool 5-4. This is also a good time to ask students if they would like to switch the role they are playing in the group; for instance, a student who was initially reluctant to take on a leadership role may find that the social connections built in the group can allow her to take on an aspect of that role.

Support effective problem solving.

When students get stuck in their efforts, help them develop effective problem-solving and decision-making skills by encouraging them to internalize a few key habits and criteria. Teach them to avoid running with the first solution that the fastest thinker suggests, or voting quickly on the first two ideas offered. Instead, they can build habits of restraint, flexible thinking, and considering consequences. Tool 5-6 provides students with a predictable set of steps that can develop habits of mind for effective problem solving. Remind them that talking about needs and interests will help find a solution that satisfies everyone. A group may need the support of a teacher to guide them through the steps the first few times. Consider using the steps with the whole class to introduce and reinforce the sequence.

Acknowledge positive contributions.

Support students to appreciate what is going well. We often stop a group to problem-solve, less often to affirm the positive efforts being made. Highlighting what students are doing well most often encourages them to continue those behaviors—and many times teens don't realize the positive impact of some of their efforts. Ask the groups any of the following questions to prompt their reflection:

- In what ways do you see someone's work style helping the group? How about your own work style?

- In what ways have you seen someone shift their style and be flexible to contribute to the group? How about your own efforts in this way?

❓ What has someone done to keep the group on task?

❓ What has someone done to help the group solve a problem?

❓ What has someone done to maintain your standard of quality for the work?

❓ What has someone done to show appreciation and support?

Support students seeking each other out as resources.

One of the limitations of teacher-centered instruction is that students do not make use of the most abundant resource in the room: their peers. We are not suggesting that students are better than teachers in delivering clear directions, breaking a task into its parts, or in referencing previous learning. However, what students often do better than teachers is to show their peers how they themselves are managing the task at hand—perhaps most importantly, how they worked through a challenge that the teacher could never have anticipated. Peers provide input and feedback without the concern that their grade is at risk. The following two approaches help students build skills of problem solving, communication, and autonomy:

- **"Ask three, then me"** requires that a student who has a question or concern about the work first seek out the support of three peers before reaching out to the teacher. We have seen this technique work from elementary classes through high school.

- **"Peer experts"** are students who feel comfortable with their skills and don't mind interruptions. They are solicited by the teacher before a specific activity, and are willing to put down their own work when a peer has a question and the teacher is unavailable at that time. Peer experts are identified for the group before a task starts.

Conflicts are inevitable; here are practices and skills that help.

Throughout the book there are many references to conflict resolution. In every chapter the skills of communicating, problem solving, and self-advocacy contribute to resolving conflict successfully, and reducing the likelihood of conflict. Here are a few practices and skills in the book you can review and reference with students when they are in conflict:

- Speak in terms of positions and interests (Chapter 4, pages 56–58)
- Conduct a round of appreciating the groups strengths and assets (Chapter 4, pages 58–59)
- Review group working styles (this chapter, page 76)
- Review their group work plan on Tool 5-4 (this chapter, page 90)
- Answer the problem-solving questions on Tool 5-6 (this chapter, page 92)
- Use paraphrasing and open-ended questions (Chapter 6, pages 100–101)
- Speak from their own perspective (Chapter 6, page 105)
- Share learning preferences and habits (Chapter 7, pages 121–123)
- Use routines for diffusing and managing challenging emotions (Chapter 8, pages 155–156)
- Reconsider negative assumptions (Chapter 8, page 157)
- Normalize the making of mistakes (Chapter 9, pages 174–175)

After: Establish reflection and appreciation routines.

A common practice after students have taken an exam is to allow them to review their answers and correct their work, so that the exam is not merely a summative assessment leading to a grade, but another experience of learning. Similarly, the writing process is dependent on students revising drafts, so that they build their skills from one essay to the next. Developing the lifelong skills of working with peers collaboratively in groups also requires reflecting on their efforts. *Doing* without *reflecting* misses the opportunity to identify the ways the students have made positive contributions. Reflecting helps students be accountable for the impact of their negative behaviors, and builds their identity as responsible members of their community.

Have teenagers self-assess on the ways they collaborated.

Given the opportunity to engage in the activities below, teenagers can be surprisingly wise and self-aware about ways their efforts impacted their learning, not just the standard academic goals, but the equally important lifelong goal of working with others. To do so, most students need more structure and support than being asked, "How do you think you did?" Consider the following:

- Tool 5-7, "In What Ways Did I Contribute to My Group?" provides a rating scale for *individual students* to assess their own contributions to many aspects of a collaborative project. If students are turning the form in to the teacher, it can be filled out anonymously, which may generate more honest responses. The teacher can then use the responses as feedback on his own efforts to prepare students for collaborative work. The aggregated responses can also be shared with the class as a way of problem solving and preparing for the next collaborative project: "Class, many of you reported that you struggled with staying organized. Let's consider what I can do, and what all of you can do, to make that part of our work more successful."

- The following "just-the-basics" questions can be answered individually, by the group as a discussion, as well as in a listening lab format:

    ❓ What are three ways we worked well together?

    ❓ What's one way we could be more effective next time?

    ❓ What's one action someone took that was really helpful for me?

- Tool 5-8 provides a structure for a *group* to assess how well they collectively worked together, helping students understand more about group processes. This reflection can be essential for students who remain on a team together, developing a better understanding of their mutual efforts, and predicting more success the next time they are teamed up. Teachers and advisors should remind students throughout this discussion that effective collaboration is a mixture of individual and group efforts.

- If a group had a conflict, even if the issue at hand was effectively managed, there may be underlying issues to finish processing. As well, reflecting on the conflict can help students secure valuable lessons learned. Tool 5-9 provides a structure for that learning opportunity. We do not recommend using the information in the handout to alter a student's academic grade as it likely would inhibit honesty.

Discussion Options for Faculty

- Which practices in this chapter seem especially important for your students?

- Which skills mentioned in this chapter are especially important for you to practice on your own or within committees, clusters, departments, or other groups?

- What structures and expectations are in place in your school as a whole now to support students learning in groups?

- What structures and expectations can you start to bring into your school as a whole to support students learning in groups?

- In what ways are you supporting a variety of student leadership styles? What else can you do? In what ways is it your job to foster diverse leadership among students?

- What criteria would you use, or are you using, to make effective learning groups: Random? Determined by learning styles? Social skills? In what ways, if any, are students providing you with input to make effective learning pairs and groups?

- In what ways are you developing with students a reliable way to solve problems when they get stuck?

- In what ways are you helping students learn to work through their conflicts in small groups?

- At the end of a learning group, in what ways are you assessing with students their skills beyond the standard academic expectations?

- Can someone who regularly has students work in groups share some of your experiences?

- Consider using a collaborative learning assessment throughout the year:

  o Keep track of the number of complaints and problems within collaborative learning groups. What are the patterns you see?

  o Keep track of the students struggling with collaborative learning. Do those students represent a small number or the majority of the class? What skills need to be taught to which students?

Practices at Home

Have your kids had challenges playing with or working with their peers? Learning the social skills to be with peers is part of growing up. Do your kids report those challenges to you, as if you have to fix them? That is often the case when kids are young; it may be less so when they reach adolescence and want more privacy—which doesn't mean they know how to work things out.

Most families teach their children to master such important skills of daily living as crossing the street safely, brushing their teeth, paying for groceries at the market, ordering food at a restaurant, and using local public transportation. Not as many adults give their children the explicit guidance to cooperate and collaborate with their siblings, cousins, and friends.

The teenage years challenge adults to find a comfortable place between micromanaging kids to make sure they have no conflicts and abandoning them to their own devices, hoping they'll figure it out on their own. Micromanaging can lead to kids waiting for the adults to set up everything, to the point that some teens may not know how to organize sports without an adult initiating and serving as a referee. Leaving them on their own is a strategy that often ends with the adults needing to step in as peacekeepers, negotiators, or powerful authority figures.

All along the way, being sensitive to how your teens are developing is critical, especially when they need adult intervention. Many parents intend to deescalate their kids' conflicts by stepping in. Intervening may prompt cooling off in the moment. However, the presence of adults can also escalate a situation. Think of adult conflicts—calling the police or lawyers can increase tension and hurt relationships. Prioritize supporting your teens to speak up for themselves and to resolve their own conflicts. You can help teenagers learn to work together effectively, and possibly spare you from having to step in to try to solve *their* problems, using the following guidelines and activities.

Prepare teenagers to cooperate and collaborate before they get started:

Ask teens to review what has to get done, and the steps that they will take. Teens can interpret what the adults are expecting in very different ways. They also may, right from the beginning, have different ideas about how to do the work—a formula for conflict. Get them to say back to you and each other what they have to accomplish and agree to a plan. Ask them how they will know when the work is done well enough so they develop self-assessment skills.

Help them decide on their roles. Teens differ greatly in the ability to speak up and to jump into the work. Some need more time to get started. Some may be good at suggesting new ideas. Others may be very good at doing detailed tasks. Help each one state the parts of the work he or she wants to do, make sure all the parts are accounted for, and that they all feel satisfied with the distribution of work.

Plan for trouble ahead of time. Prompt them to answer a few questions that start: "What should be done if . . . ?" Ask them if they can generate any questions of their own to predict problems. One last question to answer is "At what points will it make sense to get some adult help?"

Helping teenagers while they are engaged:

Checking in. Before you leave teens, make a plan for when you might check in with them. With younger teens, you may do well to impose an initial schedule of your involvement

("I'll check in with you all in about twenty minutes."). With older teens, you can negotiate what everyone thinks will be worthwhile. Don't agree not to check in if you think you should. You can say, "I'll feel better about how things are going if I get a chance to check in."

Giving them opportunities to independently manage the normal give-and-take of working together requires the adults to make some decisions. If you know that one or two of the teens have trouble collaborating, be quicker to step in. You may not have to solve the problem; sometimes an adult walking into the area is enough to get them back on track.

Here's a story of an adult, a middle school soccer coach, who kept an eye on how his group of teenagers were managing a task, stepping in only enough to help them be successful. Part of his training sessions had been to expect the players to listen to each other's ideas in order to solve their own problems, so he had very strict rules for the parents and other older family members who attended games. He'd say to them, "You may cheer. You may not yell directions or advice to them or call out to any one of them by name. They've been coached to talk and listen to each other, and I don't want them to be worried about what their parents are saying when they should be listening to their teammates." He followed his own advice when the players ran to the sideline during a time-out. They'd stand in a circle and the coach would say, "What did you notice?" and then, "What do you think we should do?" He'd give his advice when the team was confused, but most of his work was done in the practices and training sessions, preparing them to work as a team during games.

Coach your teens to self-advocate with their peers. We know a mom who told her seventh-grade daughter to stop doing all the work for the boys in her project group. With her mother's approval, the daughter told the boys that she wasn't going to carry the burden of the entire project, even if it meant getting a bad grade. This mom explained, "I want my daughter to learn to self-advocate now, before the stakes are higher in high school, or she's on a date, or she's struggling to ask for a raise in a job."

When teenagers finish:

Praise and review. From your perspective, say what looks good from their efforts. Ask a few questions: "Who did which parts?" "Is there someone who really stepped up?" "Any advice for the next time we all work together?"

When you are collaborating with your kids:

Before starting a job with them, identify together who is doing which tasks. Offer support for them to take on new challenges. Ask them, "Do you think we've covered everything we need to in order to do this well?"

Check in with them during the work. It may be hard to watch them do the task less effectively then you might if you were working alone. As long as they are not doing themselves or anyone else harm, their errors can be useful opportunities to learn to adjust their efforts. Ask, "Do you want any advice from me now?"

When you are done, tell them what they did well. Ask them if they think you, as the adult, could have helped more, or less, or differently. Then tell them ways you think they could have done better.

TOOL 5-1   Working Styles Signs

Organized
Detail focused
Methodical
Thorough
Sensible

Curious
Analytical
Deliberate
Big picture–focused
Logical

Caring
Attentive
Interactive
Inclusive
Imaginative

Active
Experimental
Ready to jump in
Inventive
Flexible

Available for download at **http://www.resources.corwin.com/PolinerBensonWholeTeen**

TOOL 5-2   Collaboration Scenarios

Scenario One

Terry and Manuel have known each other for years. They are not friends, not enemies; they've never actually spoken to each other. Their teacher thought they seemed comfortable together and paired them up for a task.

Terry jumped right into the work, making suggestions about which one of them could do which jobs, and what the final product could be. Manuel was quiet, so quiet that Terry thought Manuel was not going to do his share of the work ahead. Terry said, "What's going on? Why aren't you saying or doing anything?"

"What do you mean, not doing anything?! I'm thinking here, man, not talking-talking-talking non-stop," Manuel replied.

"That's just who I am," Terry said. "I like to get things done. I like to get good grades."

"Oh, so you think I don't get things done?" Manuel said. "You gotta stop thinking you know who I am and what I care about. I care about my grades too, but I don't boss people around. You don't even know me."

"Alright, why don't you just do your work how you want to and I'll do mine," Terry said, and turned away from Manuel. Manuel got the teacher's attention and said, "Terry won't work with me."

"That's not true!" Terry shouted back.

Scenario Two

Ed, Dana, and Lian were well along the way on their group project until the day Ed did not show up for their study period meeting to start the final draft of their writing.

"I'll go find him," Lian said.

"Don't bother," Dana replied. "Frankly, I haven't liked working with him. I think you and I get much more done without him."

"But that's not fair to work without him," Lian said. "We don't know why he's late. Maybe something's wrong. So far he's done everything he was supposed to do. I don't like him that much, but that's not the point."

"Let's work and if he shows up we'll fill him in," Dana said. "If I was late or not showing up, I'd want you two to keep working on the project so we all didn't get behind schedule. That's all I'm saying."

"That's not all you're saying," Lian said. "You said you don't like working with him. Now I see that you haven't actually been very nice to Ed. Maybe he doesn't like working with you either. But I don't want to start until he's here. I'm going to find him."

"Fine," Dana said, shrugging. "I'm going to start working on the draft anyway. We have to stay on schedule."

"No, you shouldn't work on it without us," Lian said. "We're a team."

"Well, somebody has to keep us on schedule. I'm going to start working now."

(Continued)

TOOL 5-2   (Continued)

Scenario Three

Anam and Frankie are filling out the reflection page at the end of their project. They had struggled at times to agree on the quality of the work being done; Anam had pushed them to re-read the work many times, while Frankie was sure they had already done enough to get a good grade.

Anam said, "We're supposed to write about what we could have done better. I think that means we should say something about how much more I wanted to check the work than you did."

"I don't think you have to write about that stuff," Frankie said. "It's not like we're going to get a better grade if you write about it."

"That's not the point," Anam said. "I'm just being honest."

"But if you don't write about it you aren't lying. Just skip it and we'll be done," Frankie said.

Anam sighed. "This is the same as the whole project. You're happy doing less than me."

"Right, I know that," Frankie said. "And that's not a problem; it's not something we did wrong. Our work was good. It's just how it is."

"So why can't we write about it then?" Anam asked.

"I don't see why we have to write about it," Frankie said.

"And I don't see why we can't," Anam said back immediately.

TOOL 5-3   Kinds of Leadership

1. A leader tells everyone what to do.

2. A leader does all the tasks no one else will.

3. A leader watches more than acts.

4. A leader encourages everyone.

5. A leader calls out anyone who is off task.

6. A leader does not need help.

7. Other:

8. Other:

TOOL 5-4   Group Work Plan

What products or activities must we present by the end of this group work?

_____

_____

What academic skills are we expected to learn and improve from our work?

_____

_____

What skills are we expected to learn and improve from our work?

_____

_____

What agreements have we reached about how we will work together?

_____

_____

_____

What roles are each of us planning to be responsible for?

_____

_____

What resources will we be using, including things we still need to get or develop?

_____

_____

Our time line for finishing our work:

Date: _____ Task to be accomplished: _____

Date: _____ Task to be accomplished: _____

Date: _____ Task to be accomplished: _____

Date: _____ Task to be accomplished: _____

Date: _____ Task to be accomplished: _____

TOOL 5-5   Teacher Tool for Grouping Preparation

Student: _____

Readiness: Peers with similar skills and knowledge

Readiness: Peers with differing skills and knowledge

Interests: Peers with similar interests and motivations

Interests: Peers with varying interests and motivations

Learning and working styles: Peers who work in similar ways

Learning and working styles: Peers who work in differing ways

TOOL 5-6   Effective Problem Solving

1. **Prepare** yourself to listen carefully and respectfully.

2. **Define** the problem to solve. What are the needs and interests involved?

3. **Brainstorm** several ideas that might help solve the problem—whole solutions or parts. No judgments; any idea might spark another idea.

4. **Check** that everyone has been heard.

5. **Discuss** all the ideas—separately, combined, or adapted.

6. **Choose** ideas that solve the problem; meet all key needs and interests.

TOOL 5-7   In What Ways Did I Contribute to My Group?

Actions	Self-Assessment low to high	Ways I could contribute more—or more effectively—next time
Providing ways to solve problems	1 2 3 4 5	
Keeping organized and on task	1 2 3 4 5	
Getting resources or technology	1 2 3 4 5	
Supporting others	1 2 3 4 5	
Caring about quality	1 2 3 4 5	
Bringing energy and new ideas	1 2 3 4 5	

I learned these things about myself during this group learning project:

_____

_____

_____

In what ways can what I learned help me with my goals?

_____

_____

_____

_____

TOOL 5-8   Our Group Reflects on Our Work Together

Getting Ourselves Organized

- What did we do in order to prepare for the academic task? What helped the most?

- Looking back, how might we have prepared better? How could that knowledge help in our next task?

The Roles We Played

- Did the roles change during the project? How did that happen?

- What other role changes might have helped us do the project well?

When We Worked Effectively

- What did we do to function well?

(Continued)

TOOL 5-8   (Continued)

Dealing With the Tedious Tasks

- How did we handle the tedious tasks?
- What did we learn about good ways for our team to handle tedious tasks?

When We Got Stuck or Off Task

- Who did what to get us back on track?
- In what ways might we have gotten back on track more effectively?

Making Sure We All Learned

Do we all understand the work so that any one of us can be the group's spokesperson?

If "Yes," everyone initial here:

If the answer is "No":

- Who needs to learn what? What support from the teacher might help?

TOOL 5-9   Processing a Group Conflict

What were the initial positions (demands) each person had in the conflict?

_____

_____

What were the underlying interests (needs or concerns) that drove those positions?

_____

_____

What feelings were strongest for you?

_____

_____

What feelings were strongest for others?

_____

_____

Looking at the way the conflict escalated, what opportunities were there for you at any point to limit the escalation?

_____

_____

What was the resolution (if the conflict was resolved)?

_____

_____

If the conflict was resolved, how do you feel now?

_____

_____

Are you having difficulty forgiving someone with whom you had a conflict? If so, what is still bothering you? What could you do?

_____

_____

Overall, in what ways did you help the group resolve this conflict?

_____

_____

Available for download at **http://www.resources.corwin.com/PolinerBensonWholeTeen**

6

Communicating Effectively, Not Just Mumbling, Exploding, Avoiding, or Texting

S tudents in middle school and high school need to communicate to sustain friendships, accomplish projects with peers, self-advocate with teachers, discuss issues in class, participate in clubs and teams, and engage with an increasing number of adults within and outside of school. All of these relationships—and their future learning, working, and life relationships—will depend, for better or worse, on their abilities to communicate.

Teens need to be able to listen for and ask about information, listen for and ask about perspectives, express their own information and perspectives, and choose their messages and modes of communicating. These skills are critical to developing social competence and healthy lasting relationships. These skills are critical for robust academic progress. These skills are critical for their individual interactions, for the peer culture of school, and for living in a diverse democracy.

Young people have always needed to learn the difference between talking with peers and adults, writing to family members or a public agency, interviewing for a job or for college. Young people *today* have the added decisions of choosing among many—*many*—more modes of communication, and the added challenge of having less practice in face-to-face conversation.

The Pew Research Center has found that almost two-thirds of teens ages twelve to seventeen use texting daily—and far more—than any other mode of communication, including phone calls, in-person conversations, social network site messaging, instant messaging, and e-mailing. Note that several of the other modes listed were electronic, often for brief messages, and no more interactive than texting. According to the Pew report, teens ages fourteen to seventeen sent a median of one hundred texts per day in 2011. In contrast, a little over one-third had daily face-to-face interactions (Lenhart, 2012).

Sherry Turkle (2012a), a clinical psychologist and founder of the Initiative on Technology and Self at the Massachusetts Institute of Technology (MIT), researches how people relate to technology. She says, "We are tempted to think our little 'sips' of online connection add up to a big gulp of real conversation. But they don't." When Turkle (2012b) asked teens to explain their preference for texting, "they responded that when you're face to face, 'you can't control what you are going to say, and you don't know how long it's going to take or where it could go.' But Turkle believes that these perceived weaknesses of face-to-face conversation are actually conversation's strengths."

It is true that people can have more control when writing a message—if they take time to think about their words. But even if they take the time, they have less information. They aren't seeing the person's reactions to their comments; maybe they would have altered the rest of their message. They aren't learning to observe, listen, and respond *in the moment*—key elements of true conversation.

Teacher and writer Paul Barnwell (2014) witnessed his students struggling to conduct or participate in interviews, seemingly unpracticed in the natural flow of conversation, waiting passively for questions, and not knowing how to ask follow-up questions. Innumerable important interactions will happen in person with employers, family members, friends, and others. "When students apply for colleges and jobs, they won't conduct interviews through their smart phones. If the majority of their conversations are based on fragments pin-balled back and forth through a screen, how will they develop the ability to truly communicate in person?"

Given the increased prevalence of rapid electronic messaging among teens, what should conversation look and sound like in our schools? Too often classroom "discussion" involves a teacher asking one close-ended question at a time, getting an answer, agreeing with or correcting the answer, then moving on to the next question, consistently directing the interaction, in a repeating pattern of teacher-student-teacher-student-teacher. This pinball dynamic seems far too similar to texting, doesn't it? It also remains rooted in lower-order thinking—retrieving bits of information and leaving behind students who need more time to process their deeper thoughts.

Teachers can use classroom discussions, feedback routines, and individual interactions to counter the pinball dynamics of modern communications. Because adults in schools are always communicating with students—giving directions, asking for reactions, listening for concerns—every adult in school is a teacher of communication skills. Through all the small opportunities and teachable moments in classes, hallways, cafeterias, offices, and libraries you can model effective communication.

Turkle (2012a) relates an interview: "A 16-year-old boy who relies on texting for almost everything says almost wistfully, 'Someday, someday, but certainly not now, I'd like to learn how to have a conversation.'" We disagree—it must be now! Therefore, this chapter offers skill development activities, classroom discussion and feedback practices, and practices that all adults can use and model. Exposure in all of these ways will help develop the brain's pathways for communicating, including asking open-ended questions, asserting ideas respectfully, and listening deeply in varied conversation formats. (See Chapter 4 for additional formats.) Students will learn how to have conversations, get regular practice communicating effectively, consider the modes of communication they use, and choose and use them well. The impacts will be healthy interpersonal interactions, constructive group interactions, a beneficial peer culture, and more learning. Many of the practices apply to individual and group interactions among the adults as well.

Practices That Build Skills and Habits for Communicating Effectively

Encourage teens to consider their messages, audiences, and when to communicate electronically.

Short electronic messages may be useful sometimes, but are problematic at other times. You can help students and advisees become skillful communicators in many modes, not just one or two default modes. You can also help them protect themselves and others by noting the easy and enormous amplification power of electronic messages and social network posts.

Try any of the following prompts for conversations with the whole class, advisory group, or for coaching with individual students. In addition to the prompts, watch for local or national incidents involving public figures in any field, athletes, or entertainers in which a message backfires because of its content, tone, or mode of dissemination to use as a case study. There can be significant impacts on major events or projects when public figures' communications go awry.

- ❓ What are all the modes you use for communicating with other people?

- ❓ What modes do you use most often?

- ❓ How do you choose what mode to use?

- ❓ What do you gain or lose with different modes?

- ❓ What are some situations where texting is an effective mode, and situations where it's a really bad choice?

- ❓ How often do you use social network messaging to communicate? When has that worked well? When has it caused a problem? What are some its dangers?

- ❓ When you have a conflict with a friend, how does it play out if you talk in person versus communicate in e-mail? Imagine the series of interactions involved.

- ❓ What's a question you could ask yourself regularly before pressing "send" or "post" that might protect yourself and friends?

- ❓ What are some situations where talking in person really helps?

- ❓ How should our class use any or all of these communication modes? How could texting help us? Posting? What should we save for face-to-face discussions?

- ❓ How do scholars, researchers, and innovators in our subject area communicate their ideas?

Practice patient listening. □

Listening is powerful, but is neither cognitively simple nor passive. It takes intentional focus to really hear what someone is saying—and the meaning they're not putting into words. It takes suspending your own ideas to make room to entertain another person's ideas. Listening isn't waiting someone out till you get a chance to talk, nor hearing only points to rebut.

- **Try a listening lab format in pairs** (explained in the Appendix) in which each person has a full minute to talk, and a minute to listen. They might be speaking about a question that's arisen in an academic class ("What do you think is the most important idea we've considered, and why?" "What was one thing that happened in class that helped you learn, and how so?"), or a question about themselves or about school. Students might find it challenging to explain their view for a whole minute without interruption, agreement, or reaction, or to listen for a whole minute showing attention but without reacting verbally. If that's the case, start with thirty seconds and build up, maybe even to two minutes each with rich topics.

- **In turn-and-talk or pair-share formats**, give students specific listening tasks, such as these:

  o Be able to summarize your partner's main idea. Besides encouraging good listening skills, those students who are uncomfortable offering their own views to the entire class can be less nervous when they explain their partners' views.

  o Note which of your partner's ideas were familiar and which were new to you.

  o Ask a question that helps you understand your partner's perspective, as in, "Could you say more about ...?" or "What did you mean by ...?"

- **Practice paraphrasing skills** in pairs or class discussions by asking students to explain the last speaker's view before offering their own. Coach them to not rush through the paraphrasing, and to not paraphrase in a way that denigrates the prior view. "Niki's view is ____, but I think ____," conveys that my view is better than Niki's. "But" sets up a comparison, which is sometimes intentional, but (comparison intended!) often is just a common word that unintentionally denigrates the prior view. "I can see Niki's point about ____. What also seems important to me is ____." Students will learn another way of showing respect and considering multiple perspectives.

See Chapter 4, pages 62–64, for more formats that use patient listening to develop a culture of conversation.

Practice patient speaking. □

Many teachers use think time as a regular practice, that is, asking a question and asking everyone to think for a half-minute before speaking. This is an important strategy for many reasons—talkative students learn restraint, quiet students have a chance to collect their thoughts, students who take longer to process have a chance to think, and more students will participate. You can expand on that strategy to further develop patient listening and speaking. Try any of the following options:

- **Ask students to jot down two or three ideas during think time.** Someone's first thought may well not be his best thought. Writing a few notes will surface more ideas, better ideas, and increase patience and restraint.

- **Slow down class discussions,** which can jump quickly to debate mode—point, counterpoint, polarizing a topic, simplifying it, missing the points between the poles or from a different perspective entirely, making it difficult for students who aren't the fast talkers to participate. Stay with a given point for some follow-up questions and comments before moving on to another view. "What do you need clarification about?" "What new idea are you considering?"

- **Mid-discussion, ask for thirty seconds of think time** to look at the topic from other perspectives, then continue the discussion, pausing again as needed.

Practice and model asking open-ended questions.

The questions we ask show whether we're curious, interested, and respectful, or inattentive, bored, or dismissive. They might even show that we're disrespectful and picking a fight. Questions that can be answered with a "yes" or "no" don't foster rich discussion or rich thinking, nor do questions with one right answer. Here are some practices for working on question skills that encourage conversation and exploration. Students will see that small wording changes can make a big difference.

- **Talk with students about the opening words of questions**. "Do you . . . " and "Did President Roosevelt . . . " are yes/no questions. "When did . . . ," "Where is . . . ," "Which character . . . ," and "Who said . . . " are asking for one simple response each. Moving beyond basic comprehension, there are many phrases that can start more thoughtful open-ended questions: "In what ways . . . ," "How does . . . ," "What could . . . ," "What are a few . . . ," "What are some ways to . . . ," "How might you . . . ," among many others. Make a poster or a class handout of ways to start an open-ended question, adding to it over time. Do an online search for "Bloom's taxonomy questions" to find many lists to use as a guide for yourself or to post.

- **Ask for contributions rather than complete analyses.** Instead of asking, "Why did we enter WWII?" try asking "What were some important reasons that we entered WWII?" The first question calls for a "complete" answer, which is neither likely nor necessary, and is intimidating to answer. The second example is less stress inducing, and you can encourage multiple students to contribute ideas.

- **Ask students about their thinking, not just for their answers.** Often students don't have fully formed opinions as much as thoughts. Ask, "What are you pondering right now? It doesn't have to be a complete opinion." "What seems interesting to you?" "What connections are you making?"

- **Take the charge out of questions.** Over time, listen for questions that demonstrate disrespect and take a minute to reword them together. Asking students to put themselves in the shoes of the recipient of each question will help them build perspective taking skills as well as good questioning skills. "What do you mean you didn't . . . ?" could be reworded as "Could you tell me your reasons for . . . ?" "How come you still don't know the Pythagorean theorem?" could become "Which step seems confusing?" "Isn't it obvious what Baldwin meant?" could be reframed as "I thought Baldwin was clear about . . . "

- **Conduct interviews** so students can practice questioning and conversation skills. Interview teachers, custodians, and secretaries about school issues; conduct oral history interviews for social studies units; interview a professional person in the related field in any class; interview someone in a potentially interesting career. In all of these cases, draft questions ahead, try them out in trios, revise the questions, and talk with the whole group about the best questions that each trio crafted.

Encourage multidirectional discussions.   ☐

Students can better practice communication skills if class discussions include real give-and-take among everyone in the class, rather than a back-and-forth exchange with the teacher. You can prompt more participation with pauses, body language, and statements, as well as using tools and formats explained in Chapter 4 and the Appendix, such as talking lists and go-rounds. Also, it is both symbolically and physically important that students' chairs not be in rows for real discussions. We talk to the faces we see, not to the backs of heads; rows represent that their interaction with the teacher is the only one that matters.

- **Practice your own restraint.** Pause after a student speaks to look around the group, wave your hand, or say, "This conversation is not about what I think; it is about what each of you is thinking."

- **Ask for more views when discussions become two directional.** If a point and its counterpoint are offered, threatening to become a polarized discussion, ask specifically for views other than the ones offered. "Okay, we've heard two very different views about ____. Who's got an opinion from another angle altogether?" Asking if students agree or disagree might be useful occasionally, but asking it regularly can foster polarization rather than exploration. It also raises the risk level for speaking—if it's regular practice to immediately ask, "Who disagrees?" many students will feel too vulnerable to speak.

- **Shift from the full group to pairs or trios.** After a few ideas are aired, have everyone talk in pairs or trios to consider the topic from additional angles. Think of it as using the format of think-pair-share in a rearranged and expanded way.

Practice giving feedback as well as accepting feedback.   ☐

There are many ways of giving feedback; we offer several below. In teaching any of them, have students brainstorm—ahead of time—useful and helpful feedback as well as feedback that isn't effective. Encourage some overly dramatic examples of ineffective feedback; it will add humor and will likely prevent some unhelpful exchanges. "What an awful drawing!" "You must not have spent much time on those graphs; they're a mess." "How could you possibly have come up that equation?"

Remind students that when it's useful, feedback should be encouraging while also offering insights or suggestions. The person receiving the feedback shouldn't feel personally judged or attacked, shouldn't feel defeated, or that they cannot improve and therefore should give up. To be useful, it's important not to be vague, as in "Good job." What was a good job: the research, the presentation? What was good about it: the detail, the creative approach? People who give feedback skillfully convey that the feedback is their reaction, their perspective.

Besides teaching effective feedback skills, it is crucial that you model all of the skills, and that effective feedback becomes your everyday practice. These techniques can become norms for the class, so that with a simple cue, students will be prompted to practice and build their own skills: "Okay, head back to your partners and use our feedback trios routine."

- **Start with feedback to themselves.** Besides being important that students learn to self-assess (more on that skill throughout Chapter 7), if they practice various feedback formats on themselves, they can see how each one sounds and feels.

- **Offer some sentence stems for peer-to-peer responses,** such as those on Tool 6-1, which can be a reference handout or expanded to post.

- **Start and end on positive notes:** "I think your data table for osur science experiment is really clear. Something to improve would be the explanation before the table—it seems to be missing a couple of steps. The conclusion is great; it's really convincing." Make up other three-message combinations and try giving the messages in different orders: criticism first, last, and in the middle. Many students will realize that when the critique is first, they can feel deflated and miss the points about strengths. They are also likely to realize that when the critique is last, it's all they remember.

- **Evidence-based feedback:** Rather than judgments, such as, "That's a lousy opening paragraph," students should be more constructive and specific. "Your opening paragraph could introduce the rest of your argument more clearly." For a positive example, instead of "Nice!" they could try "Strong opening paragraph! It's strong because you made the issue sound important—I wanted to read more to see what solution you were proposing."

- **Asset-based feedback:** Many students hear about their deficits frequently, in addition to having very critical self-images already, typical among adolescents. Students can note their own and their peers' positive qualities—their assets. (Tool 7-3 might help.) "Andre took a lot of care with the details in our diagrams; Karina was a really thorough researcher, and I kept us organized and on time." In the process, students will be strengthening their self-identities and appreciation of others. Your asset-based feedback is especially important. Teens are collecting reflections of themselves, trying them on. Vague or mainly negative reflections give them nothing strong to build from.

  Here's a story of using asset-based feedback from an advisor who used brainteasers as a regular ritual for developing problem-solving skills: A student who was often unengaged in classes, hood up, head on his desk, was working with a partner on a frustrating brainteaser, which took encouragement and several tries with different approaches. When the pair was finally successful, the advisor said, "Wow, Kevin, you really persevered on that problem." The student looked up and smiled, seemingly surprised to hear his name and "persevered" in the same sentence. The advisor noted that he would be able to bring up persevering the next time this student was struggling with an academic task, and it would mean something concrete, personal, and positive to the student—not an abstract unattainable command.

- **Appreciative feedback:** It's a norm to thank people when they do a favor for you or give you something, but saying a simple "thank you" does not serve the purpose of giving feedback. Sprinkled everywhere, like salt and pepper, thank yous lose their impact. When students answer a question in class, they're doing so to learn; it's not a favor to you. Using their comment to draw out more discussion or noting that they had an unusual take on the topic are meaty reactions. "Thank you" should not be as cheap as "good job." Adults can say instead, "I really appreciated the effort you took to put that idea into words" or "Here's what I liked about that insight: ... " or "I have to ponder what you just said. Thanks for sparking my thinking." Students appreciate knowing that their thinking has influenced your thinking!

- **Practice hearing feedback.** It can be hard to hear feedback; offer students practice and coaching in both choosing to be open to hearing it and responding to it. Explain that listening to feedback doesn't necessarily mean students are agreeing with it. Once they've heard the feedback, it's their information to use fully, use partly, or set aside. Use Tool 6-1 as a reference handout or consider expanding on it and making a sign together. Coach individual students who become defensive or deflated.

Students will learn best with familiar structures for giving and receiving feedback, using the skills above. Tool 6-2 is for presentation rehearsals with one peer first, then a larger group, each time hearing three things that worked well in the presentation and two suggestions for improving it. Tool 6-3 is a structure for feedback trios with self-assessment first, then positive feedback and suggestions, ending with identifying two things to add, change, edit, or polish.

Coach teenagers about how they talk with teachers, bosses, and other adults.

Students can gain or lose opportunities based on how they talk with adults, so it's an important skill to practice and improve. In any of the exercises below, watch for coachable moments to start with a greeting. "Hi Ms. Jones . . . " sets a better stage than "Hey, I need . . . " Also watch for coachable moments about being clear with requests, checking tone, and avoiding assumptions and blaming. "You weren't fair on this grade" is hardly a good conversation starter. "I've thought about my paper and this grade, and I don't understand it" shows reflection and responsibility, qualities teachers want to support. Besides coaching students when they role-play or speak with you, you can ask them to give you feedback. "Antonio, how was my tone with you then? As your teacher, I wanted to be clear about expectations and I didn't want you to feel discouraged."

- With your students or advisees, **brainstorm a tips sheet for talking with teachers**, identifying the five or six most important things to remember, such as choosing a good time, or thinking ahead about your request. You can start the process with a tip that's especially helpful to you, or work off of "10 Tips for Talking with Teachers" in Pamela Espeland's *Life Lists for Teens* (2003). Try the tips out right away by doing some role-plays of recent problematic interactions. (See the Appendix for ideas about working with lists.)

- **Use the following role-play scenarios** to consider these questions: What's the best communication mode for this interaction—in person, e-mail, phone, other mode? What's an effective message? As an example of an adult in their world, play the adult in each of these situations and share with students how their attempts strike you. Notice which words, tone, or mode prompt you to feel sympathetic to their request or unsympathetic.

  o Ask a teacher if you can do the work you missed last week.

  o You're upset with how Mr. Thompson graded your paper. How do you plan to ask him about it?

  o Ask your boss to switch your schedule. You really want to go the basketball game.

  o Your guidance counselor missed an appointment with you. You're worried about upcoming deadlines. How could you ask for another meeting?

- Turn any of the statements on Tool 6-4, "Talk So You Can Be Heard," into a question or statement that isn't blaming or commanding, since neither is likely to work well with teachers, coaches, bosses, or parents (or anyone else).

Practice respectful assertion.   □

It's important that students learn how to say what they need and express their views—effectively. Some students already express their needs, perhaps too frequently, worded as demands, and harm relationships. Other students are overly accommodating, perceiving and serving others' needs before their own. Neither of those styles represents a healthy balance of connecting with others while also building skills for autonomy.

Asserting a need can feel risky, and sometimes is risky—you're raising an issue that might surprise the person you're talking to, or prompt them to feel defensive. The key is crafting the assertion message to fit the situation. Sometimes students will use this skill to participate fully in a group project, when adding their opinion to a class discussion, or defending their recommendation for solving an academic challenge. At other times, assertion may actually protect them from a difficult or dangerous situation. Sometimes, they will need to assert a view in writing. Considering their own needs and preferences and asserting them effectively will help young people lead their own lives. Remind them that expressing their own view or need doesn't have to denigrate anybody else's view or need. Though others may forgive an insult after an apology, they may not be able to forget it, so trust may still be challenged.

- **Look at letters to the editor** in a news source, finding letters that assert a view without insults, and other letters that include insults. What's the impact on students as readers? Which views do students believe? Which letter writers would students want to talk with?

- **Identify a local issue** of concern to students, and identify a public official with authority over that issue. This task can be part of any class curriculum, making real world connections to current lessons. Craft a letter that asserts a view and asks questions, and that is respectful.

- **Use I-statements.** One option to share with students is the well-known format for an assertion message, an I-statement. "I feel ____ when you ____ because ____, and I would like ____." The challenging part is sticking to your own perspective in each part. "I feel <u>frustrated</u> when you <u>interrupt me</u> because <u>I lose my train of thought</u>, and it would help <u>if you could wait till I finish my sentence</u>." That speaker did not judge in the beginning, as in, "You're rude when you interrupt me" or judge in the middle, as in, "I feel frustrated when you're rude . . . " or judge at the end, as in, "I feel frustrated when you interrupt me, so I'd like you to stop being rude." Using an I-statement lets someone raise an issue, offer her own reaction to that issue, her own perspective on why that issue matters, and her own suggestion or request.

- **Speak from your own perspective.** Sometimes you don't need the entire I-statement format. "I'm confused when you . . . " is likely to get a calmer clarification than "You are so confusing." "I thought we'd agreed on . . . " can better lead to a renegotiation than "You agreed . . . " Discuss additional sentence stems that allow people to share their own perspectives, such as, "My view is . . . ," "What I need next is . . . ," or "What's bothering me is . . . ." The point is to represent what you know— your own experience. This skill is a powerful one for teachers to model, even if it is never explicitly taught to students.

- **Role-play** any of the following situations using perspective-owning sentence stems:
  - ○ You're in a three-person project group in which you feel like you're doing the bulk of the work.
  - ○ A friend posted a photo of you online that you don't like. It isn't a photo that could get you in trouble; it's just embarrassing.
  - ○ A student in a class discussion makes a statement that from your knowledge of the situation is not true.
  - ○ Another member of your sports team is suggesting changing the game strategy behind the coach's back.
  - ○ A member of the school department is visiting your school and you want to say that many students do not like a new proposal about school uniforms.

Coach teenagers about "place and time" choices.

As teens begin to broaden their world, they increasingly find themselves in situations that some would say require altering their usual behavior, clothing, or speaking habits—behaviors that reveal unique aspects of their family culture, religious beliefs, racial identification, or sexual orientation. Adjusting behavior can be important and useful; it might help them gain access to opportunities they want. However, it can also be challenging to their developing identities. What teens do and say holds greater meaning for them than it might for an adult with an established sense of self. There are times when people (teens and adults) choose not to compromise or suppress elements of their identity, despite potential rewards for doing so. Many teens struggle with these decisions as they are forming a deeper identification with their particular race, culture, or sexual orientation.

Have conversations with the whole class and with individual students before conducting interviews, applying for jobs or college, or even negotiating with teachers. The goal isn't to have them erase who they are and pretend to be someone else. Rather, we all have many parts of ourselves that we combine in various ways all the time. What might be the costs and benefits if they do or don't alter their usual presentation?

Rehearse interview skills for jobs and higher education.

Though rehearsing for interviews often takes place in advisory or career-related classes, any adult in a school might be in a position with a given student to help them prepare for interviews. Even if this activity does not fit into your course curriculum, you may find a student who trusts you asking for your support. Interviews for summer and after-school jobs and for postsecondary opportunities of any sort are not likely to happen via text messages or on social media. Use role-plays and fishbowl formats (see the Appendix) to practice interviewing skills.

Here are some questions to get students started:

For jobs

❓ What are the reasons you want this job? Being ready with multiple reasons can allow a student to tailor a response to the interviewer's tone.

❓ What are the skills you have that would help us?

❓ In what ways does this job fit in with your future goals?

❓ What do you think you will need help with at first to do the job well?

For college

❓ Why do you want to attend this college?

❓ What groups or activities would you hope to be involved in here at the university?

❓ Where do you see yourself after college?

❓ What are a few issues, local or in the larger world, that seem especially important to you? How are you impacted or involved?

Teach and model the steps of a good apology.

Mistakes are inevitable in the social cauldron of schools, at times interfering with a student's ability to focus on the academic task at hand. Many students do not know how to do more than mumble, "Sorry." Often they do not even do that. Without a good apology, the social miscues linger through a class period, and perhaps much longer, distracting concentration and limiting the back-and-forth sharing of ideas that is essential to a learning community.

The heart of a good apology is the desire to reestablish trust, and therefore conveys that the apologizer has noticed the impact she had, is seeing the interaction from the other's perspective, and is taking responsibility. Sometimes words and a commitment to a different approach in the future are sufficient; other times making amends involves an action. If "to err is human," then a good apology may be one of the most critical abilities to maintain not only individual relationships, but the culture of learning.

Apologizing well is a learned skill. But the sound of a bad apology, one that does not repair the relationship and the social environment, seems obvious to almost everyone when they hear:

- "I'm sorry if you felt hurt." *If* sounds like you haven't bothered to notice that they were indeed hurt or don't want to admit that you know the other person felt hurt.

- "I'm sorry for whatever I said." *Whatever* doesn't let the other person know that you're aware of what you said; perhaps you will say it again and again.

- "I'm sorry but . . . " emphasizes whatever comes after *but*, not the apologizing part. Some people tack on an insult or a threat, believing that saying "I'm sorry . . . " allows them to say anything after those words. Insults and threats overrule. The brain has evolved to protect first, and to connect only if it's safe.

- Body language matters—no sarcasm or eye-rolling.

To learn how to apologize effectively, we offer a structure with three key components:

- Identifying the specific action that was problematic
- Identifying the community value that was broken
- Offering to make amends

To support you modeling the skill, we start with a teacher apologizing after rushing a student:

- "I'm sorry I didn't give you enough time to respond. I really value giving students time to think, not rushing you. I'd like to hear now what you wanted to say, and I'll do my best to give you the time you need in the future."

The example above, of a teacher apologizing to a student, underscores how critically important it is to the culture of learning that teachers model this skill. A good apology does not relinquish teacher authority, as some fear, but reaffirms the power adults have in upholding community values in both word and deed. Particularly for many traumatized and abused students, a good apology from a teacher may be the very first time an adult has ever truly apologized to them—and can literally alter in that moment the foundation of those students' ability to trust you. They will know that you have their backs as they try to do their best work.

What does an effective apology sound like?

- "I'm sorry that I hurt you when I said you were an idiot. I don't think we should call each other names. I won't say it again."
- "Oh, my mistake. I know our project is important. I'll be ready next time."
- "I apologize. I should have asked you privately, not in the cafeteria. I know we should talk about that stuff in private, not in public."

Explain to students that apologizing well does not necessarily mean you will be forgiven. Forgiveness is the other person's task.

To give students practice in a good apology, share the structure above and have them craft apologies using the following scenes. You can jointly make up others for additional practice.

- A student mocked another student's voice in class.
- A student interrupted a lesson.
- A teacher raised her voice to a student in the hallway.
- A sports coach didn't show a student how to effectively do his or her job.

Apologizing is also a part of restorative justice classroom practices in Chapter 4, pages 66–67 and schoolwide practices in Chapter 12, page 223.

Develop class and group rituals for thanking people.

Communicating effectively is about building bridges to other people. Showing that we appreciate others is a strong way to build social connections and capital, while neglecting to thank people can burn bridges instead of build them.

Help students express their thanks, whether written or verbal, in ways that are sincere and specific. "Thank you for taking the time to speak to our class about ____.

I was especially interested in _____." Such a message is more likely to spark a return visit than writing "Thank you for speaking to our class," or not writing at all.

Thank you notes and statements can also remind students to notice the people around them—classmates who help them (see "one-minute appreciation rituals" in Chapter 3, page 46), custodians who are friendly, secretaries who deliver lunches that had been left home. When we express appreciation, we take time to feel grateful, build relationships, and learn humility and social skills—all contributing factors toward resilience. Adults take the lead here: if your class, group, team, or club has benefited from the efforts of others, show the students what it looks and sounds like to communicate thanks.

Discussion Options for Faculty

- Which practices in this chapter seem especially important for your students?

- Which skills mentioned in this chapter are especially important for you to practice?

- Where and how can you teach students about the concepts and skills in this chapter and make sure they get regular practice at:

  o Considering their messages, audiences, and modes

  o Listening patiently, speaking patiently, asking open-ended questions, giving and accepting feedback

  o Learning to talk with adults and making "place and time" choices

  o Asserting themselves respectfully

  o Appreciating others

  o Learning to apologize effectively

- What opportunities are there in your classes or advisories for students to conduct interviews as a way to build speaking and listening skills into the curriculum?

- Many teachers feel compromised when students complain about other teachers or ask them to help them prepare to talk to another teacher. What guidelines can you develop so you don't feel you are undermining another teacher and still support students learning to be assertive?

- Consider this discussion topic about technology and conversation: Teacher and writer Paul Barnwell (2014) notes, "Online discussion boards and Twitter are useful tools for exchanging ideas. But they often encourage a 'read, reflect, forget about it' response that doesn't truly engage students in extended critical thinking or conversation. All too often I've seen students simply post one (required) response to the prompt . . . ." How do you as teachers use technology while encouraging deep consideration and exchange of ideas?

- Use a listening lab among the adults. In our experience, many teachers will be surprised at how uncomfortable or unfamiliar talking and listening without interruption is. Try different lengths of time and use the format regularly in faculty meetings and workshops. It can add some extra skill building to turn-and-talk interactions.

Practices at Home

Teens need an increasing array of communication skills to navigate school and peer issues, all while their brains are changing enough that thoughtfulness and subtlety might be difficult to marshal. Research shows that today's teens are extremely reliant on communicating through technology and less familiar and skilled at conversation than prior generations. This discrepancy will not serve them well in relationships in school or life. Through conversations with you, they can practice several crucial skills.

Listening is a cornerstone of every relationship and takes a lot of practice to do well. Take a moment to think of someone who listens deeply to you. What do they do and say?

Modeling is your strongest tool to help kids learn to listen (or learn any communication skill—mirror neurons in our brains make copying behaviors the fastest way to learn). In conversations with your teens, give them full attention, ask clarifying questions, and check to see if you understood them. Instead of arguing a given point, listen to their perspective and reflect back something about what you hear.

- "I'm not sure I understood what you meant about _____."

- "Can you say more about _____?"

- "So, what you're trying to accomplish is _____?"

- "It sounds like _____ is the most important aspect to you. Is that so?"

When you reflect back their thinking, they might hear it in a different way and catch their own thinking errors. Be patient with teens' answers. They may or may not be well reasoned or well articulated. The overarching point, in addition to keeping them safe, is to stay connected while they go through their teen years—and that will keep them safer.

Make conversation a high priority at the breakfast and dinner table, in the car, and other daily or weekly routines. In an interview on National Public Radio, Dr. Sherry Turkle (2012b), founder of MIT's Initiative on Technology and Self, described the impact of parents texting at games, in playgrounds, and other places rather than paying attention to their children. Consider what she described: "Parents text at games . . . Parents are on the phones in cars, and the kids are . . . on their devices instead of having those precious moments . . . to talk to your kids on the way to school. So children grow up learning that they're not the center of their parents' attention." Turkle has observed that teens, having learned their relationship to technology from their parents, demonstrate the same inattention to parents that they've been shown.

Coach rather than lecture. Even while your non-negotiable family rules are still held strong, teenagers' need for autonomy may make them bristle when lectured. Try coaching with succinct and straightforward questions and suggestions. Your teens' rapidly changing brains are often too disorganized to pick out the main message inside a long parent lecture.

- "Did you try _____?"

- "In that situation, I would worry about _____. Is that a concern for you too?"

- "What decision will keep you safe?"

- "What's your main concern right now? How important will it be next week?"

- "Let's talk about some unintended consequences that might happen."

Give feedback. This chapter includes several techniques for giving feedback (pages 102–104), which are useful for home as well as school. These techniques support teenagers' need to develop their identities, self-awareness, and self-assessment skills.

Practice respectful assertion. Teens need to assert themselves, though few are skillful yet. It will likely help if you can take a leap of faith that they are trying to exercise autonomy, rather than being rude or defiant. When your teen has a challenge to address with another family member or with a teacher, offer to rehearse with him. If his statement prompts you to feel defensive, identify which words or phrases had the negative impact, and have him try again.

Talk with teens about "place and time" choices. They have choices about how they dress, speak, and behave in different settings. They may be unaware of distinctions between settings; they may have forgotten distinctions. They may also be exploring an aspect of their evolving identity. Short of a safety issue, coaching and questions are usually more effective than commands and lecturing. "What do you want to show about yourself?" "What are the benefits of this style?" "What might be the costs?"

Talk about technology and social media directly and frequently. Most teenagers are adept at using devices, bringing benefits and drawbacks. One challenge is that many young people have access to vastly more technology than they know how to responsibly use. They don't all keep in mind that anything e-mailed or texted can be forwarded; anything posted to social media lives forever. Urge them to craft a final check before posting: "What if my friend saw this text?" "What if Grandma saw this photo?" "What if my teacher saw this post?" Ask them to share with you the questions they ask themselves before texting or posting. Whatever question works for them, encourage them to practice it; recommend that they make it a refrain.

Since social media is a source of camaraderie as well as hurt and stress among teens, check with your kids occasionally about their online social lives. How much time are they spending on social media? Is anything bothering them? What interactions have worked well in that medium? What interactions would have been better in person or on the phone?

Lastly, model and teach that turning the devices off is actually an option, and an important one. Turn your devices off before dinner; have a drawer or basket where everyone's phone goes. Be sure to make a regular routine of turning devices off before sleeping. Whether or not a message arrives with a ping, the expectation that one might arrive at any moment disrupts relaxation and sleep. Most teens' sleep habits and needs are already problematic; don't let devices make them worse (see Tool 7-1, pages 134–136, for more information). Help them make healthy decisions about activities that should be uninterrupted—at least meals, sleep, good conversations, and homework.

TOOL 6-1   Feedback Starters and Responses

Feedback Starters

Remember key qualities to give feedback that students can USE:
usable, **s**pecific, **e**ncouraging.

- Now I understand _____ better.
- The _____ part was really clear.
- The _____ part was memorable.
- I like how . . .
- Your idea reminded me of . . .
- Now I'm curious about . . .
-

- I am not sure about . . .
- The _____ part wasn't clear.
- The _____ part confused me.
- I didn't see how the _____ and _____ parts connected.
- I want to add . . .
-

Feedback Responses

1. Take steps so you can be ready to hear feedback.

   - Take a few deep breaths.

   - Have some self-talk messages that you use over time and become your habit.
     - "I can only know how my presentation sounds to others if I hear reactions."
     - "Listening is just listening; then I'll decide what to do with the feedback."
     -
     -
     -

2. Remember that once given, the feedback is yours to use fully, use partly, or set aside. "Thanks for your feedback" can be followed by

   - "I agree."
   - "I'll think about it."
   - "Can you explain more about _____?"
   - "Wow, I hadn't thought about it that way."
   -
   -
   -

TOOL 6-2   Presentation Rehearsal Instructions

Follow these steps with the feedback partners taking notes below.

Round 1: Presenter: _____   Feedback partner: _____

1. The presenter shares his/her project, portfolio, or exhibition.
2. The feedback partner offers reactions.
   - Name three things that were clear, interesting, or memorable.

   - What are two suggestions for improving the presentation?

3. The presenter gets a chance to ask for clarification on a suggestion and/or add a suggestion of his/her own.
4. The presenter gets a day or more to make revisions and practice.

Round 2: Presenter: _____

Feedback group: _____

5. The presenter does a dress rehearsal in front of several peers.
   - Name three things that were clear, interesting, or memorable.

   - What are two suggestions for improving the presentation?

6. The presenter gets a chance to ask for clarification on a suggestion and/or add a suggestion of his/her own.
7. Closing: The feedback partners and presenter thank each other.

TOOL 6-3   Feedback Trio Instructions

Follow these steps and take notes below.

Presenter: _____

Feedback partners: _____   _____   _____

1. The presenter shares his/her essay, story, project, or other effort.
2. Everyone takes a minute or two to jot notes—silently in this step.
    - What parts were clear, interesting, or memorable to you?

    - What was unclear, disconnected, or confusing to you?

3. After the presentation, the presenter offers some self-assessment.
    - What parts went as you'd expected? What are proud of?

    - Which parts did not go as you'd expected?

4. Each feedback partner responds to the questions below. The presenter takes notes.
    - What came across well to you? (It was well explained, interesting, memorable . . .)

    - What was disconnected, confusing, or unclear to you?

    - What suggestions can you offer?

5. The presenter identifies two key things to add, change, edit, or polish.
6. Closing: The feedback partners thank the presenter. The presenter thanks the partners.

TOOL 6-4   Talk So You Can Be Heard

In each example below, you'll see a way of addressing an adult that could easily backfire because it commands or blames. Write a statement or question that would let you address the same concern, and would more likely be heard and considered by adults.

1. To a teacher: "You never think I work hard!"

In order to be heard, change to _____

_____

2. To a teacher: "You have to give me a new project partner."

In order to be heard, change to _____

_____

3. To a coach: "I need more playing time."

In order to be heard, change to _____

_____

4. To a club advisor: "You always give Dani the easier tasks."

In order to be heard, change to _____

_____

5. To a boss: "Your directions were really confusing."

In order to be heard, change to _____

_____

6. To a parent/guardian: "If I can't stay out late on Saturday it's clear you don't trust me."

In order to be heard, change to _____

_____

7

Managing Work and Developing a Work Ethic, Not Just Passing or Cramming

Every educator we've met wants students to become independent learners, able to manage their schedules, prioritize assignments, and improve their own abilities to learn. These skills and habits would prepare students for higher education as well as community roles and work life. However, the phrase, "improve their own abilities to learn," is more complicated than it might sound.

This chapter begins with an activity in which students learn about recent neuroscience research, showing that their brains are constantly changing and growing, based on the experiences they have. Students will learn that "improving their own abilities to learn" is something they can impact, that their abilities are not determined already. Via regular practice, students will also learn what tools work for them to organize, study, and manage tasks. This combination of awareness and skills fosters persistence and optimism. Helping students believe in their own ability to learn is one of the most effective strategies that teachers can use (Hattie, 2009).

The effort your students put into their day-to-day work determines their future more than standardized test scores. Quite simply, scoring well on standardized tests does not predict doing well in college. Knowing how to make the most of one's hard work, shown through success in classes, is a better predictor: "self-discipline, intellectual curiosity and hard work; that's what matters the most. Students with good grades and modest testing did better in college than students with higher testing and lower high school grades" (Sheffer, 2014).

Research on implicit theories of intelligence is another source offering insights on improving abilities. Carol Dweck has demonstrated that students' beliefs about their abilities to learn impact their success. If they believe they were born smart (or not), they demonstrate a belief that one's intelligence level is "fixed." For instance, they are good at math, or they aren't. These students believe that learning is related to predetermined ability, not trying harder. Even students who have been successful at math, upon experiencing a more advanced math class as difficult, lose confidence and stop trying. After all, if you believe in a "fixed mindset" about intelligence, having to try hard means you're not smart!

On the other hand, if students believe that they can become smarter by exercising their brains more, they demonstrate a "growth mindset." They try harder, which builds their capacity to learn. The last twenty years of brain research validates this mindset, showing that the human brain does become stronger with more learning (along with eating healthy food, getting physical exercise, sleeping sufficiently, and managing stress), so we have an important opportunity to help teenagers understand how to improve their own abilities to learn.

Dweck's research also shows that adults hold these same beliefs about intelligence. We convey the beliefs when we give feedback, and our beliefs affect students' beliefs. When we say, "good luck," we emphasize that students need luck. When we say, "I know you did the work to be prepared," or "You're juggling a lot; it's great that you're using your calming routine," or "This project showed a lot of effort and creativity," we convey that the student has made choices and taken steps to impact their performance. Helping students improve their abilities to learn requires us to believe—and convey that we believe—that students' efforts matter.

Trying harder needs to be strategic and reflective. Trying harder in the same ineffective way at the same task is not likely to be of much help. Recognizing which homework habits are effective, which aren't, and choosing the former, does help. Becoming conscious about one's learning preferences, utilizing strengths and working on weaknesses, helps. Experimenting with different ways of keeping track of assignments, finding a way that works, helps. Adults need to make a regular habit of talking with students about their habits, effort, and progress, not just test outcomes, and helping students see how their efforts impact their outcomes.

Another aspect to emphasize in helping students improve their abilities to learn is developing a positive and persistent work ethic. For example, learning to prioritize tasks is a skill for managing work. Doing so regularly, and believing that prioritizing matters, fosters a work ethic. It's the combination that is powerful—having strong skills, using them regularly, and believing that such diligence will be worth it. To be resilient, students have to believe that they have some control over their success, and they have to believe that organizing, prioritizing, and effort matter. The combination of skills for managing work and having a work ethic will help students overcome setbacks, persevere through tedious tasks, and be invested in their own learning. A story offers an example:

> We worked with an alternative high school for students with tumultuous high school careers. The faculty affectionately referred to middle-of-the-pack students who consistently put forth high effort as "pluggers"—students who dedicated themselves to studying, asked for extra help, and used their inner resources to block out distractions to complete assignments. The faculty

insisted they could clearly see a student cross the threshold: "Excellent, Isabelle is now a plugger!" Many pluggers were more successful than students whose "intelligence" test scores were much higher. But pluggers were also at risk if they studied two hours for a test in a very inefficient manner, resulting in a low score. Those students, despite their best intentions, were less likely to try again. They took the test score as evidence of their intelligence, made worse because this time they had tried.

Struggling with study skills and habits is an all too common situation for students with attention deficit disorders, learning disabilities, and executive functioning difficulties. Parents and teachers attempt to buoy up these students by assuring them that they are smart, while a lack of skills in studying result in consistently poor grades. Without understanding themselves as learners, and without developing their own unique ways to work hard, these students often become despairing, and undervalue the intelligence they do possess.

There is one more puzzle piece for managing work and establishing a work ethic. Above, we discussed becoming more knowledgeable about one's developing brain, learning skills, and building the habit of using those skills. The next piece is having and using one's own quality standards. How do you know when something is done well, or isn't yet done well? Students are frequently assessed *externally* via feedback, graded assignments, course tests, and standardized tests. Many students work on a project for several hours and stop because they've spent several hours on it, not because they had internalized a quality standard for knowing it was accurate, thorough, and polished. Other students work hard on a project without the confidence that they created something of quality, until somebody else says it's high quality, feeling anxious throughout the process. Internalizing standards of quality, and taking pride in meeting those standards, is an important aspect of having a work ethic.

It is important to differentiate having *quality* standards from *perfectionism*. Striving for quality is realistic and motivating. Striving for perfection is rarely realistic, often self-defeating, and risky to emotional health. Perfectionism often leads to problems— poor sleep, eating challenges, low self-esteem, fear of school—becoming *maladaptive perfectionism*. Psychologist Madeline Levine (2006) describes how perfectionism plays out in affluent families: "I understand the contempt of my teenage patients who roll their eyes in session when a parent says . . . the ubiquitous 'Just do your best.' Too often these duplicitous statements are used to mask a disturbing truth, that what is expected by many parents in affluent communities is not a personal best but the absolute best . . . The tendency of affluent communities to focus on and overly value external measures of accomplishment is directly related to high rates of depression and substance abuse . . . " (pp. 179–180). We must help students—in all communities— learn to self-assess, strive to do high-quality work, and take pride in that work. These internal assessments are crucial to their mental health and resilience.

Consider these scenarios—now and again at the end of the chapter—in which students don't have sufficient skills and habits to manage work and/or haven't developed a serious work ethic:

A student approaches staff with desperation in his voice, mentioning the various assignments he has in no particular order, insisting that it's not fair to be assigned so much work.

A student cares much more about her grade rather than the task at hand. Since the grade is far more important than the learning opportunity, she finds a website with papers already written on the subject and copies some text.

A student hasn't been very successful academically and stops trying. If he then isn't successful, he can blame it on not trying, rather than being stupid. Claiming the former helps him save a little pride.

A student works diligently on an assignment, turns it in, expecting it to be perfect. The assignment comes back from the teacher with a few comments appreciating the strengths of the work done, and also pointing out some aspects that could be improved. The student was sure she'd completed the assignment's steps correctly, and feels crushed at what she perceives as deep criticism.

A student has a variety of assignments for different classes, is on an athletic team, and has meetings this week for two clubs he joined to bolster his college application. He is studying late into the night, and isn't sleeping enough, though he is still submitting acceptable work in classes. He knows his work could have been better. He was tired at team practice today, so wasn't his best there either.

The students described above demonstrate not having organization, motivation, self-assessment, or prioritizations skills. Just as importantly, they demonstrate a lack of awareness that they could have those skills. Having such skills lets students manage their work; believing in the efficacy of having such skills lets them develop a worth ethic. This chapter deals with each of those aspects.

Many structures of contemporary schooling were designed based on beliefs that intelligence is narrow and preordained, rather than fluid and dynamic. Those structures have been with us so long that it may be hard to imagine an alternative. Here is one: a high-achieving suburban high school with a thousand students does not have classes divided into honors and other levels. Instead, any student can contract for honors work in any class—work that is more challenging, expands to areas of personal interest, or makes connections across classes. Honors is about the student choosing to take on a meaty challenge and the quality of the work produced, rather than a status symbol. Given that traditional secondary schools haven't changed much of their design since the 1890s, we have to be that much more conscious of conveying that all students' brains are most assuredly still growing and changing.

 ## Practices That Build Skills and Habits for Managing Work and Developing a Work Ethic

Teach students about their own brain development and growth mindset.

Musicians know that if they practice a piece of music they will get better at it. They no longer need to read every individual note; unusual combinations of notes become familiar; different segments become a whole. They may or may not know that their brains have grown new synapses, connections that did not exist until their effort made them grow. Athletes practice certain movements that might initially feel awkward and challenging, until they become natural and skillful. In the process, their brains grow the synapses to coordinate their limbs, eyesight, and breathing. This dynamic quality of the brain is called *plasticity*. Students need to know that their adolescent brains are especially plastic; what they do during their teenage years enormously impacts how their brains develop.

When music teachers and athletic coaches are helping their students and players improve, they point out improvements step by step, and also help them develop habits for practice and perseverance. These habits become built into their brains.

Whether we are teaching students history or science, we need them to know how to use their brains well, as if it were a muscle—how to strengthen and stretch their perspectives and attention, how to practice and improve how it functions. This effort starts with knowing more about one's own brain, and understanding that it changes through time and experiences—for better or worse.

Tool 7-1 includes several condensed bits of research about adolescent brain development to introduce students to some important aspects of their brains. Whether you use this activity in biology, psychology, advisory, a wellness class, a study skills class, or other part of school, all teachers will have ways to apply the information and insights to their teaching and in their conversations with students.

Use the passages in any of the following ways. With younger or struggling readers, the quotes reflection format will provide more support.

- **Quotes reflection:** Choose a paragraph to project onto the board or read aloud, and discuss it in pairs and with the whole group. Continue with another research bit afterward or on later days. Use any of these questions as they apply to the paragraph you've chosen.

    - ❓ What did you learn? What surprised you?
    - ❓ What insights did the research give you about how your brain functions?
    - ❓ What ideas did the research give you about what to do to strengthen your brain?
    - ❓ What ideas did the research give you about how to learn or study effectively?
    - ❓ How does a person become more intelligent?

- **Quotes café:** Copy the paragraphs on Tool 7-1 and cut them into strips. Follow the steps explained in the Appendix so students can read and discuss different bits of brain research. Save time to debrief. Consider splitting the research to use on more than one day.

- Use any aspect of the research that sparks curiosity for further investigation.

Help students identify and share their learning preferences and habits.

Everyone who works with teens can observe that some students show more skill and fluency with verbal tasks, others with visual, mathematical, mechanical, or physical tasks. Cognitive neuroscientists like Mary Helen Immordino-Yang and Jeb Schenck warn against seeing these abilities as fixed learning styles, explaining that anything "fixed" is a misunderstanding of brain science. Students use different learning modes and levels of effort for different tasks, different modes in different classes, and still other modes in nonacademic activities. Teen brains are changing, not fixed, and not destined to learn in only one or two ways (Immordino-Yang, 2016; Schenck, 2011).

Though students' brains and skills are still developing, they've already got some learning modes that they use more fluidly and naturally than others. Being aware of those preferences will help students take advantage of them. For example, if they are confused about something they're reading for class, does it help them to write a few summary statements, make a diagram of how several bits of information connect, or talk about the reading with a study partner?

Becoming more aware of their learning preferences and habits also allows students to work on their weaker areas—finding out what their preferred skills are doesn't release them from building additional skills. Even if diagraming concepts isn't their usual way to learn, it will likely be an important skill to use someday. The same is true for any learning mode.

There are many inventories available to help students identify their preferred learning modes. Start by asking your guidance counselors, who may have inventories, or use college access electronic systems that include inventories about learning preferences as well as interests. You can also find tools online by searching under "learning style inventory." Another resource is the book, *Engage Every Student,* by Elizabeth Kirby and Jill McDonald (2009), which has self-inventories on motivation style, multiple intelligences, and a procrastination reflection. Whatever the source, be sure to use a tool that has explanations of the styles to share with students, in language your students will understand. Make sure the tool stresses that students can strengthen any learning mode.

Taking the inventory is only the first step. The goal is to help students be aware of how they can manage their work better and advocate for themselves. Discuss the results to discern what they mean for learning best in class and at home. The following questions can be journal prompts or discussion prompts for groups comprised of students with similar preferences, and then used as debriefing questions for the whole group:

? Based on this information about your learning preferences, how might it help you to take notes or review your notes?

? Based on this information about your learning preferences, what technique might help you prepare for a test?

? Based on this information about your learning preferences, what weaker skill do you think would help you if it were stronger? What can do to practice it?

In almost any lesson in any subject, teachers can help students deepen their understanding of learning preferences and habits. After introducing the lesson and giving the directions and exemplars, give ten seconds of think time for the students to consider these two questions:

? What learning mode may be best to use for this task?

? How could you modify other modes to help you with this task?

With this short reflection and conversation at the beginning of a lesson, students can reap huge benefits. Also, see Chapter 9, pages 169–170, "Help students identify, share, and work from their strengths," for additional ways to help students use their learning preferences and habits to their advantage.

Develop skills and routines for setting short-term goals about effort and habits.

Goals range from short term to long term, outcome focused to effort focused. They are not all created equal! Let's consider a goal of losing thirty pounds, the stuff of many a New Year's resolution. Losing thirty pounds is an outcome, not accomplished quickly, and the end result of many hourly and daily steps. Losing thirty pounds is a long-term outcome goal. It will be accomplished by setting short-term effort goals, and following through on those goals, starting perhaps with walking a mile three times per week and switching two sugary drinks to water every day. In the process, those effort goals become new exercise and eating habits.

Though the parallel to school might be obvious to some, we have found that the grade-focused culture of schools is so omnipresent, that it takes many educators and students conscious effort to make the switch to effort goals. "I want to get a B in math" is a long-term outcome goal. That student cannot measure it today or tomorrow. Without concrete steps, it's just a wish, not a true goal. "I will do five practice problems three nights per week" is a short-term effort goal. That student will know very soon if she is on track, and when she does the problems, she can notice if she is confused, leading to another possible effort goal, "I will be a better advocate for my own learning by asking my teacher questions."

When trying something new becomes a regular routine, each of those effort goals becomes a new learning habit. At the end of the term, a student can see the results of her new habits—whether she understood the math concepts enough to earn the B, or at least got closer to it. She can then continue to use those habits, build on them, or try a new strategy. "My teacher gave me a B," said with blame or as if it's a mystery is replaced with "Here's what I did to earn that B."

Another advantage to a focus on effort and habits is to get away from perfectionistic outcome goals, which not only add stress, but also have been shown to reduce risk taking and enjoyment in learning. If a student (or parent) holds as a goal getting an A in every subject, every term, the student might not enroll in courses that are difficult or outside her already-established area of strength. Within classes, he might stick to noncontroversial project ideas, or even cheat.

Any teacher in any subject can try this exercise: Introduce the terms, *long-term goals*, *short-term goals*, *outcome goals*, *effort goals*, and *learning habits* to students or advisees by writing them on the board. Brainstorm examples of each that are specific to your course. Effort-focused goals might deal with study habits, attendance, participating in class, organizing tasks, using resources when they're needed, or many other efforts—the more specific, the better. Some students would benefit from participating more in class; others could be more restrained. Students could try studying before dinner, or in a quiet place, or take five-minute stretch breaks every half hour. They could try a new kind of task list, or clean out their backpack every week. For high-achieving, highly stressed students, an effort goal could be getting more sleep, or learning and practicing mindfulness or another stress-reducing routine.

Then have your students or advisees set an effort goal that can build into a learning habit. Tool 7-2, "Building Constructive Learning Habits," is a sample template. Encourage them to work on one habit at a time. Be sure to check on students' progress soon—a few days later or a week later—and make adjustments to the goal if needed.

Some teachers and advisors have found it useful to have the whole group work on a goal within one area, such as organization skills. It can become a weekly ritual to clean out backpacks, or a group effort to design a new task-organizer template. If students are comparing notes on what study habits they are trying out, it can become a norm to focus on process, not just product, to experiment and problem-solve, and to support each other's efforts. Such a classroom exercise supports a sense of "I can manage me," "I can figure this out," "I'm getting better," and "I have people around me who support me."

Help students set goals for character development.

Many students hear about their deficits more often than their assets, an outcome of test-focused schooling and traditional critique processes. (See more on asset-based feedback in Chapter 6, page 103.) Many others perceive deficits from perfectionistic media images, parental pressure, or peer competition. For all these reasons, teenagers, many of whom are self-conscious anyway, can be all too aware of their deficits, real or imagined. Recognizing one's assets and building on them is an empowering step in teenagers' identity development.

Goals aren't only applicable to tasks and work; they also apply to character. What characteristics do students think of themselves as having? What behaviors demonstrate those characteristics? What characteristics do they aspire to have? Character is based on actions. When a student learns to run a class discussion or lead her project group, she is showing and practicing leadership. When a student helps a struggling classmate, he is showing and practicing empathy and kindness. When a student works hard through a difficult course, strategically improving study habits, she is showing and practicing persistence and reflection. When a student wants to be trusted, rather than demanding it, he acts in a trustworthy manner.

Similar to task- and work-related goals, character goals are the outcome of making certain behaviors a regular habit. Developing the habits that are then internalized as character qualities supports achieving in school, developing a work ethic, and a strong sense of identity.

- **Project or read aloud this quote from author Stephen Covey**: "Our character is basically a composite of our habits. Because they are consistent, often unconscious patterns, they constantly, daily, express our character." Ask students or advisees to talk in pairs or write in journals about the question: What do you think your daily habits in this setting show about your character?

- **Find additional quotes to discuss, such as from Martin Luther King**, "The ultimate measure of a man is not where he stands in moments of comfort and convenience, but where he stands at times of challenge and controversy." Even better, have students or advisees find the quotes that say something important to them about character.

- **Identifying role models** for specific characteristics can help students picture the characteristics more fully, and aspire to them. What qualities do students see demonstrated by scientists, artists, mathematicians, historical figures, current leaders, or characters in literature? Who do they respect in school, in their families, communities, and in the larger world? What characteristics do those people demonstrate?

- **Use the character goal-setting template**, Tool 7-3, "Developing My Best Self." You can start with a reflection about a recent time when students were proud of something they did in class or elsewhere. Be prepared to encourage or suggest a quality to specific students who find this task difficult or awkward.

- **Delve into a specific character trait** when needed, for example, perseverance. You can open a conversation about perseverance by asking students to identify the person they think is represented in the statements on Tool 7-4, "Who Persevered?" and discussing their process and accomplishments. The people represented, in order, are Dr. Seuss, J. K. Rowling, Thomas Edison, Harriet Tubman, Walt Disney, Emily Blunt, and Michael Jordan. Discuss with students what each person did to show perseverance, what they might have felt, and what goals might have driven them to continue in their efforts. Ask students what they might have done in those situations. If students aren't likely to know some of the names, offer them. The discussion about character traits is the purpose of the activity, more important than guessing names.

- **Set your own character goal.** Because role modeling is so vital for teens, and because we shouldn't ask teens to do tasks that we ourselves shy away from, tell students the type of character traits you want them to perceive in you, and that you want to enhance as a professional: "I want you to see me as caring about each of you. The steps I'm taking are working on my listening skills, especially during check-in conversations."

Make improving study habits an experiment—on themselves.

Are your students certain that it doesn't matter whether they do their homework with the TV on, their phone nearby with all social networking apps sending notifications, or right after school versus late at night? Run some experiments in class or in advisory groups to test their beliefs.

You can do the following activity in a couple of ways: (1) Save some time in class to start homework, with you working at your desk in parallel mode. Or (2) find some games or brainteasers, the kind that require concentration, have time limits, and give a score, such as Boggle, Scattegories, or a memory game with cards or objects (spread out 10–20 cards or objects to remember within a minute or two; have a towel or scarf handy to cover them). If you have tablets or computers, you can use or project the online SET game daily puzzle. The game doesn't have a time limit, but you can give it one. Over time, use visual as well as verbal games. We encourage students to contribute games, puzzles, and ideas from their backgrounds. When you use this activity, on some days, have a quiet, well-lit environment. On other days, add some variables:

- Play music, especially music with lyrics, loud enough to reach the whole room.

- Set your cell phone to go off repeatedly and frequently as you walk around the room.

- Say that today will be a competition against each other and the clock. Project a large ticking countdown clock on the board or use a timer that can be heard easily.

- Allow them to work with a partner.

Have students keep track of their results and discuss the different situations.

❓ How did you score on different days?

❓ What helped you stay on task?

❓ Which distractions affected you the most?

❓ What changes to homework habits will you try?

Have the class identify ways they can help each other study.

Discuss ways students can support each other in studying. Have them try the ideas. Afterward, talk about the pros and cons. They'll become more intentional learners, and build a stronger learning community. A few options might be the following:

- In class, students can work in pairs, explaining the information they know well.

- Students can volunteer to share their notes.

- The class can brainstorm ways to study for an upcoming test.

- Teachers can assign study-buddies for a unit, who are periodically given time together in class to share their work, and who are held responsible for being first contacts when one of them is absent.

Develop skills and routines for managing tasks and time.

Most of us—over time—have found a way of keeping track of our tasks, even if we are still working on making our days manageable. Eventually students will as well, but they would be more successful in school and in the rest of their lives if they developed a system for tracking tasks sooner rather than later. Use Tool 7-5, "What I Plan to Do This Week" for students to track their schoolwork and other commitments, including teams, clubs, exercise, appointments, and socializing. Students can also use the templates in their school date book, on their cell phones or tablets, or design their own.

Some students many need extra monitoring. For example, many students have a hard time managing longer-term projects, which need tasks done consistently over time. Students who adapt their own template may need help making adjustments. Students who seem consistently overwhelmed and overcommitted may need a discussion about prioritizing. Teenage stress is at very unhealthy levels nationwide, and has lasting effects on brain development and mental health.

Teachers or advisors can include these templates in their one-to-one conferencing. These discussions may be useful at home as well as at school.

❓ When do you enter tasks in the list?

❓ When do you look at your task list?

? Where do you keep the list?

? What helps you remember to look at it?

? If you still have assignments falling through the cracks, what tool or adaptation might help?

? How do you determine priorities?

? Is there anything that you need to postpone, split into small tasks, or quit?

Consider using a juggling metaphor: If you're juggling too much, something may well drop. You can consciously set aside an item you're juggling until you can handle it, rather than having random items bounce away out of your control.

To manage time, one challenge for students is being aware of how they spend it each day. Students' assumptions are often quite different than their actual use of time. Use Tool 7-6, "Estimating a Day," to surface students' assumptions about how they are using time daily.

Then have students use the Tool 7-7, "My Daily Reality," to keep track of a real day. It might be helpful to keep track of time on two or three different days since a given day can be out of the ordinary, or be claimed to be to be out of the ordinary.

To build awareness and make choices about time, compare the two charts.

? How accurate were your estimates? Which tasks took lots more time than expected? Which tasks took less time?

? Which tasks could be adjusted?

? Were all the tasks equally important? What could you eliminate?

Self-assess work and develop academic self-improvement plans.

Are some of your students surprised when they see their grades at the end of the term? Are some students certain that they're failing—or succeeding—whether they are or not? We're sure you nodded yes to those questions, and probably pictured specific faces. Teachers and advisors can help middle and high school students learn to connect their efforts to their outcomes, and learn to monitor their own progress. In doing either, students can adjust their efforts. We offer three practices to serve these purposes.

- **Make self-assessment a regular routine.** We saw a middle school teacher use a self-assessment tool like the 1–4 scale below. On every task students handed in, from homework to classroom tasks to final tests, students considered the options below, and wrote the number on the paper in a circle. The teacher was able to organize groups for reteaches and extensions. The students quickly understood that their honest assessment and communication with the teacher helped her respond to them more effectively.

  4 = I totally understand. I could help teach it!

  3 = I understand it.

  2 = I understand some parts; others are fuzzy.

  1 = I really don't understand it yet.

- **Study routines before today's test.** Many teachers talk with students about study habits for tests, emphasizing starting three nights before the test, identifying obstacles or points of confusion, and getting help from peers, the teacher, or other sources. If you have such a conversation prior to the test, you have the opportunity to make explicit links between effort and outcome after the test. Have students fill out a self-assessment, "Study Routine Before Today's Test" (Tool 7-8), and hand it in with the test. When you give back the evaluated test, you can help students assess the impact of their study routines. Ask questions so that *they* identify the patterns, "How does your study routine connect to your test results?" "What's the one change you could make that might make the biggest difference?" You can also include the study routine self-assessment in conferences with parents and guardians.

- **Reporting my progress to myself.** The middle of a term is a key moment to take stock and exert extra effort if needed. There's evidence to look at, rather than the blank slate of the beginning of a term. And there's still time to complete, revise, or redo work. Have students or advisees use Tool 7-9, "My Progress—My Plan," to take stock and make improvement plans. Your school probably has an official "Progress Report" that goes to families. Students can learn to monitor their own progress, and be ready to explain their improvement plans to parents and guardians. Emphasize using real data rather than guessing. Do role-plays to rehearse conversations with parents and guardians.

Help students become their own problem solvers.

When students are stuck or overwhelmed, it may be an automatic reaction to give them a suggestion or a direction. However, they will more likely learn to be their own resourceful and self-reliant problem solvers if you ask questions and coach them to come up with their own options and solutions. Consider questions such as the ones below the next time you're faced with a student who seems to be asking for you to solve his or her challenge.

- What resources have you tried? What are some other resources you could try?

- How about writing down your assignments, and then tell me which are due first and which are the biggest (or hardest for you)? If writing is a challenge for a given student, ask them to talk you through what they've got due.

- What are your commitments this term (including to your own academic success)? Which are your priorities? Which can you drop?

- Where do you usually do your homework? What are some other options?

- What study routines have you been trying? What are some other options?

Try an appreciative approach to coaching students.

Imagine that a student has struggled to complete homework. If a teacher were to say to him "You don't have your homework . . . again. What's your excuse this time?" the student learns nothing more than that his deficits are as significant as he fears they are. In contrast, if he hears "Last Tuesday, you got your homework in. Let's go over what was happening on Monday night and Tuesday morning, so we can figure out what was working. Then we can see what got in the way last night or this morning."

There are three important aspects to this appreciative approach:

- It builds from a <u>specific positive</u> experience. You're not focusing on a negative, "You didn't get in last week's homework either. What's the problem?" It's too easy for a challenged teen to hear, "What's the problem *with you*?" rather than with his habits, and it's overwhelming to suddenly have to focus on a bigger, longer problem.

- It builds from a <u>personal</u> experience. You're not saying, "How did your friend Jay get his homework done?" Pointing out someone else's success often shames, deflating one's motivation, not inspiring it.

- It builds from a <u>real</u> experience that's already happened. You're not saying, "If you were a diligent student, what would your homework habits be?" Most students could offer a few ideas, whether or not they had any faith in their own ability to carry them out.

Almost all students, even those who so rarely demonstrate good habits, have their moments of showing glimmers of their strengths and skills. Whole teens in their families, at jobs, on teams and clubs, may be demonstrating many assets. By asking appreciative questions, teachers leverage those opportunities to help students build a vision of themselves doing the next task. They don't have to change overnight into a different person—they have to access one more time a skill they were once able to access.

We're grateful for this question style to the field of Appreciative Inquiry. (See Chapter 4 for an application of this approach to the whole class.)

Establish a practice of sharing information about progress on effort and work habits with families, including during teacher-parent/guardian conferences.

It is important for students to have a chance to explore and improve their habits away from judging eyes. You can help them and foster trust in you if many of the exercises and discussions in this chapter are treated as works in progress between you and them.

However, the exercises and discussions are also likely to give you information that parents and guardians would find insightful, or that you think is important to share. It is reasonable to pick specific templates to share with parents and guardians, telling students which ones, or decide with students which templates should be shared.

If your school has built a practice of student-involved parent-teacher conferences, or student-led conferences, these templates offer a lot of material for students to include. As you rehearse how they will talk with parents or guardians about schoolwork, you'll help them deepen their skills for communication, problem solving, and being responsible.

Discussion Options for Faculty

- Which practices in this chapter seem especially important for your students?

- Which skills mentioned in this chapter are especially important for you to practice?

- Use the introductory pages or other research paragraphs in this chapter or Tool 7-1 with the faculty. Use a quotes café format or quote-based conversations in pairs and with whole group.

  o Which points seem especially important for teenagers to understand about their own brains?

  o Which points seem especially important for teachers to understand about teenage brains?

  o What would you do differently if you incorporated that information into your teaching practice?

  o How consistently does your feedback demonstrate a belief in the plasticity of teens' brains?

- Practice improving your own learning or work efforts and habits via Tool 7-2, "Building Constructive Learning Habits."

- Where and how can you teach students about the concepts and skills in this chapter?

  o Understanding how their brains function and how they can help their brains get stronger

  o Understanding their learning preferences, and how to use their preferences effectively

  o Setting short-term effort goals, reviewing progress, making adjustments

  o Exploring their character traits, and building their character identity

  o Experimenting with study habits

  o Managing tasks and time

  o Assessing their own academic progress and making improvement plans

  o Flexible thinking

  o Success-based problem solving

- Try the following role-plays with the goal of coaching students to think creatively, resourcefully, flexibly, and strategically. What would be a helpful response in each scenario? Refrain as much as possible from giving suggestions or directions, since the goal is to improve *student* problem solving, persistence, resourcefulness, and sense of autonomy, not practice your own.

  o A student approaches staff with desperation in his voice, mentioning the various assignments he has in no particular order, insisting that it's not fair to be assigned so much work.

  o A student cares much more about her grade rather than the task at hand. Since the grade is far more important than the learning opportunity, she finds a website with papers already written on the subject and copies some text.

- A student hasn't been very successful academically and stops trying. If he then isn't successful, he can blame it on not trying, rather than being stupid. Claiming the former helps him save a little pride.

- A student works diligently on an assignment, turns it in, expecting it to be perfect. The assignment comes back from the teacher with a few comments appreciating the strengths of the work done, and also pointing out some aspects that could be improved. The student was sure she'd completed the assignment's steps correctly, and feels crushed at what she perceives as deep criticism.

- A student has a variety of assignments for different classes, is on an athletic team, and has meetings this week for two clubs he joined to bolster his college application. He is studying late into the night, and isn't sleeping enough, though he is still submitting acceptable work in classes. He knows his work could have been better. He was tired at team practice today, so wasn't his best there either.

Practices at Home

Most teens have more responsibilities as they mature, and want more autonomy. They need skills and practice to connect the two. There are several concepts and skills from this chapter that will help you in turn help your teens:

- Adolescents' brains change a lot. New connections are growing, which contribute to abstract thinking, and to inefficient and disorganized thinking. To gain efficiency, connections that aren't being used get pruned, so more area is available for activities that the teen is engaged in. A lot of brain reorganization happens during sleep.

- How teens perceive their ability to learn impacts their ability to learn. If they believe they were born smart (or not), they believe in a *fixed mindset*. Teens may believe that signs of struggle are signs to stop trying since they're just not smart, or at least not smart in that area. If they believe that trying hard makes them smarter, they believe in a *growth mindset*. Struggling is expected. In the long run, people who expend effort do better in life. Even the most brilliant and skillful people work hard.

- Teens will get more out of having *effort goals* and *habit goals*, than from *outcome goals*. An outcome goal, such as getting an A in math, is the distant result of many steps—attending and participating in class, doing homework, asking for help when needed. Those steps are efforts, which when done regularly become learning habits.

- Being perfectionistic tends to be self-defeating as it reduces risk taking to learn (choosing an easier topic for a project, for example); an overemphasis on the outcome makes cheating attractive; perfectionistic expectations put emotional health at risk.

- Teens need to develop and internalize their own quality standards and self-assessment skills. They are externally assessed frequently throughout their secondary school years. They'll need self-assessment skills to do well in learning and work opportunities throughout life. Self-assessment that is based in reality—not overinflated or overly critical—supports effective schoolwork and mental health.

Considering these concepts gives parents and guardians many opportunities to help their teens:

How you speak with kids shapes their belief about their intelligence. "You're so smart" or "I was never good at math either" convey a fixed mindset. Those sentences might be positive or negative; either way, they convey that what you've got for being successful will never change. "Your second draft was a big improvement" and "Have you tried doing five practice problems every night?" convey a growth mindset. Those sentences show that you believe in their ability to affect their learning.

Support teens to have effort goals and develop effective work habits. Encourage them to try different times, locations, and levels of distraction for homework (noisy and quiet spaces, phones on and off), making an experiment of their learning habits. Offer to play various roles: help them arrange a space, schedule a snack break together, work nearby on your own quiet tasks, rehearse how to ask their teacher for help. Explain that brains need exercise and sleep to integrate new concepts; support them to take a walk with you after a couple hours of homework, and to study—and sleep—for a few nights before a test. Focusing on these efforts and learning habits will impact their achievement in the near future and forever, and show that you are noticing and supporting their efforts. Conversely, pressuring them on grades alone is much less likely to help them be successful, and could harm your relationship and their mental health.

Help teens connect their efforts to outcomes. Once they're employing new study habits, emphasize those choices when they get grades on papers, tests, and report cards. If their results aren't what they'd like, experiment further with efforts. Note that reading alone isn't as effective a learning mode as taking and organizing notes, drawing diagrams and sketches, making timelines, asking their own questions about the work, thinking of examples and connections to other topics, and explaining the topic to you or a friend.

Effort and habits apply to building character as well as doing schoolwork. What character trait do they and you think they demonstrate well? What do they do that shows it's a real part of them? What's another character trait they'd like to have in their identity? Help them think of some ways to practice building it into their regular tasks.

Help teens try different organizational tools—calendar templates, binders, task lists. There are several tools in this chapter to use or adapt with your teenager. Talk with them about your own attempts to manage time, tasks, and priorities. Help them prioritize and split big projects into smaller steps. Over time, be sure they become their own time managers.

Help your teens spend their time well and sleep enough. How they spend their time will change their brains, and impact their success in and out of school. Help teens keep track of how much sleep they are getting and how much sleep they think they need to do their best—many researchers say that teens need at least eight hours per night. Don't be surprised if their weekend sleep schedule is both late-to-bed and late-to-rise. The hormones that regulate their daily rhythm are different for teens than for children or adults.

Support teens to learn to self-assess through homework and chores. If they ask you if they can stop doing homework, or ask you if their homework is done, turn the question around. "What was the assignment? What are the signs that it's done? What are the signs that it's done *well*?" If their chore is clearing the table after dinner, rather than telling them if you think it's done, ask, "How will you know when you're done clearing the table?" The same logic applies to any chore or responsibility. "What are the things you need to check to make sure you're ready to leave the house?" "What will it look like when you're done _____?" Offer suggestions or ask questions when their standards are not yet developed enough.

Encourage teens to be resourceful when they're stuck. "It looks like you've been trying to fix your bike from the instructions for a while now. Is there another way to approach it?" Your teen might think of a friend who could help, or an online video. You are a resource too: "Is this a time I can give you advice or ideas?"

TOOL 7-1   Brain Research and Mindset Key Concepts

| 1 | It used to be thought that humans' brains didn't physically change much after early childhood years. The last twenty years of brain research has dramatically altered that understanding for all age levels, with particular insights for the teenage years. Among other changes, teenage brains grow enormous numbers of synapses, connections between brain cells, which many researchers refer to as *wiring*. "When you learn something, the wiring in your brain changes . . . The brain is constantly learning things, so the brain is constantly rewiring itself" (Medina, 2014, p. 86). "[T]he most amazing new discovery about the brain might be that *human beings have the capacity and the choice to be able to change our own brains*" (E. Jensen, 2005, p. 10). |

| 2 | "Because humans have so much uncommitted brain tissue at birth . . . our brains have an extraordinary opportunity to become customized by life experiences . . ." (E. Jensen, 2005, p. 15). "For example, playing a musical instrument consistently over time can literally remap the brain's 'real estate.' It's as if there's a big 'Texas land grab' going on . . . an autopsy on a renowned violinist . . . found that the area of the brain responsible for hearing reception . . . was twice as thick as normal . . . It's as if the brain said, 'We need more space for what you're doing . . .'" (p. 12). The amazing and crucial opportunity for teens is realizing that their brains will change—*depending on what they spend lots of time on.* |

| 3 | The teen years are especially important for learning because teen brains are so adaptable; they can grow the synapses they need. Neuroscientist Frances Jensen explains, "That creates a huge opportunity—an optimal time window when teenagers can grow their cognitive strengths and work on their weaknesses" (Perkins-Gough, 2015, p. 17). Our brains do not see this flurry of synapse growth as all equally useful. Our brains eliminate connections that we don't seem to need. " . . . although this nearly exploding brain has more choices, it is often paralyzed by inefficiency . . . [T]he adolescent brain relies on pruning of synapses for more efficient decision making . . ." (E. Jensen, 2005, p. 30). The growing and pruning of synapses in our brains is called *plasticity*—what we do tells our brain what synapses to grow and keep. |

| 4 | The vast rewiring that the adolescent brain is doing creates some challenges. "On a gross anatomical level, most areas of the brain are under major construction during adolescence . . . The frontal lobes . . . the area of the brain responsible for thoughtful, reflective reasoning capabilities, are the last areas of the brain to mature" (Jensen, 2005, p. 30). So, one challenge is that the part of the brain that teens need to delay gratification and make good decisions isn't completely wired in yet and won't be till their twenties. Also, just as a brain at this age is more open than during adult years to grow the wiring to play a musical instrument or learn a new language, it is also more open to grow the wiring involved in bad personal or learning habits, and addictions. |

(Continued)

TOOL 7-1   (Continued)

5 | "If you ever get a chance to listen in on someone's brain while its owner is slumbering, you'll have to get over your disbelief. The brain does not appear to be asleep at all. Rather, it is almost unbelievably active during 'rest,' with legions of neurons crackling electrical commands to one another in constantly shifting, extremely active patterns" (Medina, 2014, p. 41). "It is during [sleep] that memories appear to be reactivated, reorganized, enhanced, and consolidated into more stable forms (Rasch & Born, 2008)" (Schenck, 2011, p. 253). In other words, during sleep the brain shifts experiences into long-term learning. Brain researchers consistently emphasize the importance of sleep—most say teens need eight hours or more. "Students who don't get enough sleep do worse than students who do (Thatcher, 2008). Even students who load up on caffeine . . . don't do better than students who get more sleep (Harrison & Horne, 2000) . . . " (Schenck, 2011, p. 253).

6 | We're more likely to remember new information if it's repeated, builds on something we've learned before, view it as important, or see how it connects to a larger concept. "The brain pays more attention to the gist than to the peripheral details . . . Normally, if we don't know the gist—the meaning—of information, we are unlikely to pay attention to its details" (Medina, 2014, p. 114). Also, "the more personally involved adolescents are with the learning process, the more their attention, emotional systems, and working memory are involved . . . " (Schenck, 2011, p. 271). When more neural networks are involved, more learning happens. This means being active—asking questions (of others or themselves), diagramming notes, creating examples, talking it over with a partner, making drawings to represent the topic, connecting new information to a big interesting issue.

7 | "Multitasking, when it comes to paying attention, is a myth . . . [The brain's] steps must occur in sequence *every time* you switch from one task to another. This takes time. *And it is sequential*. Three researchers at Stanford University [studied 'hyperdigital users' and 'low-key users.'] . . . The researchers called the first category of students Heavy Media Multitaskers. Their less frantic colleagues were called Light Media Multitaskers . . . In every attentional test the researchers threw at these students, the heavy users did consistently worse than the light users. Sometimes dramatically worse. They weren't as good at filtering out irrelevant information. They couldn't organize their memories as well. And they did worse on every task-switching experiment" (Medina, 2014, pp. 115–116).

(Continued)

TOOL 7-1 (Continued)

8	Researchers used sensors to measure how people react physically and emotionally when they spend time online. "Interruptions stress us out and keep us from properly concentrating, which stresses us out further, disrupting our concentration further, and on and on." Additionally, they found that people had become so accustomed to being interrupted that their attention spans were quite short. Without notification pings or other external distractions interrupting them, they interrupted themselves (All Tech Considered, 2016). Another impact of having devices nearby and turned on is that we develop a readiness for interruption, guiding conversation, concentration, and reflection to be shorter and more shallow (Immordino-Yang, 2016; Turkle, 2015).

9	It is an outdated notion that intelligence is innate, you're born smart or you're not, but some people still believe in this "fixed" idea about intelligence, which has impacts on them. "In the fixed mindset, students care first and foremost about how they'll be judged: smart or not smart. Repeatedly, students with this mindset reject opportunities to learn if they might make mistakes . . . They believe that if you have the ability, you shouldn't need effort, that ability should bring success all by itself . . . When they hit a setback in school, they *decrease* their efforts and consider cheating" (Dweck, 2007, pp. 35–36).

10	Evidence now shows that " . . . the brain is like a muscle—the more [students] exercise it, the stronger it becomes. They learned that every time they try hard and learn something new, their brain forms new connections that, over time, make them smarter. They learned that intellectual development . . . is the formation of new connections brought about through effort and learning" (Dweck, 2007, p. 38). "[for students with] the growth mindset, effort is a *positive* thing . . . In the face of failure these students escalate their efforts and look for new learning strategies . . . [W]hen we have followed students over challenging school transitions or courses, we find that those with growth mindsets outperform their classmates with fixed mindsets—even when they entered with equal skills and knowledge. A growth mindset fosters the growth of ability over time" (p. 36).

TOOL 7-2   Building Constructive Learning Habits

Think about the habits that lead to the outcomes you want. They might be habits for being on time for class, attending school, participating in class constructively, keeping track of assignments, doing homework, destressing occasionally through the day, or other habits that support effective learning.

1. What habits do you demonstrate well on most days or every day?

_____

_____

2. What habit would help you be more successful in school or make learning more enjoyable?

_____

_____

3. What are two steps you could try this week to begin to build that learning habit?

_____

_____

4. What might get in the way of implementing that learning habit? What could you do?

_____

_____

5. Monitor how you're doing on that learning habit:

Monday: _____

Tuesday: _____

Wednesday: _____

Thursday: _____

Friday: _____

Weekend: _____

TOOL 7-3   Developing My Best Self

When I'm my best self, what are three character traits I demonstrate?

_____

_____

_____

How do I demonstrate those character traits? What does it look like?

_____

_____

_____

What gets in the way sometimes of being my best self?

_____

_____

What character trait would help me be my best self more often?

_____

_____

How would that character trait help me?

_____

_____

What are two steps I can take to demonstrate the new character trait and practice it regularly?

1. _____

2. _____

The character traits below might give you some ideas. Add other character traits as well.

Adventurous	Creative	Kind	Patient
Assertive	Curious	Levelheaded	Persistent
Balanced	Dependable	Lively	Practical
Brave	Diligent	Meticulous	Purposeful
Calm	Expressive	Motivating	Respectful
Cautious	Generous	Open-minded	Responsible
Collaborative	Gutsy	Optimistic	Sensible
Confident	Idealistic	Organized	Supportive
Conscientious	Inventive	Outgoing	Well-adjusted
Other _____	Other _____	Other _____	Other _____

TOOL 7-4 Who Persevered?

 After starting out as an illustrator and a cartoonist for magazines and advertisements, this person wrote his first children's book, which a few dozen publishers rejected. He was ready to burn it when he finally got a publishing offer. Over his life, he wrote many more books about cats, Sneetches, a Lorax, and other odd characters, selling over six hundred million books.

 This person was a secretary when she got an idea for a book. In the next few years, her life included tragedy, turmoil, and poverty. Despite those challenges, she wrote the book (on a manual typewriter). Twelve publishers rejected it; the thirteenth agreed to publish it, but only one thousand copies, and he said, "I told her she wouldn't make any money at children's books, and she should get a day job" (Blais, 2005). Her books are now the best-selling book series in history.

 Teachers said this person was "too stupid to learn anything." He was fired from his first two jobs. After many tries to invent a light bulb, a reporter asked him if he would give up. His reply: "Why would I ever give up? I now know definitely over 9,000 ways an electric light bulb will not work." After 10,000 tries, he invented the light bulb, among many other things (wanderlustworker.com).

 Born into slavery in the 1800s, this person escaped, then returned again and again to help hundreds of other slaves escape via the Underground Railroad. During the Civil War, she served as a nurse, spy, and scout, and led an armed raid that liberated hundreds more slaves. After the Civil War, she worked for women's voting rights. She did all these efforts despite a brain injury in her teens that caused seizures, dizziness, and pain throughout her life.

 A newspaper editor fired this person because he "lacked imagination" (wanderlust worker.com). It took 302 failed attempts to get financing before he got funds to build his fantasy park for Snow White and Mickey Mouse.

 This person had a bad stutter from age seven to fourteen, making it difficult to even have a conversation. A teacher suggested she try out for the school play, and try different accents and character voices. By the end of her teens, she'd overcome the stutter and became a successful actor, eventually acting in *The Devil Wears Prada* and *Into the Woods*.

This NBA legend was cut from his high school varsity basketball team because of "lack of skill." He said, "I've missed more than 9,000 shots in my career. I've lost almost 300 games. Twenty-six times, I've been trusted to take the game-winning shot and missed. I've failed over and over and over again in my life. And that is why I succeed."

TOOL 7-5   What I Plan to Do This Week

Think about tasks for school, commitments to friends and to yourself. Circle the priorities.

	Monday	Tuesday	Wednesday	Thursday	Friday	Long-term project due dates
What do I plan to do each day? Include when you will hand in work.	___ ___ ___ ___	___ ___ ___ ___	___ ___ ___ ___	___ ___ ___ ___	___ ___ ___ ___	
What parts of long-term projects need to be tackled this week?	___ ___	___ ___	___ ___	___ ___	___ ___	

A few tips if you're overwhelmed:

- Look for tasks that you can divide into smaller chunks. Get the first chunk done.
- Look for a few tasks that you could accomplish quickly so you can have more attention for a bigger task.
- Have you committed to doing too much? Look for tasks you can postpone or eliminate.
- Don't eliminate sleeping enough or eating nutritious food. Keeping yourself healthy helps you get things done.

TOOL 7-6   Estimating a Day

	In a typical 24-hour weekday, how much time do you estimate that you spend on each of the activities?
Eating, including preparing food	
Personal hygiene and getting dressed	
Attending school	
In transit to/from home, school, and other activities	
Playing sports or exercising	
Participating in clubs or bands, including preparation and practice	
Working at a paid or volunteer job	
Doing house chores	
Studying and homework	
Sleeping	
Socializing with friends (in any mode—in person, over the phone, texting, or other medium)	
Reading, journaling, playing music, drawing, or other personal interests	
Other	
Other	
Total	24 hours

TOOL 7-7   My Daily Reality

On these weekdays, how much time did you spend on each of the activities? Note actual times.	Date:	Date:
Eating, including preparing food		
Personal hygiene and getting dressed		
Attending school		
In transit to/from home, school, and other activities		
Playing sports or exercising		
Participating in clubs or bands, including preparation and practice		
Working at a paid or volunteer job		
Doing house chores		
Studying and homework		
Sleeping		
Socializing with friends (in any mode—in person, over the phone, texting, or other medium)		
Reading, journaling, playing music, drawing, or other personal interests		
Other		
Other		
Total	24 hours	24 hours

- How accurate were your estimates? Which tasks took lots more time than expected? Which tasks took less time?

- Which tasks could be adjusted?

- Were all the tasks equally important? What might you need to eliminate?

TOOL 7-8   Study Routine Before Today's Test

1. What day did you start studying? _____

2. What did your studying look like—where, how long, with what resources? What were you doing—reading, reviewing notes, sorting information, making diagrams?

   _____
   _____
   _____
   _____

3. What did your studying look like after the first night?

   _____
   _____
   _____

4. What questions or challenges arose while you were studying?

   _____
   _____
   _____

5. What did you do to resolve those challenges or questions?

   _____
   _____
   _____

6. How well did your studying connect to what was on the test?

   _____
   _____
   _____

7. On a scale of 1–10, how well prepared did you feel? What were some gaps?

   1 2 3 4 5 6 7 8 9 10
   _____
   _____

8. How do you think you did? _____

   _____

TOOL 7-9 My Progress—My Plan

It's the middle of the term. Take charge of your progress. How are you doing in your classes? There's still time. What can you improve?

Class	Current status on homework, quizzes, tests, papers— Done? Grades?	Improvement plan—what needs to be completed, revised, redone

8

Developing Emotional Skillfulness Proactively, Not Just Reactively

Many elementary educators we've worked with intentionally help their students develop skills for managing emotions. They help students learn to calm themselves, and to use words to express how they feel, instead of acting out. They guide students to notice others' feelings. They believe that helping students participate effectively in class is an expected part of their teaching role. For those teachers, learning *how* to help students build emotional competencies is the question, not *whether* they should.

Views have varied more widely in the middle schools and high schools we've worked with. While some of the secondary educators we've met are fully aware that students are still developing skills for managing their own emotions and responding to others' emotions effectively, others say that students should have learned these skills already. Some say that it's just not their job.

Let's put one of those views to rest quickly, that teens should have learned emotional management skills already, implying that they should be done developing that skill set, and that childhood emotional competencies are sufficient for adolescence and beyond. Are all the teens and preteens you know emotionally stable? Are they all skillful at self-motivating, self-calming, expressing their emotions effectively, and choosing healthy emotional outlets? Are they adept at perceiving others' feelings, empathizing, and being responsive? Do their emotions support their academic focus?

We're certain you answered "no" or possibly something stronger. In fact, as adults, we're all still learning to manage emotions; it's a lifelong task. But it is particularly challenging for teens because of what's happening as their bodies change, their brains change, and their psychological and social needs change. The teenage brain is changing dramatically, making processing the complex interplay of their cognitive, emotional, physical, and social activity inconsistent and inefficient. The contexts around them change as well, often not aligning with their developmental needs. Managing emotions is even harder for students who've experienced trauma, or who were raised in unstable environments or without enough consistent and caring attention; more on those challenges below.

When secondary educators are unaware of the need to support students' emotional development, it often leads to a reactive approach—catching students after they've exploded in anger, are crying in distress, or have retreated in defeat—none of which help them learn academics, self-management, or relationship skills. In too many of these cases, the reaction becomes a disciplinary action or a counseling referral. Special adults step in at this later stage to help manage the students' behavior, rather than the students learning to manage themselves in a more proactive way.

In contrast, teachers can help students in their classes and throughout school develop awareness and skills for managing their emotions so they can be more conscious of what they're feeling and how those feelings are impacting their behavior and learning. Adults can help teenagers become more aware and skillful in noticing and responding appropriately to others' emotions. In addition, they can learn more in class and be more insightful about academic content. Students learn best in an environment shaped for "relaxed alertness," fostered by positive relationships with peers and the teacher, and engagement.

We are focused in this chapter on understanding emotions, how they impact teens' thinking, behavior, and learning. The field of cognitive neuroscience has shown that emotions are inextricably involved with all of those functions, and that ignoring emotions produces obstacles to thinking, behaving, and learning effectively. We are also focused on how teens can learn to be more skillful with their own and others' feelings, including understanding factors that inhibit effective emotional processing. Third, we focus on routines teachers can establish so the whole teen, even the emotional parts, can fully enter their classrooms.

So, what's going on in whole teens' brains that can make emotions hard to manage? Understanding adolescent brain development helps both educators and students. The first activity in this chapter offers research on how the brain processes emotions, and how emotions impact thinking and learning. Students will learn about helpful and harmful factors in emotional and cognitive development, and the need for social interaction and environments that feel safe. The chapter then offers ways for adults who work and live with teens and preteens to foster their emotional skillfulness by acknowledging their emotions, helping them identify their emotions, teaching them about emotions and the role of emotions in thinking and learning, establishing routines for managing emotions, and ensuring a safe learning environment. This chapter builds on the understandings about brain development in Chapter 7, on the communication skills in Chapter 6, and adds another layer to classroom community building from Chapters 3 and 4.

It is important that schools have an effective student support team and a health and wellness program (not just a half-year class in Grade 7 or 10). However, even with counselors and wellness classes, schools will do best to send a consistent message that all adults care about the whole teen. For any student who's experienced instability or trauma, having the teachers they see most frequently notice and support them, in addition to the specialists they see less often, is especially important.

While several of the practices in this chapter help to deal with stress, it is unfair to expect students, relying on their own still-evolving skill set, to compensate for the ever-increasing array of stress being put on them by high-pressure, high-stakes education policy and practices. Adults feel the pressure too, and often communicate that pressure to the students. In every way that school staff can build a culture that is emotionally healthy, through their words, actions, and policies, every person in the school will learn better. We discuss stress and school policies impacting stress further in Chapter 12.

Practices That Build Skills and Habits for Emotional Skillfulness

Teach students about how their actions impact their brains, their brains impact their emotions, and their emotions impact thinking and learning.

For hundreds of years, there was an assumption that human beings were rational, thinking individuals. Emotions were thought to be extras—appreciated when they were positive, challenging when they were negative, but either way, separate from thinking. Emotions were thought to be a process of the body, not the mind, and the mind could take charge. Recent research has proven those assumptions to be wrong, flat out wrong.

If we want students to manage their emotions, to know the value in self-calming, to know when they need emotional support, to value and uphold a safe learning environment, to perceive others' emotions and be responsive, it will help them to know more about their own brains. We may be aware of our emotions via our beating hearts, tight stomachs, clenched fists, and active sweat glands, but it's our brains that process and make sense of everything, including emotions.

Thinking as well as feeling happen in the brain. Both are cognitive experiences. And while different parts of the brain specialize in different kinds of activity, the parts are interconnected. They inform each other; they spark each other to react to situations. It might help to think of emotions as a sixth sense in addition to seeing, hearing, smelling, tasting, and feeling physical objects. Feeling emotions gives you information. Emotions tell you when you're safe or threatened, or whether you're curious and interested, or bored and disengaged.

Some people experience emotions as sudden and in charge; the emotions are managing them. With more skill, they would be able to manage more of their emotions. For example, when people are aware of and use emotional vocabulary, their brains process emotional experiences differently (Lieberman et al., 2006). With greater awareness, they can more easily notice an emotion before it becomes intense, think about it and deal with it. Is their emotional reaction reasonable or an overreaction? When they are bored, what can they do to pique their curiosity or persist? When they're feeling impatient with a project partner who needs more time than they need, what can they do to be patient? When they're frustrated with low grades, what can they do to not feel defeated? All of these insights and choices are part of emotional skillfulness—using emotions to inform decisions and actions.

Emotions give people information, and emotions help people to remember things. To say that emotional memories are stronger than nonemotional memories probably seems obvious. The biology behind that process is less obvious, but useful to know for students who want to remember information, and for teachers who want students to remember and incorporate new academic information and concepts. Emotions may be visible and conscious, or not—they can be so subtle as to be "nonconscious," perceptible only with medical devices. Either way, they are guiding the brain to be open and learn, or to shut down in vigilant self-protection mode.

The part of the brain that processes strong emotions such as fear, the amygdala, is older in evolutionary terms than the more rational frontal lobe, and gets "wired" more fully to the other parts of the brain before the frontal lobe does. The amygdala had to develop early in our evolutionary history if we were to survive as a species. In order to keep us safe, it reacts quickly; it doesn't wait for nuance, varied perspectives, or weighing consequences. (We'd be dead by then!) Knowing how the brain handles strong emotions, short-term stress, and long-term or traumatic stress can help teens communicate better, monitor themselves and their friends, use helpful strategies, and seek help when needed.

Students can also learn about the value of having a safe learning environment, and their role in keeping it that way. When their emotions are telling them they aren't safe—maybe they're new at school, or someone in class has been intimidating them, or they're struggling with the work, or the teacher doesn't seem to know or care about them—their brains are likely to be in more vigilant states, not the best for learning. We can help students sustain a positive classroom environment for themselves and others by reminding them that everyone has a role in making and sustaining a positive learning environment.

Use the paragraphs on Tool 8-1 in quote-based reflections in pairs or with the whole group, in a quotes café format, or for journaling. (Formats are explained in the Appendix.) With any format, save time to debrief. The research can be split into more than one class period, and might prompt further research ideas for students. With younger or struggling readers, provide more support by choosing one or two passages and use them in a quotes reflection format.

While this activity can fit easily in advisory or wellness class, with some passages fitting certain science or social studies classes, we encourage all adults to learn about brain development and incorporate this knowledge into their practices.

The questions below are prompts for conversations and/or journaling:

- ❓ What insights did the research give you about how your brain develops and deals with emotions?

- ❓ What information surprised you?

- ❓ What's great about how your brain processes emotions? What's hard about it?

? What's really important to remember and act on?

? What information prompted you to think of an experience you've had? How is it connected?

? What insights did it give you about how you learn?

? What are some of the stressors in your life that feel motivating?

? What are some of the stressors that impact you negatively and for a long time? How have they impacted you?

? What are one or two things you could do to be a good caretaker of your brain?

? When do emotions get in the way of learning in school? What techniques or habits might help you with your emotions in school?

? When do emotions get in the way of constructive relationships? What techniques or skills for managing emotions might help you with classmates, friends, or family?

Help students identify their emotions.

Teens' emotional vocabulary and statements often sound limited: "I'm fine," "I'm bored," "I don't know." Or, they sound dramatic: "I hate you!" "This is the worst day ever!" They might name an action rather than the emotion: "I'm never taking another math class!" Or, they sometimes blame someone else, as if the other person is in control of their emotions and actions: "He made me mad, so I had to . . ." None of these expressions is particularly helpful. Naming how you feel, and claiming it as your own feeling, are important steps in managing emotions. (We're not parsing the difference between feelings, moods, and attitudes.)

Many people can recall calming down once they'd named how they felt, or recall witnessing a four-year-old who learned to say (ferociously), "I'm frustrated!," instead of throwing a tantrum. There have been studies showing that the brain does indeed function differently when we express emotions verbally—different parts of the brain—less reactive parts—become engaged in helping to process those emotions (Lieberman et al., 2006).

Only a few emotions seem to be consistent across cultures, such as happiness, fear, anger, surprise, disgust, and sadness, perhaps hardwired into our brains to help us survive and thrive. The rest are taught and learned as part of the culture around us, and vary across both culture and time (Watt Smith, 2015b). Below are two ideas to help teens become more conscious of their emotional vocabulary, expand it, and use it. The first could be useful in any classroom; the second will fit many advisories and wellness classes.

- There are many lists of feelings vocabulary online. Choose one to download and post in your room, the same way that you might have a poster of grammar rules or the periodic table of elements. There are innumerable times during the school year when you can actively reference it to help you and students identify feelings: during the study period before a test, after completing a project, beginning to read a new book, saying goodbye at the end of the year.

- Use Tool 8-2 to have students identify emotions they might feel in a variety of scenarios, and hear how their peers might feel. Brainstorm additional situations. You can explain that their brains are better at learning when they're calm; they're more likely to have vocabulary for emotional situations if they build it deliberately. You can have students work alone first, then compare reactions in trios, or start in trios if you think they'll be as forthcoming. During the activity and the debriefing with the whole group, there are several important insights to draw out:

o There are no right or wrong responses about feelings, and contrary to some popular beliefs, happiness isn't the "best" emotion. Cultural historian Tiffany Watt Smith explains, "stronger physical and mental health is correlated with experiencing a range of emotions instead of just being happy or content all the time. It means allowing yourself to feel sad, angry, irritable, bored, and frustrated" (Lofthouse, 2015).

o Emotions can change; they might identify feelings in the first moments; other feelings later in the same situation. This insight can be important for teens who expect every difficult emotion to last forever.

o Students might imagine they'd feel more than one emotion within a given situation. For example, dealing with peer pressure often involves both fear and excitement. Because their brains are developing in ways that handle abstraction, adolescents can perceive having more than one emotion at a time. Feeling multiple emotions can create inner conflict. Explore how they might handle that conflict. Which emotion will impact their actions more?

o If the words they tend to use to express feelings are not appropriate for use in school, you'll know the activity is especially needed. Highly charged expressions might rev them up further, not help them calm down or act in ways they would otherwise.

o They are likely to have emotional reactions in common with their peers as well as different from them. The latter can be a surprise—that others would feel differently in the same situation. Encourage students to consider whether their own emotional reactions might be the same or different in the future, as sometimes hearing other's reactions prompts them to look at situations differently— maybe they'd have more empathy in the future, or less fear.

Use these debriefing questions to encourage more exploration.

? What were the situations where you had different feelings from your partners? What are some reasons for having different feelings?

? What were the situations where you had more than one feeling? How would you imagine managing both feelings?

? As a result of our discussion, in what ways might you notice and manage your own emotions in similar situations?

? What were some of the feelings words that you use frequently? Less often? Might be useful?

Attend to emotions when you're talking with students.

Teenagers in highly emotional moments are often not ready to hear rational suggestions; the emotions have to be attended to first. An upset student might just need you to listen (and model patient listening). If she pauses or seems stuck, you can draw more of her story out with short statements or questions: "What happened next?" "How did you feel?" "Tell me more about ____." You can show that you're hearing the emotional impact: "Wow, that sounds overwhelming." To reinforce an expanded and nuanced emotions vocabulary, your questions can include some variations from mild emotions to medium intensity to strong feelings. "So, were you a little annoyed, fairly aggravated, or really furious when Jared took over the group?"

Once a student has described her experience and what she felt, in the process diffusing some of her emotions, her brain will be in a better state to hear your suggestion. You can check if she's ready: "That sounds complicated. Would you like a suggestion, or do you have a plan already?"

Besides helping students learn to name and manage emotions, you'll show that you're listening and that you care, necessary steps to help teens build trust with you (Quaglia & Corso, 2014). That trust means they are more likely to consider your feedback, and in class, more likely to take on an academic challenge you present to them.

Establish regular classroom practices for managing emotions.

Students come to your class with feelings, which impact their learning. "Negative emotions tend to have a 'narrowing effect' on our thoughts. . . . Fear and anger and disgust give us sharp focus—which is the same thing as putting on blinders. [Psychologist Barbara] Frederickson argues that, in contrast with the narrowing effects of the negative emotions, positive emotions are designed to '*broaden* and *build*' our repertoire of thoughts and actions. Joy, for example, makes us want to play. We become willing to fool around, to explore or invent new activities . . . we are building resources and skills" (Heath & Heath, 2010, p. 122).

As you and your students understand how all of our brains react to curiosity or enthusiasm versus fear or stress, it's important to put that knowledge to work. Some of the routines below might be effective in faculty meetings as well (see Chapter 13 for improving faculty culture).

- **Help students identify what motivates them to attend and be engaged in class.** In addition to designing compelling and lively classes, making student participation more likely, you can engage students as partners identifying what motivates them. Is there another student they like working with? Is there an overarching question that they find intriguing? Can they see any connections between this class and others or issues in the world? What skill does the class include that might be useful in their out-of-school activities or a career?

- **Talk about emotions that are blocking effective learning and work.** When students are feeling frustrated with a concept, overwhelmed with their workload, or unmotivated to write a third draft, what can they do? For example, some students will find deadlines to be short-term motivators; others will find them to induce panic and unclear thinking. The latter group may need help to figure out how to spread work out, especially large tasks like studying for tests or working on projects. Students' emotional blocks vary, as will steps that clear the way for learning and working.

- **Monitor moods as students enter the room, and help them adjust.** Arriving to class agitated about something that happened in the hallway or in the prior class can be an emotional block to being in a good learning state. Consider routines you could establish to help students calm themselves—journaling for two minutes near the window, walking briskly twice to the water fountain, practicing some self-talk messages, taking a few deep breaths, or visualizing a calming location or image (their own mental "screensaver"). Trying these out and having students make choices—before there's a need to use the routine—will likely give you more instructional time and will help students practice routines that could benefit them for life.

  Monitoring moods is not only for when students feel agitated. Most students will appreciate a moment to adjust to their next class, especially in high school when each period of the day involves a new collection of peers. Many teachers have a "do now" on the board that is a bridge into the academic expectation. One teacher we've worked with starts every class with a half-minute of silence, and then asks, "Does anyone need to take care of something so that you can focus on the work? If so, take care of yourself for a minute while others start the 'Do Now'; raise your hand if you want to check in with me. I want everyone to feel ready and focused to dive into the work ahead."

- **Identify and use strategies that help students focus when entering class.** For students entering class a bit frazzled, spending one minute making a list of the things they're worried they'll forget can help shift their focus to the current class. For students who enter passively waiting for teachers to energize their thinking, you can help them craft a curiosity-piquing question that they can follow throughout the current unit, adding a couple of notes to it every day as their "do now" upon entering the class.

- **Demonstrate and regularly use stress-reducing brain breaks.** They can be done at natural transition points in a class when students are moving from one task to another and probably need some brain activation and social connection. Students can use these same brain breaks while studying. The mini-activities energize the brain because they involve quirky and challenging movements. See Tool 8-3 for a few examples.

- **Introduce a mindfulness routine to use in class or for students to use independently.** Mindfulness is the calming awareness of the present moment that comes from paying attention on purpose, nonjudgmentally. It reduces stress and supports focus. Mindfulness routines vary in format and length of time. Even if you only have limited time, here are a few ideas that are easy to do with your students.

  o For thirty seconds, pay attention to your breathing—as it enters, flows through, and leaves your body.

  o Listen to the noises in the classroom for twenty seconds, then listen for noises outside the room in the hallway and other rooms for twenty seconds, then listen for noises outside the school for twenty seconds.

  o For one minute, direct the students to look at something really carefully—all the parts of a pencil or pen, shades of light on a book or desk, how an ant or spider moves, the nuances in a poster, the dust in the air.

  o Choose a simple action, like raising a hand or standing up and sitting down, to do in slow motion. Tell students to try to be aware of what their bodies are doing to prepare for the movement, and what different parts of their bodies are doing at each tiny segment of the movement (Rechtschaffen, 2014).

We've worked with a district in which the high school English teachers surveyed students, found that many struggled to focus and frequently felt guilt, fear, and nervousness. They introduced mindfulness practices, making participation optional. Most students did indeed participate, often requesting the routine. Over time, many students reported using the practice at various times in the school day or on their own, feeling more focused, less stressed, and more supported by teachers.

Help students find emotional connections to their academics.

Lots of teachers wonder how they can entice their students to be more motivated. Two considerations: emotions drive learning; teens have lots of emotions. Below are examples of engaging students' emotions in academics. Discuss explicitly with students how their emotional connections impact their learning, so they learn to harness this enormous source of motivation.

- **Algebra theater:** A teacher described a class of students struggling to learn algebra concepts. Demonstration and repetition weren't helping sufficiently; students were not remembering the principles and didn't care. He announced they would do algebra theater—make up skits that demonstrated an algebra concept. For example, one group of students crafted a sibling rivalry drama in which children needed to be treated equally or the family would be in chaos—every time one child got something, the other had to as well. The students experienced the project as interactive and funny (two emotional connections), as related to their real lives (third emotional connection), and as a way they successfully remembered the math concepts (fourth emotional connection). The concepts stuck.

- **Authentic discussions:** Many students are aware of the issues in the world around them, possibly feeling inspired, curious, confused, or scared. Too many of those students experience school as a place where they cannot talk about real issues, which can be seen as off-curriculum or too political. When schools don't offer opportunities for students to talk about the real issues they care about, educators lose the chance to connect to powerful motivators, and they send the message that only part of the teen has a place in school. They also lose the opportunity to support students who are only beginning to make sense of larger issues—and do so with rigor and support. These real-world issues can be found in every curriculum area, and may also be important to the teacher, whose own desire to learn about the issue can increase student focus. Assess the culture of conversation in your class in order to choose a format that feels safe, the most basic emotional state for taking risks and sharing what matters. To maximize safety, try a listening lab structure. For groups ready for a little more risk, try an opinion continuum. You'll see other formats in Chapter 4, pages 62–64; instructions are in the Appendix.

- **Search for practical and personal applications:** For any skill in any subject, students can search online for an aspect of the lesson they care about. "Photosynthesis, practical application," can connect to a current issue, an application to a future career, or an intriguing photo or video. All are all emotional motivators. A student interested in history can search for "photosynthesis history." A student interested in graphic design can search for "photosynthesis images." Help students find out what they're curious about.

Build emotional awareness of others through any subject area.

Every piece of literature has characters with perspectives and emotions that drive the plot, and a plot that drives perspectives and emotions. Novels, plays, and biographies are rich material for understanding more about the connections and consequences between emotions and actions. Words to describe feelings and attitudes (whether they appear in the text or not) are a category of vocabulary, worthy of expanding for its own sake as young people build language skills, as well as the personal growth that comes with it.

Whether students are reading Steinbeck's *Of Mice and Men*, Taylor's *Roll of Thunder, Hear My Cry*, Shakespeare's *Macbeth*, or Tan's *Joy Luck Club*, the following questions or adaptations can be useful:

- **?** What emotions do you think the characters are feeling? Encourage specific and nuanced responses, not just angry, more angry, and really angry. Be careful to ask questions that allow several possible responses: "What *emotions* do you think . . . ?" rather than "What *emotion* was . . . ?"

- **?** What in the text led you to name those emotions?

- **?** How do you see those feelings driving the next steps in the plot?

- **?** What other emotions might have had a different impact?

- **?** What do those emotions show about the character's perspectives?

- **?** What might you have felt in that situation? What actions might have followed?

- **?** Focus on the unlikable characters and antagonists. What are they feeling? How is the plot unfolding from their perspectives? Build and stretch empathy skills to notice that even the nasty characters have feelings and perspectives.

Music and visual arts use emotions powerfully. What are brush strokes, dance steps, and musical phrases that express various levels of anger? What about optimism and pessimism? Or delight, amazement, or inspiration? Or awkwardness, shame, or fear? How are musical and visual elements combined to produce emotional reactions in film and video? How do advertisers use emotions to promote a product?

In history class or when studying current issues, students can consider what leaders might be feeling, how those emotions are impacting their decisions and actions, and what their constituents are feeling. People are not purely rational decision makers in their personal lives, nor are those who become public figures. Emotions are still in play. How are leaders connecting and communicating with constituents? How did/ does that leader's emotionality or restraint impact public reaction? In contemporary election cycles, are voters preferring experience, calm, and detailed policy from candidates, or is an emotional connection a priority?

A focus on emotions in curricula is not a tangent, and doesn't weaken or soften the academic content. Quite the opposite. When focusing on emotions, students will be observing carefully, gathering evidence, interpreting, noting different experiences and perspectives, identifying connections, supposing alternative scenarios, and considering relevance to their lives. These are important and rigorous habits of mind.

Consider this exhibition from *Horace's School: Redesigning the American High School* by Theodore R. Sizer (1997):

An Exhibition: Emotions

Select one of the following familiar human emotions: fear, envy, courage, hunger, longing, joy, anger, greed, jealousy.

In an essay, define the emotion you choose, drawing on your own and others' experience. Then render a similar definition using in turn at least three of the following forms of expression: a written language other than English; a piece of drawing, painting, or sculpture; photographs, a video, or film; a musical composition; a short story or play; pantomime; a dance.

Select examples from literature, journalism, the arts, and history of other people's definitions or representations of the emotion you have chosen. These should strike you as important and arresting, even if they do not correspond with your own definition.

Physical education is enhanced by integrating an awareness of emotions. The greatest athletes in the world are susceptible to the emotional stakes of competition. They train to visually imagine themselves performing well and to harness their emotions to maintain their efforts. They gain energy from fans who cheer, as even the richest professionals can play poorly under the pressure of a championship moment.

Our students walk into the gym or onto the field with emotions that often determine their participation. Many students feel embarrassed and incompetent in sports; others are inspired to raise their game by the words of their teachers and coaches. Some students, who can at first seem unmotivated and anxious by team sports, will commit to a rigorous training regimen if it involves monitoring their own progress in fitness activities, rather than being part of a competitive game. Like the world's greatest athletes, whole teens bring their emotions along with their bodies into physical educational classes. A few simple questions from a PE teacher can help all students be more ready to do their best:

❓ What is one word you would use to describe how you feel going into this activity?

❓ What challenge are you ready to take on today?

❓ When things aren't going well for you when you play sports, what can I do to help you stay focused? What can your peers do?

Establish routines for diffusing and managing challenging emotions within class.

During a discussion, a small-group activity, or an individual task, students might feel frustrated, discouraged, embarrassed, overwhelmed, or other distracting emotion. In those moments, it will be very challenging for the student(s) to learn, so it's worth establishing routines and agreements. For example, adapt the entering-the-room routines above so students know that when they need a chance to compose themselves, they can ask for a minute to breathe, journal, draw, or pace outside the door. Here are a few more options:

- When discussions get heated, have the whole class pause, breathe, and think about what they could say—less dramatically. (See Chapters 4 and 6 more tips on productive group discussions.)

- "Be soft on the people, hard on the problem," is an important agreement for negotiating (Fisher, Ury, & Patton, 1991, p. 13) and for discussions and projects. It means that people should focus on the issue and assume that the other person has reasonable intentions. "You only have that opinion of Cuba because you're . . ." is being hard on the person. "I disagree with ___ part of your opinion because . . ." is focusing on the issue.

- Once students are calmer, use the moment to build perspective-taking skills. Have them describe what happened from their own point of view and from their classmate's point of view. Note, when students are upset, the other perspective too often sounds like their own, as in, "She always wants to be the boss," and "Her perspective is that she always wants to be the boss." It can take practice to *really see things from someone else's perspective*, as in, "Well, from her perspective, I guess she really thinks the best first step is ____." Asking students to identify their interests and the other student's interests will help as well. "My interest was getting started fast. Maybe hers was planning carefully first." (See the explanation of "positions and interests" in Chapter 4, pages 56–58.)

Talk about healthy and unhealthy coping strategies.

Make a practice of checking on coping strategies via periodic conversations in advisory groups or individual check-ins. You may be the adult who a teen trusts, so even if these conversations aren't in your syllabus, you may have opportunities to rise to the occasion to support a student.

- Make it a normal practice to **talk about self-care and supporting others**, which reminds teens that they're not alone, and that they have choices. Here are some questions and prompts that can help:

  - ❓ When are you patient with yourself? When are you impatient?

  - ❓ When you do something you regret, how long do you feel bad about it? What helps you resolve your feelings? (Healthy steps might include apologizing, making amends, journaling, talking with someone, learning something from the situation.)

  - ❓ It's testing season (or holiday season, football season . . .). What are you doing this weekend that's healthy? Who's sleeping eight hours each night?

  - ❓ Who's an adult you can talk to about things that matter? When did you last check in with them?

  - ❓ How do you show friends that you're supportive? What do your friends do that supports you?

(?) Who are the people around you who believe in your success? Who drags you down?

(?) I do some pretty stupid things when I hang out with. . . . I make smarter choices when I hang out with. . . .

(?) I stick up for myself pretty well when. . . . It's harder to stick up for myself when. . . .

- **Establish a ritual for identifying positive things** that happened (our brains focus on the negative out of self-protection). This can be done in classes to bring closure to a unit or a week's worth of work. What's a good thing that happened this week? Name two things you're grateful for. What good thing will you make happen next week?

- **Identify people who are or have been helpful.** Thinking of these people reminds teens that they're not alone, that they are worthy of positive attention, and gives them role models. What elementary teachers did you especially like? Name a few people outside of school who've taught you something valuable.

- **Help students reconsider their negative assumptions.** In the book, *How Doctors Think*, Dr. Jerome Groopman, suggests that patients ask key questions of doctors to make sure they aren't deciding on a diagnosis too quickly, rather than considering other possibilities. Among other questions, he suggests asking, "What else could it be?" and "Is there anything that doesn't fit?" These are great examples of the kind of questions that protect against thinking errors, such as assumptions and biases (and incorrect diagnoses). For young people to be emotionally self-aware and constructive, they need to catch their own thinking errors, which can be their own worst enemies, leading them to ruminate, feel helpless, and alienate people. Consider these patterns of behavior and questions that you can ask, make explicit, and encourage students to ask themselves:

  o A student jumps to conclusions—"What information have you not considered?" "What else could explain . . . ?"

  o A student expresses helplessness, blames others consistently, perhaps assuming unintentional harm was intentional—"Is there really nothing you can do? You have no power to act at all?" "What are possible explanations for what happened that could be unintentional?" "Is there anything you did that contributed, even in a small way, to the situation?"

  o A student overgeneralizes and overdramatizes situations: things are always this bad, they last forever, the consequences will be life altering, situations are all or nothing, or the mistake someone made is a permanent personality flaw— "What's a less dramatic way this situation could play out?" "What would the other person's perspective sound like?" "In what ways has that person acted differently at other times?"

  o A student is consistently negative, self-critical, self-blaming, dismissive of positive feedback and support—"Can you repeat to me the positive feedback you got?" "Tell me three of your positive qualities." "What's an accomplishment that you're proud of lately? What does it say about you?"

Discussion Options for Faculty

- Which practices in this chapter seem especially important for your students?

- Which skills mentioned in this chapter are especially important for you to practice?

- Use Tool 8-1 in a quotes café format or quote-based conversation pairs.
  - Which points from Tool 8-1 seem especially important for teenagers to understand about their own brains?
  - Which points from Tool 8-1 seem especially important for teachers to understand about teenage brains? What would you do differently if you incorporated that information into your teaching practice?

- Where and how can you teach students about the concepts and skills in this chapter?
  - Understanding how their brains process emotions, and the interaction of emotion and cognition
  - Expanding their emotional self-awareness, vocabulary, and facility talking about emotions
  - Managing stress in healthy ways

- What routines can you establish in your classrooms or advisory groups to
  - help provide motivation and teach self-motivation?
  - diffuse challenging emotions?
  - help students focus and learn to self-focus?
  - model reducing stress in healthy ways?

Practices at Home

As your son or daughter grew into their teens, did you wonder if he or she had been hijacked by a sullen or volatile stranger? If so, you're not alone. They won't be stuck in that phase forever, though they could be impacted by it long term. There are things you can do to help. Even if your child's teenage years are not filled with drama and tumult, they are still having experiences that will significantly impact the sort of emotional adult they will become.

Your teen is a whole person—cognitive, emotional, physical, and social. Their brains are changing dramatically so the connections among those aspects can be inconsistent and inefficient, sometimes resulting in being moody or short tempered. They need practice to build the brain connections for emotional awareness and self-management, and awareness of and responsiveness to others. Here are some practices you can put in place at home to support your teen's development of emotional skillfulness.

Model using words that identify *your* emotions and model diffusing strong emotions. Teenagers learn to handle their emotions in large part by watching and hearing how the adults around them do so. Be direct with stating your feeling: "I am sad right now." Model processing emotions as well: "I had a frustrating day at work; I think I'll take a fast walk around the block a couple times to calm down." (Invite them to join you.) Naming and diffusing an emotion doesn't solve the issue that upset you; it's taking care of yourself and helps to put you in a mindset where you could solve it. "Solving" it while still being upset might make things worse. By identifying and diffusing your emotions, you'll help your teens have vocabulary for their feelings, and a model of someone who takes responsibility when they are emotional.

Help teenagers share their feelings. Teenagers can come home upset, which might look and sound as different as crying, swearing, or sitting in sullen silence. There is no single way to help them put their feelings into words. Some teens will respond well if you say, "I am interested in how you feel." Other teens may need a bit of help finding the right words to get started: "I am guessing that you are really angry. But maybe you are more anxious than angry. Am I close to reading you right?" The point is not to be right, or to change their feelings—it is to let them know you want to hear how they are doing. Expressing the feeling will often start to diffuse it.

Design a place at home to calm down with your teens, to use when they are upset. They shouldn't have to leave when they're upset, which would be a risk factor. The place at home could help them be quiet and nap, draw or write, exercise, or do other activities for processing and calming down. They might even talk with you there. When they're upset, they might need a reminder to use the routine, as in, "It looks like you had a tough day. Do you want to talk or use your music routine?"

Help your teens self-motivate. Some people can be bored by even the most dynamic book or movie. A passive brain can be bored by anything, never mind the tedious tasks in life. Since emotions, such as curiosity and anticipation, drive attention and memory, help kids find a skill or concept that connects to something of interest in their schoolwork as a motivator. What character or historical figure could they identify with? What overarching question about fairness or quest against the odds might be in play? What skill might connect to a future career option? Let them know what strategies you used when you were unmotivated in school; it might give them hope and ideas. Teenagers are good at catching adults being hypocritical, so your suggestions will carry more weight when you acknowledge that some things are indeed not interesting.

Encourage teens to be involved with other people. Persuade them to have face-to-face conversations, asking them what friends and siblings were feeling and what their perspectives were. Use their involvement in activities, clubs, teams, volunteering, or work to chat afterward about how they felt, how they remained patient, how they got over their nervousness, and so on. Since teens' brains are changing so much, every experience helps to build the architecture for what a given teenager understands and can do. Spending time engaged with people helps build wiring for empathy; spending a lot of time playing with violent video games fosters wiring for aggression (Schenck, 2011).

Support establishing routines to manage stress, including sleeping eight hours per night and relaxing in structured and unstructured ways. We've worked with high-pressure schools in which students' definition of *downtime* was not a healthy sign. They reported two modes of activity: (1) performances, presentations, championship games, and tests; (2) all of the preparation for those high-stakes experiences. They had such structured lives that even downtime included relentless expectations. Stress, like all their experiences, impacts their brain development—it is serious. For some kids, yoga or mindfulness practices will help; for others, it may be regular exercise, cooking, art, music, or reading for pleasure. Partner with your teens to craft realistic goals. Prioritize and streamline their schedule. If their stress is chronic, ask your school counselor or doctor about services.

Help your teens avoid thinking distortions that impact their emotions and reactions. Listen to patterns in their emotional reactions. Do they overgeneralize or blame? Are they overly self-critical or express helplessness? The segment of this chapter, "Help students reconsider their negative assumptions," on page 157, includes questions that can help them reconsider a situation and their reaction. Help teens stretch their perspectives and interpretations to better manage their emotions.

Be aware of the signs of substance abuse and addiction and get help. Teenagers' brain circuitry is changing more than adults'—for better or worse—based on their experiences. Their rapidly developing brains make them more susceptible to addiction than adults' brains. The greatest risk of alcohol and tobacco addiction occurs between the ages of twelve and nineteen (Jensen, 2005). Teens "often see drugs as harmless . . . and tend to believe that they can survive anything . . . [T]ake a positive, brain-building approach by helping students see that they can be proactive in developing the 'the brain they want.'" (Jensen & Snider, 2013, p. 22) If you have any concerns, find services in your school or community.

TOOL 8-1　How Emotions, Thinking, and Actions Impact Each Other

1	Some people have "school smarts," "street smarts," "tech smarts," or other set of insights. They have the knowledge and skills to understand how a system works, and how to reach their goals within that system. What would it mean to have emotional intelligence? How could it help you? You'd be aware of what you were feeling, and would have words to express feelings without exploding, blaming, or going silent. With words, different parts of the brain get involved with processing emotions, not just the fast-reacting parts (Lieberman et. al., 2006). You could use your emotions like a sixth sense—getting a sense of the level of safety or tension in a group, sensing how others feel about something you said or something that happened. You'd be able to calm yourself when you need to, or motivate yourself. Likewise, you could help others with their ups and downs. Being emotionally skillful lets you improve relationships and make good choices.

2	How do emotions impact thinking? Researchers studied people with brain injuries whose IQ scores hadn't changed but their emotional processing was damaged. Those patients offer an example: "Instead of becoming more rational and logical when their decisions were free of emotion, these patients did not care what other people thought . . . , were unable to learn from their past mistakes, and did not stop and change course when it became clear their current actions were leading them astray . . . [The brain researchers] argued that, without emotion, all decisions and outcomes are equal—people can have no preferences, no interests, no motivation, no morality, and no sense of creativity, beauty, or purpose . . . Emotions are, in essence, the rudder that steers thinking" (Immordino-Yang, 2016, pp. 27–28).

3	Healthy physical habits—eating, exercising, and sleeping—help teens academically and emotionally. "Although the brain is only a fraction of our body's weight, it consumes approximately 20 percent of our energy, which makes good nutrition a critical component of learning" (Cozolino, 2013). Physical exercise improves brain function by impacting alertness and memory, and stimulating the growth of neurons and synapses. "John Ratey, of Harvard Medical School has said that, 'exercise is the single most powerful tool you have to optimize your brain function' (2008)" (Schenck, 2011, p. 57). " . . . sleep loss cripples thinking in just about every way you can measure thinking. Sleep loss hurts attention, executive function, working memory, mood, quantitative skills, logical reasoning, general math knowledge" (Medina, 2014, p. 48).

4	All learning involves *attention*—focusing on something—and *memory*—connecting the new understanding to brain networks. Since emotions drive both attention and memory, emotions drive learning. "Emotions drive attention, create meaning, and have their own memory pathways (LeDoux, 1994) . . . emotions give us a more activated and chemically stimulated brain, they help us recall things better and form more explicit memories . . . Curiosity and anticipation [emotional states] are known as 'appetitive' states because they stimulate the mental appetite. They are highly motivating states . . . when we anticipate and are curious about a subject matter, our learner response goes up (Kirsch, 1999)" (E. Jensen, 2005, pp. 69, 77).

(Continued)

TOOL 8-1   (Continued)

| 5 | When we feel fear, anxiety, or anger, it's hard to think, learn, or make good decisions in or out of school. In school, we learn more when we feel comfortable with classmates and connected to a teacher. When we experience bullying or other forms of intimidation, our brains can't focus on learning. "Evolution has shaped our brains to err on the side of caution and to trigger fear whenever it might be remotely useful. Fear makes us less intelligent because amygdala [part of the brain that processes strong emotions] activation—which occurs as part of the fear response—interferes with prefrontal functioning [part of the brain that considers nuances and weighs consequences]. Fear also shuts down exploration, makes our thinking more rigid . . ." (Cozolino, 2013). These processes in the brain that protect us can hijack rational, careful thinking. |

| 6 | Do you wonder why laughter and yawns seem contagious, or why you cry and cringe for others' experiences? Our brains have mirror neurons that prompt us to observe and imitate other people. Mirror neurons evolved beyond copying behaviors; they connected with emotional networks, which give us a sense of another person's emotions, almost as if we feel them ourselves. The upside is empathy: "Empathy is an idea you develop about the experiences of others based on the emotions you witness them having, the context they are in, and the emotions evoked in you" (Cozolino, 2014, p. 7). Empathy is a guess about how others feel; it helps us feel connected, and helps unify groups. "Emotional attunement has a downside; it makes us susceptible to . . . the negative feelings of others. This is why both joy and depression feel contagious, and why fears, anxieties, and phobias can be passed from one person to another" (p. 141). |

| 7 | Our brains need to be interacting with other brains; we evolved as a social species. We survived by cooperating, not by outrunning or fighting off tigers or mammoths by ourselves. However, our need to protect ourselves produces assumptions. "We analyze others but not ourselves . . . Our brains have evolved to pay attention to the behaviors and emotions of other people. Not only is this processing complex, but it is lightning fast, shaping our experience of others milliseconds before we even become consciously aware of their presence. We automatically generate a theory of what is on their mind—our ideas about what they know, what their motivations may be, and what they might do next. As a result, we are as quick to think we know others as we are slow to become aware of our own motives and faults" (Cozolino, 2013). |

(Continued)

TOOL 8-1   (Continued)

| 8 | Everyone's life involves stress, which can motivate us to overcome a challenge or accomplish something. When stress is intense and lasting, though, it resets the body's emotional state to be vigilant rather than relaxed enough to learn. "We're built for stress that lasts only seconds . . . The saber-toothed tiger either ate us or we ran away from it—or a lucky few might stab it, but the whole thing was usually over in moments. Consequently, our stress responses were shaped . . . to get our muscles moving us as quickly as possible out of harm's way. These days, our stresses are measured not in moments with mountain lions, but in hours, days, and sometimes months . . . Our system isn't built for that. And when moderate amounts of stress hormones build up to large amounts, or hang around too long, they become quite harmful. That's how an exquisitely tuned system can become deregulated enough to affect a report card . . . " (Medina, 2014, p. 63). Managing stress is important—exercising, meditating, cooking, drawing—even reducing commitments. |

| 9 | Since teen brains do so much rewiring—which happens based on good experiences and bad experiences—both types of experiences have the capacity to make lasting impacts. Neuroscientist Frances Jensen explains, "The clinical research shows that binge drinking, substance abuse, and stress all tend to have a stronger effect on teenagers than on adults. Addiction is actually a form of synaptic plasticity. When a reward circuit gets repeated exposure to a drug, that circuit starts to build stronger synapses. So sadly, the teenager can become more strongly addicted than the adult and have a much harder time shedding that addiction later" (Perkins-Gough, 2015 p. 18). |

| 10 | The experiences we have change our brains and our emotional states—especially if the experience is repeated and frequent, and active rather than passive. We're often lighthearted after a funny movie, or somber after a sad movie. What's the impact of playing violent video games over time? "There is fairly strong evidence that increased playing of violent video [games] is associated with and contributes to higher levels of later aggression and violence . . . The general pattern of increased exposure and increased violent or aggressive behavior seems to start early and even affect other cultures noted for their nonaggressive public behavior, such as Japan." The impact is not necessarily direct or immediate, but over time, and over large numbers, research is increasingly showing a connection between violent video games and an increase in aggressive behavior and its partner, a decrease in empathy (Schenck, 2011, pp. 131–132). |

TOOL 8-2   Imagine What You'd Feel

Imagine you're in the situations below. What feelings do you think you'd have? Remember:

- There are no right or wrong emotional reactions.
- You can have more than one feeling at the same time.
- Feelings can change—quickly or slowly.

1. You've gotten an A- on a test.	2. You've gotten a C on a challenging project.
3. Your team won the game, though you missed your shot.	4. Your team lost the game, though you hit more shots than usual.
5. It's up to you to pick three classmates for a project team.	6. You asked a classmate to work with you, and he or she said no.
7. Your teacher praised your effort in front of the class.	8. Your teacher says he is going to call your home about your progress.

TOOL 8-3   Energizing Brain Breaks

Ear and Nose Switch

1. Stand up.

2. Take your right hand and grab your left ear.

3. Now take your left hand and touch your nose.

4. Put your arms back by your sides.

5. Move your left hand to your right ear and your right hand to your nose.

6. Switch back and forth as fast as you can, lowering your hands to your hips each time.

Arm Wrap

1. Stand up and put your right arm straight down at your side, then tuck that arm behind your back so that it's resting on your lower back. It should be bent at a 90-degree angle.

2. Follow these instructions while closing your eyes, keeping your right arm bent behind you.

   a. Use your left ring finger to touch your right pinkie finger. Put your left arm back by your side.

   b. Use your left middle finger to touch your right thumb. Lower your left arm.

   c. Use your left pinkie finger to touch your right ring finger. Lower your left arm.

3. Then, switch arms so that your left arm is behind your back and your right arm is at your side. Repeat a, b, and c.

Elbow to Knee Stretch

1. Stand up.

2. Hold your ears with your hands.

3. Tap your right elbow to the top of your left knee. Now tap your left elbow to your right knee. Repeat five times.

4. Bring your left knee up and have your right elbow tap the top of your knee and then tap the side of the same knee. Now do the same thing with the other knee and elbow. Repeat five times.

Source: Adapted with permission from Sladkey (2013).

9

Becoming More Independent, Not Just Alone

Perhaps more than any other developmental task of the teenage years, leaving behind one's childhood in order to establish an identity as an independent young adult is the most powerful task of all, fraught with risks and opportunities. The opportunities include discovering hobbies that will last a life time and perhaps become a career, identifying one's attraction to potential romantic partners, following unique interests in the arts and sports, and sorting through the news of political campaigns and social justice issues that draw one's participation. Old friendships wither away as new friends emerge who share similar worldviews. Sixth graders are still children; twelfth graders are young adults.

The profound changes during those seven years are spurred by an equally profound cognitive development, the teenager's exponentially increased ability to think abstractly. No longer is the world bound by absolute rules; events happen in a context that must be taken into account. People's emotions must be taken into account. One must consider an array of actions, and then take actions in an imperfect world and without absolute assurance of outcomes: "How much do I care if people make fun of me if I wear this shirt? Will this afternoon job at the hardware store drain too much of my energy for school? Do I want to continue my religious studies? Should I ask that person out on a date? How important is this class to my plans? Is it too late to safely go to that part of town? Will my parents approve of my choice for college?" Adults also make many decisions, but teenagers are making their decisions without a lot of personal experience and wisdom to fall back on. They are developing wisdom by learning from the decisions they make.

The risks of unwise decisions during these years are well documented: affiliations with destructive peers and gangs—more so with teens because they are looking for where they belong; experiments with alcohol and drugs that grow into addictions—more likely to become addictions than at other ages because their developing brains are so susceptible to being transformed by their experiments; loss of faith in civic institutions—the complications of history and politics may lead to seeing all the good done by government and organizations as insubstantial; self-destructive behavior—as their access to dangerous substances and situations coincides with their cognitive and emotional instability.

The research on resilience is critical here—the vast majority of teenagers, even those who have grown up in very traumatic circumstances, are eventually able to create a stable and healthy independent self-identity. Their schools and communities play a huge part in hastening those healthy outcomes. Teenagers require intentional adult support to develop the skills of autonomy and the responsibilities of independence.

Adult support is critical because independence is not all or nothing. It is much like any curriculum in school. We expect sixth graders to write essays and twelfth graders to write essays; every year their teachers provide different challenges and modes of support. Independence is no different. Adults must steadily provide students with opportunities and feedback to learn skills they need as they become more independent. Will the teenagers make mistakes? Absolutely. The degree to which they learn from those mistakes depends greatly on how often adults have engaged with them, and learned with them all along the path of their decision making.

Opportunities to develop the skills of autonomy are abundant in school. As we saw in Chapter 4, teachers who set up their rooms, routines, structures, expectations, and agenda by incorporating student input and decision making, and allowing students varying degrees of autonomy, are leveraging a tremendous resource for having high functioning classes. The practices in Chapter 4 focus on setting up the overall culture and expectations for the class; in this chapter, we are looking at ways individual students can have their independent identities emerge from that foundation.

Independence is not the same as being alone. In schools, independence means having the opportunities to develop partnerships with adults and peers, while being able to work with less oversight, and to have more choices. The common school opportunity for "independent study" doesn't have to require the student to labor all by themselves; students can make independent decisions to work collaboratively, or to seek out the support of coaches and mentors.

Independence is also not just for high-achieving or well-behaved students. Students who seem initially resistant to teacher efforts can often be engaged when given choices. Student motivation is generated when adults recognize the unique ways even resistant students can buy in through developing their own interests and abilities.

Buy-in builds trust. When teens trust adults, because the adults support appropriate independent decision making, teenagers will share their experiences and hear feedback. Schools struggle with student buy-in when teenagers' only experiences of decision making are in opposition to the adults. The students may take action behind the adult's back because they feel trapped by all the absolute adult rules—and there are a lot of absolute requirements and mandates for everyone in schools. Instead, when adults take the time to listen to students' stories and hear how they considered options, teens stay connected to adults, while developing an independent young adult identity. They are more independent, but they are not alone.

Independence and decision making help students handle mistakes, setbacks, and emotional turmoil. There will be times when they feel badly for having let down a friend, or prioritized poorly their studies, or spoken too harshly during a heated class discussion. Most of them will suffer losses in sports on a team they chose to join, not get a job for which they interviewed, fail to achieve straight As on final exams for which they have studied, and have a college application rejected. Maturing into an independent young adult requires consistent chances to take risks. Through successes and failures teenagers discover emerging and evolving beliefs. Perhaps most critically, they learn who will be there with them when they inevitably have a failure, so that they can continue on their journey, with increasing wisdom: independent but not alone.

Critical in the practices below is that there are no specific right or wrong answers in the usual way one might find them on a multiple choice test. In the absence of a right-and-wrong rubric for assessing the skills of autonomy, students can be given feedback on the thoroughness of their responses to your prompts and questions, on their ability to identify the competing interests that drive their decisions and the decisions of characters in books and histories, on their evaluation of the moral behavior of the people they are studying, and the costs and benefits of others' behaviors. Academic lessons become safe places for teens to practice their developing beliefs, prior to then behaving on such beliefs as independent adults.

Practices That Build Independence

Help students identify, share, and work from their strengths.

Almost all schools require that students successfully pass courses in major subject areas. Many high school graduation requirements also include mandatory credits in the arts, world languages, physical education, computer literacy, and health. The exposure to such a wide variety of curricula, starting in middle school, can support the development of well-rounded young adults. Through their efforts in their courses, teenagers have the opportunity to identify particular areas of strength. These strengths can form the foundation for investing in hobbies, career training, personal development, and the decision about where to go to college. Every teen is not expected to have the same interests, career or vocational aspirations. The range of required courses in schools is only one way to support the development of broad and strong academic and cognitive strengths. The following activities allow teachers to foster teen's individual exploration and reflection. (Also see Chapter 7, pages 121–123, "Help students identify and share their learning preferences and habits.")

- **Provide options for displaying understanding using a variety of modes.** In language arts, when wanting to assess students' understanding of character development, or in history when exploring notable people, offer these options:

  o Drawing a visual character sketch that can be annotated with quotes from the text

  o Organizing a flow chart of key events that shape the character

  o Creating and annotating a playlist of songs that the character would find compelling

  o Writing a standard three-paragraph essay.

Offering options that leverage students' interests and strengths increases their investment—and they begin to make suggestions of other ways they can demonstrate their learning. They become collaborators. When developing lessons, use Tool 9-1 to brainstorm with individual students and the class a variety of ways they can choose to explore the task.

- **Point students to academic options they may not see and give them choices.** Some students initially get distracted by choice. Other students, whose skill sets are not yet solid, may be attracted to tasks that are likely to overwhelm them. We know of one teacher who identifies, appreciates, and supports unique student interests when she distributes to the class multiple options for a task. She quietly says to one student, "I was thinking of you when I included the music option. Do you want to try it?" or "Take a close look at the flow chart idea. You might like that one from what I've seen of your work so far. Let me know."

Here's a story from a teacher who took the above option to another level:

> My students were struggling on tests; some were even outright giving up on them without completion. We spent a class session discussing and asking each student to identify both their test taking strengths, and weaknesses. For the next test, I put together folders, each of which contained different styles of assessment (multiple choice, open response, identification, essay, matching). Each packet was assigned a point value (20 pts, 10 pts, 40 pts). Students were instructed to go to the "buffet" and construct an a la carte test that totaled 80 pts. Student buy-in went through the roof, and the average score for the class increased by 12 points. Was it extra work? Yes and no. Yes, it took some time and care to create the different styles. But, I did not have to fight students to finish the test. I did not have to make calls to support staff and home. Preparation for our next test has been far more enthusiastic as well.

- **Provide support in choosing big projects.** It is common in many schools to offer students choices for big projects and papers. After distributing the assignment, ask students to share with the class their choices and the reason behind their choices, reasons that include their areas of interest. This reinforces that the school cares about their independent thinking; it also helps students who have not yet identified their unique interests to simply have more ideas from which to choose.

- **Advisory is a good place to share hobbies, skills, and interests.** Advisors and advisees can make presentations of their unique interests the main theme for a month or a term, or make them a weekly ritual if advisory meets frequently. We've worked with schools where advisees have shown their photography, played a musical instrument and taught a song, taught their favorite card game, or shared the volunteer work they do.

Help students identify and strengthen their emerging values and beliefs.

We live in increasingly complex and diverse communities. Even teens who grow up in small homogeneous neighborhoods are exposed through the media to innumerable perspectives, advertisements, and cultures. Constructing a stable young adult set of beliefs and values from all of this input requires time to ponder one's reactions, to weigh new ideas with the expectations of family and community, and to reflect on one's emerging beliefs with trusted peers and adults. Safety to talk *and* access to adults who truly listen are both imperatives.

There will be times when adults must do more than listen. Adults have an obligation to take their turn to articulate and underscore the values of tolerance, justice, and education. They do this most effectively when they refrain from long one-sided lectures and judgments, and instead share their beliefs and some of the journey they took to become who they are. Adults will then be role models who invite further dialogue. These essential dialogues can happen at teachable moments throughout the school day.

- **Highlight the parts of lessons in every subject area that require students to assert their opinions and beliefs.** In science class, underscore how evidence from experiments leads scientists to draw conclusions and publish papers, skills developed in writing lab reports. Book report expectations can include everything from what makes a specific character one's favorite (a middle school-level task), to writing to the school committee to advocate for a book to be a required text (a high school-level task). Research papers in history classes ask for a thesis statement and a summary of the research. Students in vocational arts have to make choices in developing blueprints, leading to the skill of winning contracts in a business. Students on sports teams can make suggestions to teammates; coaches show they value student input by making time for student observations of teamwork. In all of these settings, adults develop the whole teen.

- **Include in all courses of study exposure to historical figures who took decisive actions**. In almost every subject area, teachers introduce students to a vast array of noteworthy people, some famous, some obscure, some fictional. Teachers highlight these individuals so that students are historically literate, to offer them role models, or to warn them of the dangers of following tyrants and demagogues. Offer students a chance to discuss the people they find compelling:

  - In an historical era, whose actions do you admire, and in what ways do you think you would have done the same? What are the risks and rewards for taking such actions?

  - If you could insert yourself into a novel, what role might you play?

  - What advice would you have given to Galileo, to Robert Oppenheimer, to Rachel Carson? What social forces should influence a scientist's decisions?

  - Would you have taken the risk to hide Anne Frank, and how would you have weighed your decision?

  - If you were the great football player Jimmy Brown, would you have retired so young?

  - To what degree would you have suffered to make great art as Michelangelo did to paint the Sistine Chapel?

- **Assign homework and projects that support students to identify heroes in their family and community.** As students learn about noteworthy people in a course of study, they can find connections between those historical figures and the people they admire in their lives. Having relationships with accessible role models is a significant factor in building confidence and sense of identity, and in making positive choices. Younger teens can be asked to interview people to learn the basic biographical information; older students can be asked to more deeply analyze the efforts of their interviewees, and note the qualities they'd wish to emulate. At any age, students can ask people at home or in their neighborhoods about recent eras referenced in literature and history. How did they manage during the Depression or the recent significant recession? Did they play an active role, including a local role, in the labor movement, the civil rights movement, the women's movement, the environmental movement? How did those movements affect them? Did they ever invest their time and energy in a political or social movement that ultimately disappointed them?

- **Have conversations about beliefs in any academic subject.**

  - ❓ What seems important to your generation in this subject?

  - ❓ What problems do you think your generation will tackle in this area?

  - ❓ What issues do you think leaders in this field should focus on now?

  - ❓ What ballot initiatives from this subject would compel you to vote in a local or state election?

  - ❓ What issues do you hope to work on someday (or are working on now)?

  - ❓ What are the most important movements these days related to this subject?

  - ❓ In what ways are ideas from this subject making an impact in the world?

  - ❓ In what ways are ideas from this subject making an impact in your own life?

Help teenagers manage setbacks and frustration to build an internal locus of control.

In a culture of high-stakes testing, and in their everyday efforts to learn, we have to help teenagers normalize making mistakes. A growth mindset is critical here: teenagers who see their mistakes as experiences of learning—as explorations—continue to put forth effort. Quite simply, they will try again. But they won't try again if their fear of making a mistake is accompanied by a belief that they must be perfect or that the mistake represents an insurmountable weakness. Many teenagers do not yet have the ability to measure accurately the implications of their imperfect decisions, and they can imagine that irreparable harm has been done. They need trusted adults to provide an alternate perspective on the situation.

As well, they need trusted adults, and trustworthy peers, who will bear witness to their pain when they have failed. The emotions of anger, frustration, and dejection are by-products of caring and trying. It can be helpful for an adult to say, "You should feel your feelings. It's okay to feel badly when you didn't do as well as you wanted." Learning usually requires the acknowledgement and integration of feelings into growing wisdom. Brain research continues to make the integration of emotions and cognition ever clearer: the neural networks of learning are activated when students are emotionally engaged in the lesson—and learning is diminished when a student's emotions flood and overwhelm the cognitive processes.

Our recommendations here emphasize supporting students realizing their own locus of control over what happens to them. With support they can see that they have more control than they originally believed they did. Within themselves, they can be encouraged to consider other steps, other perspectives, and other tools. They can be encouraged to identify resources as well—both specific people and organizational structures—that will help them try again, and do so with a better chance of succeeding. This is another opportunity to reinforce that readiness for autonomy is enhanced by being in a network of support; teens grow independently, but they are not alone. (See also Chapter 8, pages 156–157, "Talk about healthy and unhealthy coping strategies.")

- **Provide structures and rituals that help students process their inevitable disappointments on the road to academic success.** Start a class conversation by asking, "What helps when you don't do as well as you wish you did?" The question lets students know that it is inevitable to have difficult times. Many teachers, anticipating that their students will have rough days, set up a space for reflection, post the steps to get help, and make available books that support reflection and balance, such as *Chicken Soup for the Teenage Soul*.

  Deciding together to build that support space in class brings teenagers into the conversation as central players, making it more likely that the final decisions meet their particular needs (see the "consult" and "collaborate" options in Chapter 4, page 56, to consider the level of student participation you want in making decisions). To prompt the conversation, ask these questions:

  - **?** If you are frustrated because you didn't do well on a test, what routine can we put into place for you to get support to do better?

  - **?** Where in our room can we set up a space for students to go if they just need a little distance from everyone, a little space to focus on their own and not be disturbed?

  - **?** What phrases and pictures can we post around the room that have helped you when you were not happy with how things were going?

  When we ask teens these age-appropriate, open-ended questions, we continually underscore our belief in their growing ability to learn from their decisions.

- **Practice self-talk that helps students problem-solve their struggles.** Many teenagers will quickly blame others, or denigrate themselves, when they fail a test, miss a deadline, or encounter one of life's inevitable disappointments. Listening to one's own self-talk, and hearing when it's negative and self-defeating, is a first step in shifting mindsets. Then, practicing alternative, constructive self-talk is a way to avoid getting stuck and overwhelmed. As with many skills to be employed in the face of disappointments, this one is best practiced when students are feeling good; the skill can then be prompted in difficult times. Teachers can engage students in the following activity prior to beginning a challenging project, in one-to-one coaching, or in advisory groups. Coaches on sports teams may also find this exercise very useful.

  1. Read one or more of the following quotes and ask for a few reactions. What do the students hear in the quote?

     - It's part of life to have obstacles. It's about overcoming obstacles; that's the key to happiness. (Herbie Hancock, musician)

     - If Plan A isn't working, I have Plan B, Plan C, and even Plan D. (Serena Williams, tennis player)

     - Failure is an event, not a person. (Zig Ziglar, author)

- o I don't think of myself as a poor deprived ghetto girl who made good. I think of myself as somebody who from an early age knew I was responsible for myself, and I had to make good. (Oprah Winfrey)

- o Life consists not in holding good cards but in playing those you hold well. (Josh Billings, author)

2. Ask students to brainstorm the positive and negative phrases students say to themselves when they haven't done as well as they hoped on a test, challenge, or game.

3. Ask students to consider the situations on Tool 9-2, think of the negative phrase someone might be saying to themselves, and craft a positive phrase they could say. Explain that "positive" in this case means moving them forward. Being positive is not about glossing things over. Some students may benefit from doing this activity with a partner; others may be more successful writing quietly on their own.

4. To summarize, offer the following prompt and ask for several responses: *When things aren't going well, I can . . .*

Help teenagers manage setbacks and frustration by using supports.

When students need information and resources, they should be able to access those supports efficiently, as part of the landscape. They should be able to have access without shame, and with the option for privacy.

- **Have conversations about community resources that support long-term success.** Many teenagers don't know where to find help. They can believe that seeking help is a sign of weakness, as opposed to a mark of independence and strength. Reference the availability of counselors, student-run support networks, tutors, and community organizations. Keep a list up in the room. Have the students brainstorm additional resources.

- **Make connections to colleges and universities for role models.** Many colleges make connections between their students and local middle and high schools, whose students need tutors and mentors.

See Chapter 12 for schoolwide structures that offer support systems and resources.

Create routines that normalize errors along the path to learning.

Many teenagers struggle to put their setbacks in a rational light—they can think their future has been sealed by one misstep. This all-or-nothing mentality can be countered by a school culture that not only gives students safe places to be counseled, but actively acknowledges all the mistakes everyone is making on their path toward wisdom.

- One great practice we've seen in a middle school classroom is a "**Mistake Board.**" The teacher gives all the students a stack of forms with three sections: (1) My mistake was ____, (2) What I learned is ____, (3) What I can do differently next is ____. When students make mistakes, they can fill out the form and give it to the teacher to post anonymously, or they can post it themselves. The teacher posts her own mistakes with a great flourish.

- **Include in the curricula examples of famous people whose success was the result of much work done over time.** Teenagers seek role models, and the history of every school subject is filled with stories of people whose success was earned through great effort. Going beyond the examples of perseverance in Chapter 7, provide students with a list of names to research as short projects, extensions, extra credit, or homework.

- **For homework, have students interview adults in their community about how they overcame setbacks.** Success is not only found in the famous; it is a capacity every person can develop, including the people with whom our students live every day. Have the class brainstorm an array of questions to ask the adults in their lives. Offering a few examples of questions can help students generate their own; for example, "In what ways do you wish you had done things differently when you were in school?" "In what ways did you struggle to have the family life you now have?" "Was your career path direct or did you try a few different things until you settled on your career?" "What job or community project do you wish you'd done differently?" The subsequent interviews will help students find unexpected role models, make connections that build their support networks, and expand the options they can choose from when they need to persevere through hard times.

Help students differentiate and separate as well as connect.

Teens need many experiences to find the balance between the need to belong and the need to be an individual. That's not an easy balance for a teen to establish, as everyone in the peer group is searching for a stable identity. This collective search for identity is often demonstrated by large numbers of teenagers adopting similar tastes in fashion, music, and movies—teenagers seem to be the quickest to pick up on and then discard fads. It is sometimes common for adults to tease teenagers for their "group think," an adult response that rarely diminishes that behavior.

What the observing adult cannot see are the teenager's mirror neurons that physiologically and nonconsciously connect their emotions to their peers. Many teens will rush to stand up for a peer whom they perceive has been treated unfairly. As their understanding of complex political realities develops, so does their empathy for those oppressed, from world genocide to the smallest endangered animals. Their empathy provokes righteous beliefs, and connects them to the struggles of people all over the earth. These intertwined cognitive-emotional connections are admirable traits, and can lead to much social responsibility.

Those empathetic connections can have a dangerous component, far riskier than buying a pair of jeans that suddenly are no longer in fashion. Without practice in both connecting and separating, the empathetic mirror neurons can contribute to shared teenage fears, unsafe sex, substance abuse, and in extreme cases, increases in suicide. Sadly, group think has a neurobiological basis. In these contagious ways, the teenage years are particularly vulnerable times.

With ongoing opportunities through school curricula, connections with role models, and chances to reflect, teenagers can find a more stable self-identity in this very difficult process.

- **Include in curricula examples of famous people in every subject area who resisted pressure to conform.** Bring out in discussions that there is a tension between fitting in and standing out. Students can be motivated in answering such questions as

  - (?) What were the factors that prompted this person to act?

  - (?) What were the social and professional risks for this person?

  - (?) In what ways might this person have done better in life by fitting in more?

  - (?) In what ways do you think her success was enhanced or diminished by taking her own path?

  - (?) What evidence tells you that this person was satisfied with the path she chose, or regretted it?

  - (?) How does this person's strategies compare with other people's strategies in the same field and era?

- **Include in project assignments reflection and discussion related to the reasons the teenagers each chose their topics.** Offering students choices in curricula supports them to follow their own areas of interests, which is a key character trait for developing a sense of purpose tied to a growing sense of self. Students can be prompted to answers questions such as

  - (?) What were the main reasons you made your choice?

  - (?) What would you like us to know about you from your choice?

  - (?) In what ways does this choice reflect ideas that are important to you?

  - (?) What might have been your second choice?

  - (?) What if everyone in the class thinks your choice is an odd one?

- **Advisory groups are also a good place to talk about decision making**:

  - (?) What were a few recent decisions that were easy to make?

  - (?) What decision was harder?

  - (?) What's great about making your own decisions?

  - (?) What's challenging about making decisions on your own?

  - (?) What's something positive about disagreeing with your friends or making a different choice than they made?

- **Use an "opinion continuum" to help students establish their own beliefs among a range of peers.** (See the Appendix, pages 249–250, for instructions.) There are opportunities in every subject from Grades 6 through 12 to get the students standing up and seeing where they stand in relation to their peers. Crafting a half-dozen questions related to your current lesson can spark curiosity about perspectives and self-reflection. Opinion continuum formats are useful in any area of study, as you can see from this array:

  - o I'd want to be friends with the main character in the story.

  - o Drawing helps me relax.

o The government should fund science research that is not tied to a product.

o I am learning something important about how I learn in the study of math.

o It would be fun to do a dance unit in phys ed class.

o You can't judge historical figures using modern beliefs.

- **Prepare for difficult situations.** When emotions are strong, clear thinking usually isn't. Below are scenarios that students might experience and find challenging. Being prepared will help. The scenarios are examples for classes, advisories, or one-to-one conversations, which can be used for brainstorms, role-plays, turn-and-talks, or writing prompts.

  ❓ You're feeling stressed with too many assignments. You tell your friend, who offers to do some of your work for you. You take pride in never cheating. Is there another way your friend could help?

  ❓ You're hanging out with some friends and a few of their friends. Someone you don't know well is paying you a lot of attention, making you feel uncomfortable, maybe even a little afraid. You've set up some code phrases with a friend ahead of time and a promise that using them means you'll leave soon and together. What are the phrases you'd choose? Which friend will be your reliable exit partner?

  ❓ Tomorrow you will be walking into class to take a big test. What are some ways you get yourself ready to do your best?

  ❓ It's party season. Your friends have been drinking; you don't want to be with them, or get a ride home with them. What do you do? What could you say?

- **When more than one student misbehaves, speak to each one individually to support each taking responsibility as an individual**. Pull aside teenagers to talk one to one, especially when they are part of a group. This strategy is as important for building relationships and supporting responsibility as it is for decreasing group influence. Refrain from addressing, "You guys"—a situation in which the students look to each other for connection. The goal is to help each teen develop the capacity to accept responsibility and reconnect to community norms. Reach for the connections students have with you, even the most slender threads, when their behavior most communicates a rejection of your beliefs. You make those connections one to one. Also see information about restorative justice in Chapter 4, pages 66–67.

Help students experience personal mastery and success.

Many teenagers are accustomed to turning in an assignment on Tuesday because it's due on Tuesday, not because they checked, revised, and polished their work. If it's C-level work, so be it; it's due and therefore "done." The student moves on to other assignments on Wednesday. The sense of being done comes from an external source, the deadline, not an internal source, a personal sense of mastery or a self-assessment of quality. The student isn't developing the skills to *fully* complete a task, or the criteria to know when it's as good as it can be.

For some students, that C-level work is all anyone expected of them; being done with the work was the only pressure they had faced. Madeline Levine, in *The Price of Privilege* draws attention to demanding, affluent parents, who pressure their children for a level of traditional achievement, to such an extent that the kids do not develop almost any personal criteria for mastery. The situation often is exacerbated by the drive to get into prestigious private schools and colleges. This relentless demand to meet external measures of success led two parents to realize "that they had neglected the . . . important task of stepping back and allowing a safe space in which [their son] could develop his own likes, dislikes, interests, and priorities" (2006, p. 90). Their son turned to drugs and alcohol to get relief from his parents' relentless definition of success, one that was not his own.

Teachers can help students develop the higher-order skills of personal mastery, informed by the students' unique goals, interests, abilities, priorities, and resources. Of course, to be successful in higher education, and in life in general, they will have deadlines to meet, and they will have to deal with other people's expectations. What is also true is that they'll become more successful and more self-regulated because they will be motivated by an internalized sense of pride and mastery. (Also see Chapter 10, page 188, "Assign a project or task where the focus is by choice and connection to one's future," and Chapter 7 for organizational skills and tools.)

- **Develop with students self-assessment rubrics for mastery.** There are self-assessment practices in Chapter 7 (pages 127–128). Many teenagers can be supported to create more context-specific mastery self-assessments for themselves. Teachers can establish certain mastery expectations for the entire class in an activity, and also offer students a menu of options for picking two or three elements of mastery they each would like to work toward. Student self-assessment contributes to responsible independence and healthy self-identity; student participation in shaping self-assessments is even more powerful.

- **Have at least some projects or tasks that have to be fully completed and polished.** They are done only when they're really done, not when a deadline has arrived. This expectation is as important for struggling students as it is for those who have well developed academic skills. In fact, struggling students need to hear that mastery is the baseline for them as well. For instance, in a high school program for students with learning disabilities, students have to answer correctly every item on their tests. Those students who do not achieve that absolute criteria meet with their teacher, an assistant teacher, or a tutor to talk through their errors, get a reteach, and demonstrate their new understanding in the one-to-one sessions. One-to-one meetings may be necessary to support some students in identifying reasonable personal goals, always underscoring the message that their work has to be driven by their interests.

- **Hold exhibitions** of student work with people from the community with experience in those fields. Students can also post their work to the class' online site, inviting community members to look at their postings.

- **Develop student portfolios.** There are innumerable resources for supporting students to develop portfolios of their work. We encourage portfolios that are largely determined by student choice of work and their attention to personal mastery. Be sure to look for portfolio resources that include student self-assessment.

Help students connect with traditions, their heritage, and causes.

For most teenagers, integrating their families' heritage into their emerging adult beliefs is a critically important step to a stable self-identity. If independence is supported by our social connections that lend support and perspective, there is much to be said for the support and perspective teenagers can gain through knowing their heritage. Marcus Garvey famously said, "A people without the knowledge of their past history, origin, and culture is like a tree without roots." Conversely, connecting teens to their roots, ranging from school to community to the larger world, can have a profound impact on their stability. An extreme example of such deep roots is found in the autobiography of computer innovator An Wang, who grew up in China in the early 20th century. His family followed a local custom of having someone from each generation keep a written history of the family. Wang was given those books as a young man; the books traced his family story as far back as forty-eight generations! He writes, "I grew up with a sense that my culture and my family had been around a very long time."

Even if you can research only a couple of generations, the connection to cultural and family heritage matters. Unlike An Wang's extraordinarily stable community, most students' family histories have at some point been lost or severed. When asking students to engage in family history exploration, be sensitive to individual contexts. Offer alternatives, such as researching a particular culture's traditions, or interviewing a trusted adult about her background. The following activity is an example of a way to allow students to choose to work with their own family's history, or to do research independent of knowing that history:

- One high school history teacher begins the year by having each student develop a personalized fictional character based on a handful of potentially powerful background traits: race, religion, national origin, economic class, occupation, sexual preference, geographic location. As the class studies an era of history, the students develop a portfolio of how their character might have lived, and struggled, through that time; for example, during the years leading up to the Civil War, a student's character might have been a slave, a freed slave, a teacher in the North, an abolitionist religious fanatic, a southern blacksmith. That same character returns to experience World War I.

- In advisory groups or in social studies units on culture, students can explore the many groups they are part of, the many aspects of culture that influence them, from family culture to clubs and teams, school, neighborhood, regional, national, historical, religious, political, and other influences. What aspects feel woven into their identity already? What aspects do they struggle with?

Also see page 175 and the Chapter 10 activities on page 191 that support students interviewing people in their family and community.

Discussion Options for Faculty

- Which practices in this chapter seem especially important for your students?

- Which skills mentioned in this chapter are especially important for you to practice?

- When in your teenage years were you given new responsibilities? Did that timing seem right on schedule, too soon, or too late? How can those reflections inform the decisions you are making in your school?

- In what ways are you currently giving students opportunities for making decisions? How can you do more?

- How are you helping students to use their opinions and beliefs for academic exploration and success? What else could you do?

- Who has projects going on in class that allow students to demonstrate a variety of intelligences and interests?

- What jobs are students doing in the school now? What else can you ask of them?

- In what ways are you giving students opportunities to set personal goals for improvement and mastery?

- What structures and rituals exist in classes or in the school that encourage students to analyze how their errors help them improve? What else can you do so that errors are first and foremost seen as part of learning?

- What are opportunities in the curriculum to help students understand peer pressure as it is applying to the work in class?

- There are many cultures and diverse family heritages in the school. In what ways are you giving students opportunities to make positive connections to those cultures and heritages?

Practices at Home

No doubt it provoked anxiety when your kids were toddlers, moving and exploring near staircases, corners of tables, and cabinets. The anxiety was for their safety; you probably didn't feel your authority was in question as they stumbled forward. You may have felt exhausted chasing them but otherwise felt positive about their curiosity and energy.

Your teens are exploring the world, including the world of ideas and self-identity. This exploration can raise concerns for their safety at times, and can feel like a constant challenge to *your ideas and self-identity.* How can you let them explore *and* keep them safe? How can you make sure that the lines of communication stay open so you hear the next idea they're trying? How can you see their explorations as another positive and curious experience? Besides, what's the alternative—that they don't learn to be independent? Or that they hide their actions from you?

There is no exact right time to give a teenager more independence, no specific age to allow them to stay out later, hold a job, go on a date, or drive on their own. What is absolutely true is that at some point teenagers need opportunities to do all these things. They need adult support to develop skills for making wise decisions. Of course, they'll make mistakes. With adult support, their mistakes can provide learning experiences. The skills of autonomy develop gradually, year by year.

One of the most difficult tasks teenagers face as they explore independence is managing the competition for allegiance between peers and family. Most families want their children to have friends and to not be overly influenced by their friends. Teens may want to be exempted from family dinner or events as they develop their independence, but those are not times to disconnect from family. In *The Courage to Raise Good Men,* Olga Silverstein and Beth Rashbaum (1994) urge parents, and all the meaningful adults in the lives of adolescents, to remain connected and involved, while embracing the "dozens of opportunities every day for validating a child's sense of himself, and thus allowing him to come into the fullness of his autonomy" (p. 147). The primary influence for teenage boys to become men, or teenage girls to become women, should not be groups of teenagers! Adults must still take the lead in remaining connected.

Brain research offers important insights about teens. The last part of the brain to fully connect to the rest of the neural network is the frontal lobe, where humans weigh risks and benefits, consider options, and self-regulate. Those connections are not completed during adolescence. The brain learns skills for independence by having real-life experiences and learning from them. Parents can assess their teenagers' readiness for more independence by spending time together, talking and planning together, and reviewing events. Those conversations and activities can include many of the following practices:

Talk with your teens about the ways you are independent, interdependent, and dependent on others. Let teens hear your own considerations of other people's needs and feelings. Let them hear when and where you need support. Your kids will learn from your deliberations, and recognize that decision making and independence are complex and worth talking about.

Talk about what you hold firm and what you can negotiate. There may be family rules, such as no smoking, that are firm. Be clear about the rules that won't change, and the rules and guidelines that can be adjusted as teens grow older. You can have this conversation when planning family traditions, such as Thanksgiving—there may be parts of the event that will not be considered for change, and other aspects that may be altered. Ask your teenager, "Is there anything you think we could add to the event?"

In Chapter 4, pages 55–56, read about the "tell-to-collaborate continuum." Notice how often you tell your teens what to do, compared to how often you consult with them, or how often they are given the chance to share in decisions. By letting them know your approach—"I'm in 'tell' mode now" or "I want to consult with you"—you help them cooperate in ways that build your relationships.

Share family stories and struggles. Teenagers are exposed to many "heroes" through the media. It is likely that people in the family have done courageous and impressive acts: emigrating from another country to make a better life, holding multiple jobs, advocating for a community improvement. The hard work of putting together a home, job, and community is part of every family's history. Most teenagers will be interested when you say, "Did I tell you about how your Aunt Mary . . . ?"

Support initiatives to earn more independence. Many teens say, "My other friends' parents let them do this. Why can't I?" You do not have to do what other parents do; talk with your teenagers about what you want to see and hear in order for them to get more privileges. Be straightforward, realistic, and encouraging. These moments are great opportunities to set expectations about shopping, cooking, cleaning, and other tasks within teenage capabilities. Once the criteria are set for earning independence, be their cheerleader and resource. They will be able to gain their independence and your trust, two huge accomplishments in the family.

Help them realize that mistakes are inevitable. We are not suggesting that breaking a family rule is inevitable, or happens without consequences. However, life is filled with errors and bad decisions—from how teens use their time on weekends, to which friend they lent money, to losing their phones. Help your teenagers make sense of mistakes, recover stability, and learn. Tell them about errors you made growing up, and lessons you took from those situations. Help them use their errors to develop their own wisdom, and to know that you will help them along that often difficult path. Read about restorative discipline in Chapter 4, pages 66–67, if your teen has broken a family rule.

Support them to take care of themselves more. When children are young, we have to show them how to put a plate in the sink, or how to hang up a towel. Teenagers can take on varied responsibilities, developing a sense of independence and mastery that they'll need as adults. Show them how to vacuum, do the laundry, and run the dishwasher. Teach them to cook a few meals, and then make meals together. Work with them to fix things that break, do basic car maintenance, and care for the yard. Many teenagers will be excited to find out they can take of themselves. If you've got teenagers who are extremely responsible, ask them about another aspect of self-care—relaxing. Sometimes a few minutes sitting together looking out the window and chatting about the day can give you and your teenagers a chance to slow down, and you a chance to hear how they are managing all the expectations of kids their ages.

TOOL 9-1   Learning Activities

Reading		Writing	
Watching (Media)		Role-Playing	
Listening		Building	
Collecting/Finding/Cataloging		Observing	
Online Research		Drawing/Graphing	
Interviewing		Other	

TOOL 9-2 My Self-Talk

How can you shift self-defeating messages to self-talk that that gives you energy and ideas?

Scenario	Negative Self-Talk	Positive Self-Talk
1. You are on the bench throughout most games, or are named an understudy for the school play.		
2. Your project group partners criticized your work.		
3. You have no opinion when asked to share one in a discussion.		
4. You promised a friend to be a study partner but forgot about it.		
5. You applied for a part-time job and didn't get it.		
6. Your own scenario:		

10

Connecting Lessons to Life, Not Just to Tests

When students are engaged and excited to learn, the effort teachers put into crafting lessons and organizing activities feels so worthwhile. What can schools do to more consistently access teen motivation? One answer has been to expect them to complete required courses and pass high-stakes testing. This double-barreled expectation of students—pass required courses and tests—has been seen by many as the pressure point to increase student motivation. Some adults believe there is little choice but to force teenagers into compliance to do their schoolwork.

We take a different perspective, supported by the research on healthy adolescent development, including brain science and our years working in schools. When schools provide outlets for their students' interests, strengths, hopes, and dreams, rather than depending on compliance with adult demands, engagement and learning increase (Bernard, 2004). Even without a complete radical restructuring of schools and curriculum, our classrooms can ascribe to the belief that "a child's need to know is a drive as pure as a diamond and as distracting as chocolate" (Medina, 2014, p. 255).

That drive to know is leveraged by connecting teenagers to the larger world, which must be a central objective of schools. Teens are beginning to develop aspirations for hobbies and extracurricular passions, for jobs they will hold, for families they will build, for communities they wish to join, for character traits they wish to grow into, for colleges and vocational programs they hope will accept their applications. These aspirations, among the many elements of what goes into adulthood, are powerful incentives for each person's motivation to learn. Compliance as a day-to-day strategy of schooling is not nearly as robust as connecting to those personal aspirations and building commitments to one's life goals.

Some teachers believe that goals imply only college and vocations, and that the guidance department is solely responsible for those pathways. In this chapter, we are talking about much more than getting applications in on time—necessary but not sufficient help for students, especially those who aspire to be the first in their family to go beyond high school. The Bridgespan Group (Bedsworth, Colby, & Doctor, 2006) looked at supports to help low income students make the leap from high school to a successful college career. They found that one of the least significant supports was merely helping those students with the procedural paperwork, such as filling out applications. These first-in-the-family students need the whole school to help them make connections to their future aspirations.

Everyday within the standard curriculum are innumerable opportunities for whole teens to connect to the greater world, and to appreciate how the gifts and skills of others build society. Helping students find relevance in today's lessons builds character traits—they are literally being asked, "What do you care about? How do you want people in your community to see you? What do you need to learn to become the person you want to be?" Providing opportunities for teenagers to connect to their community through schoolwork gives them a head start in their adult development, and helps them realize their growing power to be influential citizens.

We have heard from many teachers how annoyed they feel when students ask, "Why do we have to do this? Will I ever really need it when I grow up?" Most students don't bother to ask the question; that alone should give teachers pause. When the vast majority of students seem quietly content to comply, is it worth teachers' efforts to ask for active personal engagement more than compliance?

Yes, especially when we consider our schools as the most important institution that will support democracy for the next generation. In the 2014 midterm election, only 36 percent of eligible voters exercised their rights at the ballot box, a figure that has been steadily decreasing for the last fifty years. Through connecting the curriculum to the world beyond test scores, our schools ask students to play an active role in our collective future. Developing a sense of purpose that bonds them to the larger society is a contributing factor for resilience.

As well, we know that the lack of a high school diploma is a barrier to adult success. The US 2012 nationwide rate of Black students graduating was 69 percent, the rate of Hispanic students graduating was 73 percent, and the rate of White students was 86 percent (National Center for Education Statistics, 2015). As a nation, we are leaving millions of young adults at risk, a strong reason to consider the connection of the curriculum to the aspirations of all students.

Edward Fergus, Pedro Noguera, and Margary Martin (2015) express the concern that many Black students believe that "expending effort to succeed in education will not result in access to good jobs and upward mobility later in life" (p. 16). In their study of schools for boys of color, the authors saw inconsistent results from merely including Black history as required content. More engagement happened when the curriculum encouraged the students to understand how historical struggles for freedom were impacting their own concerns and choices as they approached adulthood. For students who come from underserved communities with low graduation rates, connecting their curriculum to aspirations for their world, one with more equality and justice, can be a profound motivator.

Too often that drive to know in teens has been muted by years of compliance with an imposed curriculum disconnected from their particular worlds and needs. As noted in Chapter 2, for many students who do not come to schools from the dominant culture, with all of its implicit beliefs and rewards, or who face barriers to learning, the lack of real personal relevance in the curriculum is a large hurdle to overcome every day.

As well, many students from the dominant culture have developed the skill of compliance that mimics engagement. We observed a high school honors class in an affluent suburb. In the fifty-minute period of instruction, there was not a single discipline problem—and just as telling, only one student *one time* asked a question that he really was interested in. All the other questions from this elite class were only to make sure they understood what the teacher expected them to write down, or what they might be asked to reproduce on the exam.

In a school context that so often drains the curriculum of student passion, many adults think of teenagers as lazy and easily distracted. But watch them when they are focused on something that matters to them—everything from the arts to cars to sports to politics to relationships to spiritual quests to the latest big movie to video games to service projects—and it is apparent that the "need to know" drive is still accessible in teenagers. Not surprisingly, those activities are integrated with playing, competing, moving about, problem solving, engaging with others, and passionate conversations about interests; they involve the whole teen. Schools can leverage student passion. Teachers can implement lessons that maximize motivation.

The alternative is too well known: many teenagers going compliantly through the motions in school, a small number displaying actual enthusiasm, and far too many drifting away from the adults. The emphasis on compliance also makes many of our most willing students more stressed than is healthy or motivating. Imagine for a moment working at a job in which your supervisor watches over you every minute of the day, compares all of your work to the other workers sitting near you, and continually monitors your compliance to a set of expectations few could fully master. Compliance alone is exhausting for everyone.

For many students, the emphasis on compliance compared to personal connections is debilitating. Author Ta-Nehisi Coates (2015) writes of growing up poor in West Baltimore: "I remember sitting in my seventh grade French class and not having any idea why I was there. I did not know any French people, and nothing around me suggested I ever would. France was a rock rotating in another galaxy . . . Why precisely was I sitting in this classroom?" (p. 26)

Many students like Coates do not have a family history of everyone going to college. They don't have a large group of peers going to college, or the vital experience of having been on a college campus. They have not been exposed to the ways a college education leads to careers and financial stability. They lack the support systems to navigate the college application process and the money to go to college. Without those supports, we are asking much of the teenage brain and body to sit through innumerable hours of disconnected lessons to get the diploma that allows them to take the next step into more formal education. What schools can offer students, whether or not college is an aspiration, are lessons that matter, activities that connect school and community, and inspirational relationships with teachers.

Connecting school work to one's life work and character, and not just to tests, is among the most powerful tools we have to realize the potential in our curriculum and the potential within each of our unique whole teenagers.

Practices That Connect Lessons to Life, Not Just to Tests

Help students identify their current goals.

Goals are helpful when they aren't just wishes, but connect to the efforts and actions that bring them about. Russell Quaglia and Michael Corso (2014) emphasize that aspirations include dreaming *and* doing—images of the future linked to actions in the present. Aspirations for a few teenagers are very clear: they pursue particular courses, jobs, relationships, and hobbies with tremendous focus. They know where they want to go and who they want to be. Aspirations for many others are very much in formation: most teens are still in the process of piecing together their image of themselves as adults. Some are dreaming with no actions toward those dreams; some are feeling and acting on pressures to achieve without a vision of where all that action could lead; yet others are neither dreaming of their future nor doing in the present. Helping students realize their aspirations is a huge—and often untapped—source of motivation for schoolwork.

- **Talk about and learn about student aspirations**. At the beginning of the school year, give your students the Tool 10-1 survey and make it anonymous. By doing so, you will get an honest look into the breadth of aspirations among your students. Asking them to put their names on the survey would potentially draw unwanted attention to the students who aspire for jobs, families, and colleges that are atypical among their peers. As noted in Chapter 2, the pressure on teens in certain communities to conform to a common set of hopes and beliefs is powerful enough to undermine their honesty. The goal of the survey is for the teacher to know how to connect with, expand upon, and support the range of aspirations in class. At other times and through other means, certainly have conversations with individual students that allow them to share their own particular aspirations.

  Aggregate and list the student responses. Post the lists around the room, not asking any student to self-identify their contribution—it is the range of ideas that matters. Refer to the lists regularly as possibilities emerge from lessons. This activity can be done in classes and in advisory. (See "Sense of Purpose and Future" on pages 16–18 in Chapter 1 for how one teacher uses the responses from this survey.)

- **Assign a project or task where the focus is by choice and connection to one's future.** Have students complete Tool 10-2, "My Project—My Future," an array of questions about their personal and academic goals. Collect and reference these student-identified goals throughout the project. Look for opportunities to support and give feedback to individual students.

Within and beyond the walls of the school, expand their goals.

Students often do not know what they are capable of learning and doing, nor of the many opportunities in life that would be well suited to their strengths and goals. They may circumscribe their aspirations due to long-held prejudices that lead them to think, "People who look like me aren't allowed to do that" or "I will be rejected because of my beliefs." Early struggles in school may lead them to prematurely decide that their goals must be curtailed. Other students know only fragments, often distorted and narrowed by movies and TV, of what certain professionals really do on the job, and the qualities of character that are needed to be part of a team. The activities below support students in knowing more about their goals, and provide teachers with many stimulating lessons tied to various subjects.

- **Take trips to postsecondary institutions with classes and advisory.** Visiting colleges, universities, and training programs can happen throughout the teenage years, connected to a particular class or advisory project; for example, a tour of science labs, robotics department, the gymnasium, the art studios, the libraries. For some students, such a trip will literally be their first steps into those worlds. After the trip, debrief together what looked interesting or daunting, and how the trip could connect to their aspirations—not just for careers, but also for the communities they want to be part of, and for the contributions they wish to make to those communities.

  A teacher in the Boston area took her predominantly minority students for a day of reading in the tree-lined inner courtyard of Harvard University. One student turned to her and said, "I didn't know that any minority students went to school here."

  That unexpected vision of seeing a potential peer group on a college campus parallels the experience of a student interviewed in *First in the Family* (Cushman, 2005). The student grew up in a rural Black and Latino neighborhood in Texas. He was watching a University of Texas baseball game on television, which he realized was close to his home. Seeing student athletes prompted him to picture himself in college. He says, "College was this abstract thing that people talked about, but seeing it on TV, with the same skyline as my city . . . I was like, 'Wow, maybe I can attend that university'" (p. 2). The next step would be for students like him to set foot on the campus, and schools can provide them with that opportunity, within the standard curriculum.

- **Help students plan explorations to expand their visions—and skills.** We worked with a school in which advisory groups were given small budgets for field explorations that had to include postsecondary learning, career connections, and cultural or civic institutions. Students needed to discuss their aspirations and ideas to craft plans, make all the calls (after rehearsing), schedule the tours and visits, and figure out a budget. They also had to recruit two more advisory groups to their plan, or merge plans, in order to spread the cost of the school bus across three groups. This is a wonderful example of synthesizing students' growing ability to problem solve, experience autonomy with the safety of adult guidance, and develop their personal goals. As in the stories above, it was enormously eye opening for students to see people who looked like them in their visits.

- **Make use of museums and organizations in your area.** Many cities have museums that highlight the histories of their citizens: African American; indigenous communities; immigrant groups. These visits can provide role models and let students know that their work and hopes are part of the long march others have taken. Students who connect to their cultural histories, and see the paths others have taken, develop a deeper sense of purpose as they pursue their many goals.

  Career readiness is not only a set of basic math and language arts skills, but knowledge of how various businesses and industries contribute to society. Many students will find motivation in a path that does not always go immediately through college.

Museums can get teens excited about inventing, running a business, working in industries, and working for social justice. Visiting a textile museum, a farm museum, a clock museum, or a replica of a whaling ship stirs ideas. Many museums and organizations have education departments, which will plan school visits and also bring people and materials to classrooms.

- **Attend plays.** Theatre companies often sell reduced priced tickets to schools for afternoon matinees. We've worked with a high school that twice a year took advantage of such an offer. After attending a rather dull version of a Shakespeare play, one group of students were having an animated conversation about the electronics involved in the lighting and sound production, and another about stage sets. Going to the theatre is not just for the language arts department. It exposes students to possibilities and the interdependence of arts with technology and trades.

- **Use every environment to expand ideas about jobs and professions.** You and your students are always surrounded by an environment that resulted from the effort of many minds and hands. Start a discussion by saying, "Look around this room. How many different professions and jobs were necessary to build this room and to make all the objects in it?" The list should be enormous; you may need to prompt answers by pointing out certain features: "Have we considered the walls? What about the floor? Did anyone get us thinking about the heating system? How did the books in the room go from the author's ideas all the way to our shelves?" With the list on everyone's mind you can then ask, "How does the work we are doing in class relate to the work done to build this classroom, and all its objects?" One great benefit from doing this activity in class is how it can be revived any time you go on a field exploration, prompted by your question, "Look around this area. How many jobs and professions made this all happen?"

- **Connect qualities of character with the future.** In addition to the traditional academic learning objectives many teachers post in the class, for example, "Students will be able to understand the structure of the periodic table of elements," post the characteristics of the whole teen that are being developed in the lesson: "Students will seek out resources to improve their final drafts," or "Students will understand someone else's perspective on this topic." Brainstorm with students how improving their skills beyond the standard curriculum expands their potential to succeed in all aspects of their lives.

- **Provide students with case studies.** Through short readings and internet searches in every subject, students can become familiar with contemporary and historical issues that connect the curriculum to the world beyond the school's walls. Students can summarize the facts, compare and contrast competing arguments, and suggest ways they would like to see the situation addressed. A case study can be integrated into the standard curriculum as an on-going activity, and be an option for extra-credit work.

- **Use project-based learning.** Project-based learning promotes the integration of skills and ideas, opening the possibilities for experiencing the ways courses of study influence each other. Project-based learning pulls students into the larger world, where the boundaries between subjects disappear as the students use all of their learning to make sense of a real-life problem, the kind they will face as adults.

Too often lessons in school come in discrete chunks. Students learn one skill or idea, and then another, and then another. For many students, this fragmented approach to education requires a stoical compliance with expectations.

Because brains develop webs of connections, schoolwork that integrates facts, skills, and concepts develops deeply held understanding. Project-based learning allows students to exercise their strengths and interests, and in that process, consider once more if their aspirations match their willingness to put in the effort it takes to be successful. Because most teenagers are still exploring their futures, project-based learning gives them opportunities, within the safety of the classroom laboratory, to connect their efforts and interests today with their hopes for the future.

Here's one example: A school district was working with community partners to raise awareness of lead poisoning. "A school-to-career class wrote a play about a parent's experience with lead poisoning and presented it at neighborhood elementary schools. Nutrition classes wrote a nutritional guide and cookbook with recipes full of important nutrients that help prevent lead poisoning. The book was distributed to elementary classes, preschools, early start programs, and parent support groups. Students in a media class learned how to design PowerPoint presentations illustrating the critical points of lead poisoning. In an ESL class, students learned English by interviewing each other about lead poisoning on videotape and created pamphlets and posters in their native languages" (Smith, 2003).

Many of the projects listed below make connections between schoolwork and the communities students must learn to navigate. Some projects will explicitly include direct service to others, or offer service as one component of the project. As noted in Chapter 2, students who are often marginalized in the dominant culture of schools may also find passion in focusing on projects that explore the racism and discrimination so many of their communities have faced. And because teenagers in all communities are subject to particular pressures, encouraging all students to explore the issues that mean most to them can spark curiosity and commitment. Some problems may be societal and others very personal. In all cases, such projects work to enlist students' internal motivation.

- Study the usage patterns of a local park or playground and suggest renovations.
- Investigate the barriers and supports people face obtaining health care coverage.
- Analyze the projects of national environmental groups on local concerns.
- Investigate and make a guide for the voter registration procedures in your area, including an advocacy plan to convince people to vote.
- Report on your district's and school's budget changes in the last decade.
- Investigate hiring practices for local civil service jobs, such as police and fire fighters.
- Interview senior citizens regarding the evolution of the neighborhood.
- Identify a ballot initiative or candidate in the coming election and research the varied perspectives that are informing people's voting decisions.
- Analyze the data from various high schools on college acceptance rates.
- Help a well-loved local business initiate an advertising campaign.
- Help increase recycling rates in school or the community.
- Explore historical and current local employment data and draw hypotheses about the future.
- Compare and contrast the work conditions of particular trades.

Help students explore pathways to reach goals.

Some students will have the good fortune of coming from homes and communities that are rich in resources, where they have been exposed to many possibilities. Unfortunately, that exposure does not mean they know how to find a path from all the possibilities to a desired future. Other students come from communities in which the possibilities seem limited—prompting the need for the exploration sections of this chapter. Unfortunately, even with a goal, the pathways may be extremely limited. Every adult in the school has the ability to provide some information about pathways from aspirations to accomplishments. The actions below can be done in classes, advisories, and in one-to-one dialogues with students.

- **Hang teachers' diplomas and certificates up in classrooms**. Doctors, lawyers, real estate agents, and mechanics display their diplomas and certifications. Teachers should do the same. Students can then engage in meaningful conversations about how the choices their teachers made when they were younger brought them to their current professional status.

- **Invite alumni to talk about their post-high school experiences.** Many schools hold an alumni presentation day every year that is well received. To offer a wide array of pathway ideas, choose alumni who graduated within the past two years, those who are finishing college and training programs, and those in the first years of their careers or having a family. Include alumni who went into rehab programs and those in the military. These alumni can tell stories of their secondary school years and link their school stories to the lives they are now leading. If you can't put together such a diverse panel, even one graduate coming to your class provides a first-person account into the ways *now* connect to *later*.

- **Extol the benefits of attending all types of postsecondary learning opportunities.** In many communities, possibly more so in affluent communities, there is a lot of pressure on teens to be accepted into prestigious colleges, even if those schools are not a good fit. Much of this chapter, and indeed a large portion of this book, is dedicated to supporting teens finding their unique strengths and building an adult identity in harmony with their skills and strengths. It makes no sense to abandon all of that hard-earned personal wisdom only to be dazzled by the fame and celebrity of a famous college. One benefit of teachers hanging up their own diplomas is to give students access to their diverse experiences in colleges and universities.

There are pressures in all communities to attend certain colleges and programs; those pressures can come at a teen from any adult. One high school senior reported to us that every adult asked her the same question: "What are your plans for next year?" Whatever she said, the adults gave her advice. Being a polite young woman, she patiently and respectfully listened. She said no one asked her about anything else in her life that mattered to her. She had been reduced to a partial teen.

Another student was accepted at a prestigious university as well as a small, less-well-known college. His principal, with every good intention, pressed him to go to the larger, more highly regarded institution, conveying that students should believe in themselves, take on challenges, and grab opportunities that would open the most possibilities. A teacher worried that this particular student needed the support systems of the small college, and that the student would feel lost and out of place among the larger and more affluent study body of the university. The student took the big challenge, enrolled in the university, but dropped out in October. The principal, for all his good intentions, may not have seen this particular whole student.

All adults can help students understand that how they fit into a college is one of the most important insights for their decision. Maybe the right fit is a big university, or maybe it's a small college; maybe a city would expose them to options, or maybe having a suburban or rural campus would help them focus. Fit is complicated, including everything from the price tag to what programs are offered, from level of challenge to the level of diversity. Getting in is only the start; completing school is what's ultimately important, and the right fit will help.

The range of colleges reflects the diversity of student needs and aspirations. Share with them the following quote from organizational development experts Margaret Wheatley and Myron Kellner-Rogers (1996), from their studies of nature and systems. They turn our notion of survival of the fittest on its head, writing,

> There is no such thing as survival of the fittest, only survival of the fit. This means that there is no one answer that is right, but many answers that might work . . . There is no ideal design for anything, just interesting combinations that arise as a living thing explores its space of possibilities. (p. 16)

Then ask the students, "In what ways does that quote relate to going to college?"

- **Invite local professionals and trade workers to class**. Students need to hear about the diverse pathways adults have taken to their current professions. Most of the students in a science class have no intention of being a physicist, but listening to the effort these adults exerted to achieve their careers affirms characteristics of the whole teen. Don't forget to invite professionals in jobs related to your subject area whose stories include a range of post-high school years of study. Students should see the many pathways to vocational and career success.

   Unfortunately, many television shows and movies that teens watch present a narrow array of unrealistic, highly dramatized versions of professions. Teens need access to real people doing the work, to hear what the routine activities of any job really are. What are the tedious tasks lawyers and scientists and firefighters deal with? What sustains their commitment? Students will be more prepared to choose and last in a field with reality-based knowledge. As school staff know from their own jobs, success is not usually measured in glamour and riches, but in the pride of fulfilling day-to-day responsibilities that have meaning—not as exciting as what jobs look like on television, and still very valuable.

   Other adults can bring wonderful stories of having had multiple jobs. United States Representative Stephen Lynch was a steel worker who became a lawyer and then was elected to Congress. Students will benefit from hearing that no specific job or particular profession is required to fulfill their future success—because success includes being a lifelong learner and having a commitment to admirable character traits.

- **Explore biographies in every course**. Learn about historical and contemporary leaders in every field. Focus student attention on the paths these people took to become exemplary role models:

   ❓ What obstacles did they face?

   ❓ What character traits helped them persevere?

(?) What critical decisions did they make?

(?) In what ways did they find people to provide support?

(?) What visions of their future sustained their effort?

(?) In what ways did their formal education help?

Help students nurture their own goals within the peer pressure to conform.

Adults often talk about the impact of peers on making safe choices, less so about the ways peer pressure can impact a teen's deepest goals. One outcome of our work in a wide range of communities is that we've seen how the pressures on teenagers vary greatly depending on where they live. Chapter 2 details many of the ways that teenage development is intricately woven with family and community economic levels, histories of oppression, access to resources, and presence or absence of stable social networks. Peer pressure is another context-based force.

While no teen is an exact prototype, and no neighborhood is without diversity, very powerful forces make certain peer pressures most probable in particular communities. In affluent suburbs, we have too often seen the anxiety from relentlessly high expectations amid the abundance that does not bring relief, and the competition that can undermine long-standing friendships. In poor rural and urban communities, we have seen the despair of limited resources and role models, and the lack of a cohort of peers planning for college, a factor more important than encouragement from parents, general encouragement from adults, or help with paperwork (Bedsworth et al., 2006).

Discuss and brainstorm ways to respond to peer pressure. Tool 10-3 features a series of quotes based on conversations with students from varied communities. Some of the quotes will be pertinent to your students; others may seem very foreign. Please work with the examples that match the pressures your students are experiencing. Read a pertinent quote with your students and ask them

(?) In what ways do we see this happening in our community?

(?) In what ways have any of you felt like one of these people?

(?) What resources and supports are in our community that could help these students?

(?) What advice would you give the student in this scene?

Support widespread student leadership.

Not every student wants to be a leader in the traditional sense of consistently speaking out in public and initiating actions for others to follow. But all students have the capacity to do so at various times. That capacity for leadership may emerge when teenagers' commitments and sense of values are at issue—in situations that range from publicly organizing a rally, to privately reaching out to a student who has been bullied. Schools develop the leadership ability in all teenagers by providing them with multiple opportunities to have voice, make decisions, and manage the outcomes of their actions. The leadership actions students take are learning opportunities about problem solving, social connections, autonomy, and a sense of the future—literally the whole teen.

Work with your school mission statement. □

Brainstorm with students how they can build the mission statement into their own goals. Most mission statements describe much more than academic success as a desired outcome for the years children spend in the school. Mission statements often include reference to leadership and civic responsibility. Most mission statements would fit very well into the resiliency framework in Chapter 1. Fergus et al. (2015), investigating schools whose mission statements are crafted with particular students' needs in mind, write that, "Knowing the mission of the school . . . served as the glue that provided students with a sense of community and civic responsibility" (p. 11). Referencing the mission statement is a resource for students who want to build community-wide support for their leadership efforts.

Help students learn to access a range of resources and supports. □

The future can be a very hard concept to grasp, especially for teens who see the present world as chaotic. Their connections to the future can be established by helping them navigate the institutions of government and civic organizations that impact them today. School staff may wrongly assume that teens have learned how the world works from their family and community relationships. Many unfortunately don't know how to make the best use of government and civic institutions.

Here's an example of adults overlooking a common lack of student experience: students with limited family and community resources who have not travelled far from their neighborhoods. In a school with very impoverished students in a town just north of Boston, many students were the first generation of their family born in the United States. When the staff were preparing for a trip into Boston, they realized that almost none of the students had spent more than a day or two in the big city, and needed lessons on how to pay for the subway.

As part of projects and homework, schools can support students to

- Obtain a library card—the authors have worked with a number of teenagers who lost or stole a library book when they were very young, and have never stepped in a library again, for fear that the fine would be astronomical, or that they would be charged with a crime. Their teachers have needed to reassure them that libraries would be very forgiving. In one case, a peer of a very nervous student volunteered to walk with her to the library.
- Register to vote.
- Obtain a public transit card (many schools have free or reduced fare programs for their students) and/or plan trips on the buses and trains.
- Observe court proceedings.
- Write a letter to the editor of the local newspaper.
- Go to a government meeting, hearing, or community forum.
- Explore the town hall or city hall and report on the offices and services available.
- Visit the offices of their local, state, or federal elected officials.

- Locate and visit the nearest health clinic.
- At a local bank, get information about various accounts and services.

Support students to be of service to others.

"All resilience-based community change approaches have as a bottom line getting youth involved as partners in the change effort" (Benard, 2004, p. 103). Involvement breeds commitment, and sustained involvement breeds confidence. Being of service to others shows teens that problems do not disappear through wishful thinking, but are resolved through effort.

When schoolwork compels students to be in service to their community, we enhance the development of the whole teen. Cognitive neuroscientist Mary Helen Immordino-Yang (2016) states that humans are motivated to do tasks that are not only personally meaningful, but that have intrinsic worth to others. Schools can leverage the human desire to be of worth.

Serving others, rather than only being the recipients of adult care, is often a critical experience for teens on their pathway to active citizenship. Connecting teens' capacity to learn through service, and bringing that experience into our curricula, motivates learning and builds whole teens.

Some of the opportunities below fit well within standard curriculum tasks. Some can be done as an entire class, or as an advisory group, after-school club, or as a sports team. Other opportunities will likely arise through the on-going relationships adults have with teens. You may be the right adult at the right time and place to say to a student, "I have a really good idea for something you could do."

- Support students to introduce themselves to a new student (incoming to a specific class, grade, school, advisory), offering encouragement and strategies for becoming part of the school community. Suggest that students join or begin a committee to welcome all new students. Ask them to sit next to a new student at lunch—remind students that service takes many forms—service to others can happen in a minute during an ordinary day at school.

- Set up peer tutors. In specific classes and advisories, teachers can match a willing student tutor with a peer who may not be easily able to access support. (We also encourage peer tutoring schoolwide in Chapter 12.)

- Suggest students act as allies by supporting individuals who are struggling or being intimidated.

- Lend adult support to students who want to join or begin a group such as a Gay-Straight Alliance or diversity club.

- Conduct studies, surveys, and service projects within the school and in the community, with reflection about the service, how it felt, what students learned about themselves and others, and how well they followed through on commitments.

- Help students expand the possibilities of traditional school rituals. One school turned spirit day from celebrating the football team into a schoolwide service day. Advisory groups chose a community service from a list of options, everything from working with the town's maintenance department sanding and painting fire hydrants, to visiting with Alzheimer's patients, to recording audio books for the blind, to helping the elderly in town with garden and yard chores. The results were more students more involved with peers and the community, and more people in the community with positive experiences with teens.

Discussion Options for Faculty

- Which practices in this chapter seem especially important for your students?

- Where and how do you already talk to students about their hopes and aspirations? What else can you do?

- What have been the best community explorations you have taken? What connections did students make between the explorations and their futures?

- What community explorations are in your plans for the year? How can you build into the lessons leading up to the explorations the ways students can make connections to their aspirations?

- Who can discuss the ways they have integrated project-based learning and community service into their curricula?

- Who would be willing to experiment with displaying your college diplomas? Your certifications? What sorts of questions do you think your students might ask you?

- What recent alumni would be great to invite back to talk to your current students?

- What organizations can you partner with that connect your students to the community?

- What tasks are you giving students to explore community agencies, government offices and services, and other resources they will find useful now and in their futures?

- In what ways are students supported to be of service to others in the school? What else can you do?

Practices at Home

In elementary school, students are learning basic facts about the world, and the basic skills of reading, writing, and math that they will see adults use every day. Early elementary students often draw, sing, and run around in gym and recess. The elementary school years may not be the best time in every child's life, but the curriculum is generally close to what children need to master.

As teenagers move through middle school and high school, the curriculum can begin to look very unfamiliar to the adults at home. Many parents have the experience of not being able to help their kids with the assignments, and of not being able to provide guidance on how to prioritize all the school responsibilities. When teenagers ask, "Can you help me with my homework," adults can feel inadequate.

The good news is that the adults at home and in the community can help teenagers do more than just pass classes. Adults can talk to their teenagers about hopes and dreams, both the ones the teenagers have and the ones the adults have had, and perhaps continue to have. The chance at home to talk with adults about goals, and to get personal support to build those goals, is a great supplement to the day-to-day challenge of being a middle school and high school student.

In all of the "Practices at Home" sections of this book, talking to teenagers, and listening to teenagers, is the highest recommendation. The conversations about hopes, dreams, goals—and how to achieve them—are among the most important conversations you can have.

Share histories of hopes and goals. The teenage years are time to give your kids more stories about how you grew up. Who helped you? What paths opened up because you made the effort? Which paths were not available? Tell them the stories of other family members, or elders in the community. If you know someone who has a good story about getting through school, or starting a career, find a way for your teen to have a talk with that person. Tell stories, too, of people who made a difference in the lives of others because of their personal qualities. Role models in the family and neighborhood can help develop the whole teen in many ways.

Listen to their hopes and goals. Even if you think you know your child well, changes happen in the teenage years, and long held dreams can disappear. We know a man whose daughter always wanted to be a forensic scientist, because she had watched television shows that made the job seem exciting. But as middle school turned into high school, the daughter showed little interest in science classes, and the dad was worried that his daughter's dreams would never be realized. He began to pressure her to take more science classes, even as she was barely passing her current courses. Finally, she told him that she had long ago given up on being a forensic scientist, had developed a passion for photography, and was getting high marks in that course. "Why didn't you tell me?" he asked. "I didn't want to disappoint you. And you didn't notice that I had changed," she said. It was after this conversation that the dad shared with the daughter that he too had been interested in photography.

In addition to academic and career goals, find opportunities to ask your teens about the family they want to start, the places they'd like to go, and of critical importance, the type of person they'd like to be.

Help them expand their career and vocational goals. From going together to buy groceries, or to a movie, sports event, museum, or trip out of town, opportunities are abundant to share observations about how the world works, and who does the work. The settings, from landscapers working outdoors to nurses serving patients in clinics, offer opportunities to compare observations: "Would you want to work in a place like this? Could you imagine yourself doing this kind of work?" Talk about what you see. Ask your teens for their reactions. Help them see where they might find their niche.

Get onto a college campus together. Whether you go on a formal trip to look at universities, or one day hop on the bus to walk around the local college campus, it is important that teenagers set foot onto the grounds of higher education. You can do this with students in middle school as much as high schoolers. Go on a tour offered through the college admissions office. If you don't need an ID card for entrance, stroll through the library, gym, and student center. Ask your kids what they see that they like; begin to help them figure out what would be a good fit for them, should they be interested in higher education.

Help teens resist peer pressure to do what everyone else is doing. The conversations about goals are a good start to support your teenagers doing what is right for themselves. If you're concerned that their friends don't have worthy goals or admirable personal qualities, don't expect that your kids will abandon their friendships because you point out the weaknesses of those friendships. You will support your teenager by asking them about their friends' goals, and which friends are helpful, and not so helpful, for reaching their own goals. Tell your own stories of feeling pressured by peers: when did you give in to peer pressure? When did you resist? What helped you stay on your path?

Help them be connected to the greater world. Many teens need the company and support of an adult they trust to step into, and beyond, their community. Consider volunteering with your teenager at a local community agency, such as a senior center. Take your teenager with you when you vote, and help them register to vote when they turn eighteen. Make sure they have a library card. Go together to a political rally or public forum. Offer to go with them to the local bank to open an account. Tell stories of your first steps into the greater world. Make engagement with the world a motivation to build passion and reach for goals.

TOOL 10-1   My Aspirations

1. Which careers or jobs now interest you?

2. What study skills would you like to improve this year?

3. What character traits would you like to develop this year?

4. Where in the world are you interested in living? What images do you have about you in your future community?

5. In what ways would you like to see the world improve?

TOOL 10-2   My Project—My Future

1. What academic skills do you aim to improve from your work on this project?

2. What information would you like to learn from your work on this project?

3. What study and organizational skills can this project help you improve?

4. What personal characteristics can this project support you to develop?

5. In what ways can this project move you toward your vocational or professional goals?

6. For each answer above, what evidence will show your efforts and growth, both during your work and after your work is done?

TOOL 10-3 Peer Pressure Can Change Your Path

1. "I don't want to go to college, but everyone talks as if that is all that matters. I want to be a car mechanic."

2. "The college I want to go to is very hard to get into. My best friend wants to go there as well, but she doesn't know all the things she should do to get accepted. I'm not telling her what I know because they might take her instead of me. But I hate keeping this secret from her; we've always been like sisters."

3. "The guys on my street believe that doing well in school means you think you're better than everyone else, better than them. I never show them the books I'm bringing home to do my work. I don't think I'll let anyone know that I want to go to college. Maybe the guys are right—college isn't for us."

4. "My girlfriend offered me her ADHD medicine so I can stay up late with her to write our essays for college applications. I don't know what to do. I can't stay up that late without taking something. I'm ahead of her on the applications, and I have a research report I have to work on for my history class."

5. "I'm probably the best athlete in school; everyone is telling me I don't have to worry about my future, that I'll get a college scholarship and have a chance to be a professional. I'm already getting letters in the mail from colleges. My friends will think I'm crazy to study more than practice my game."

6. "I don't know what I want to do for a job or school or anything. I'm just a kid, not a grown-up. I do know that I want to do things that help people. I don't say that to anyone when they're talking about all the stuff they want to buy when they make a lot of money."

7. "My boyfriend dropped out of school. He is pressuring me to do the same, but I will not drop out of high school. I am interested in college, and I'm afraid of losing him."

8. "I have way too much to do; I won't get a good grade in English without a really good paper. There's this student who you can secretly pay to write your book reports, and I know other students who have paid the money. They seem fine with it, and I know some of them are applying to the same colleges I am trying to get into."

9. "My friends don't know that my grades and test scores are too low to get into the colleges they're applying to. I sit with them at lunch and pretend that I am also applying to those schools. Truth is, there's this program at the community college that looks great for me but I'd never say anything about it to my friends. There's this other student who I know is going to the community college but no one likes that kid."

10. "My friend is taking the hardest classes, running two clubs, and applying to lots of colleges. I really want to do well in life too, but is that the only way? She's in tears every other day."

PART III

The Whole School Surrounds the Whole Teen

Whole teens attend whole schools. They experience many different classes, hallways, the cafeteria, arts and athletic events, clubs and teams. They experience interactions with peers and adults. One teacher using practices to support the whole teen will make a difference for her students; all adults using those practices make more of a difference. When all aspects of school are aligned, the practices are mutually reinforcing and more likely sustainable. New teachers or students come into that school and sense immediately, from the hallway signs to the teacher language to widely used routines, that they are in a school that cares about the whole teen.

What does it take to extend best classroom practices throughout the school, and into the school district? Leaders—of many sorts. If you are the lead teacher on your middle school team, you can set a tone at meetings that fosters problem solving and reflection. Classroom practices that you discuss are more likely to be used by your colleagues, and experienced by a hundred students, multiple times per day. If you are a high school department head, the ways in which you talk and engage teachers in conversations about students and curricula will influence the program.

All adults involved in hiring processes communicate, through their questions and recommendations, if the whole teen is the focus of the community. Teachers who serve on committees, chair committees, or who are sought out for advice advance the vision. Union representatives, by working toward such reforms as teacher evaluation practices that align with the whole teen, further the conversation about best practices. Every supervisor prioritizes in their conversations what is most important.

Structures that place the whole teen at the center of school functioning are critical to the work of every person in the system. The fractal nature of organizations, discussed in the introduction to Part II, reveals the substance of the entire organization in every aspect. Schools can't effectively teach the whole teen in a system that is only partially aligned to that mission. Administrators oversee structure and alignment. When administrators pursue structural changes and robustly model best practices, staff and students get the message: all adults support the whole teen.

Chapter 11 focuses on the habits of leaders, who inevitably serve as role models—as one principal said, "Watch me to see how we roll around here." Chapters 12 and 13 focus on structural and faculty culture practices that will need the robust support of leaders with organizational authority—principals and assistant principals, superintendents and assistant superintendents, curriculum coordinators and coaches, among others—in order to become part of the school infrastructure. Chapter 14 focuses on supporting novice teachers, which is a responsibility shared by many—another iteration of the fractal nature of the school—marking how well the system will ultimately serve the whole teen.

11

Leaders Set the Tone for Themselves and Others

We were with an elementary school principal in a second-grade class. He asked the students what they thought a principal does. A student raised a hand and said, "You fix everything." While the rest of us had a hearty laugh, the principal sighed and looked heavenward.

It is said that schools lie at the intersection of infinite need and finite resources, making it impossible to "fix everything," as much as the second grader, and perhaps even leaders themselves, think they should. We have an unsustainable model of leadership. "Twenty-five thousand (one quarter of the country's principals) leave their schools each year . . . Fifty percent of new principals quit during their third year in the role" (School Leaders Network, 2014, p. 1). Teens are whole people; so are principals, who are at risk in a fragmented environment that doesn't support the whole administrator.

Almost all of us are all susceptible to the hope that our leaders will be superheroes and visionaries. Their failure to match those models erodes the confidence of leaders themselves, and the rest of the school community. School leaders need the protective factors of strong connections, high expectations with support to meet them, and meaningful participation in the community as much as any other person in the school. As many an administrator can say, finishing required paperwork is essential to the school running smoothly, but it does not do much for feeling that you are cared for and part of the life of the school.

In the fractal view of schools, how leaders thrive can express how the entire community thrives. The good news is that there are many ways leaders can be resilient, many rituals, relationships, and habits that sustain good leadership. In all those ways, school leaders build their professional skills. Simultaneously, because all actions leaders take are a form of communication about what is important, leaders who thrive model for everyone the importance of social competence, problem solving, autonomy, and a positive vision of the future. Administrators, through their daily practice, are the lead actors in setting the tone for a school that attends to the whole teen.

Practices for Leaders to Set the Tone for Themselves and Others

Articulate your interests.

In Chapter 4, we discussed the importance of not getting stuck in a debate about a single proposal, strategy, or position—instead, start by defining deep interests. This is an essential step to unite a community around its goals. For leaders, invoking interests has the benefit of building communities that solve problems and nurturing the autonomy of its members.

A principal we worked with embraced the language of "positions and interests" in his everyday communication. When a staff person or parent came to his office with a demand that he take a specific action right away, he said, "First, please tell me your interests. Maybe your idea is the best solution. Maybe there's an even better course of action." He convened a teacher meeting to help a particularly challenging student, and started by saying, "Let's list our most important interests." Once the interests were posted, including two of his (stay in budget; keep the parents informed), he was able to say to the teachers, "As long as you meet those interests, I trust you to come up with strategies. Let me know if there is a role for me in this." Then the teachers continued the meeting without him. He learned that he does not have to have the stress of micromanaging his team if the interests are clearly defined. Before introducing an initiative to the entire staff, he'd say, "Here are the interests that I had to meet in this proposal. There were also a couple of interests that I just couldn't squeeze in; we'll get to those in a different way." By starting with interests, he found that his initiatives were better understood, and that staff input was more on point.

Demonstrate a growth mindset at the leadership level.

If your greater intentions include growing on the job, and fostering a growth mindset in your school community, mistakes are part of the school leader being an active learner. A principal we've coached embraced this belief in a particular way. At the beginning of the monthly faculty meeting, she would energize the team by reminding everyone of the recent accomplishments of students and faculty. Then she would say, "Here are a few things I could have done better, and what I am taking from those experiences." She chose her items carefully; the errors she shared were never ones that could be interpreted as putting the school at risk. They were often how she had wished she had taken more time to listen to a particular parent, or had missed an opportunity to give thanks, or had scheduled a day so that she had no chance to eat lunch. Her strength in identifying her errors and making commitments to improve her own practice in the presence of her staff was unmistakable, as was her determination to model a growth mindset.

Talk about the books and articles you are reading. Share what you're pondering about being an educator. We know a secondary school principal who wrote an occasional memo directly to students, sharing ideas about educational issues, including the questions on his mind. He'd sit with students at lunch, inviting them to share their reactions to his thinking.

Fully attend and participate in professional development initiatives. Principals who do not sit with the faculty for workshops, or who leave part way through, are sending the community a clear message about what is prioritized. Of course, there will be times when the school leader must attend to a special responsibility. If so, inform the staff about it ahead of time: "I have to leave at 4:15 to meet with the building inspector. I will get back as soon as I can, and I've asked Ms. Ramos to fill me in on what I miss."

Read more about growth mindset for students in Chapter 7; for faculty culture in Chapter 13.

Listen.

One of the most basic needs of people is to be heard. Because leaders represent so much to members of the school community, the simple act of listening supports a culture of social connections. We recommend closing laptops, putting down pens and papers, and coming out from behind the desk. Keep a couple of comfortable chairs where they can be easily accessed. Some leaders keep a bowl of fruit and a pitcher of water by the chairs. One benefit of slowing down conversations to listen is that you may not have to be the one to solve the problem, as much as to be a sounding board. Most leaders are aware of other available resources in the community that may be well positioned to support the person, which can build that person's support system and social connections. Chapter 6 has many practices to support all members of the school community to be strong listeners.

Express your emotions to model and inspire.

We urge students to use I-statements and speak from their own perspectives in Chapter 6. School leaders also have feelings and perspectives. Using very specific words that identify your emotions minimizes staff wondering what you were really feeling—which is as pertinent to everyone else as are your explanations and directions. You also are role modeling that being passionate about teaching and learning and children inevitably provokes us to feel. In every moment in a school just about all the emotions that humans can experience are being felt by somebody, in some room or office or hallway. Leaders show that strong feelings can be communicated with respect.

We recommend practicing this skill when your feelings are positive: "I felt so pleased with the direction of this school when I saw your students working passionately on their projects." If all you ever do is the positive feeling part of our recommendation, your school will be a better community. With enough experiences of sharing positive feelings, and staff hearing you do so, the practice of sharing other strong feelings will seem less difficult: "I was very discouraged with the lack of student input into the field day, and I'm curious to know more."

Speaking from your own perspective is also a key component of the next practice, initiating difficult conversations.

Model social competencies and problem solving by initiating difficult conversations.

Administrators can use their authority to stop people in the hall and ask provocative questions or give critical feedback. They can also leave staff unsure of their standing by ignoring a conflict and walking past them, avoiding eye contact. Even the best of administrators can forget how the power of their position influences the ways they talk with others, especially when there are sensitive or contentious topics to discuss. Here is a three-step formula for initiating a difficult conversation (adapted by John D'Auria, from Stone, Patton, & Heen, 1999):

1. Make your intentions known: "I'd like to talk with you about yesterday's staff meeting."

2. Start with curiosity: "I am puzzled about . . . . I am curious about . . . . I want to hear more about . . . . I have a concern with . . . ." As mentioned above, sharing your perspective means being honest without being blunt or unkind; letting people know what is prompting you to initiate the conversation is an opportunity to respectfully identify your perspective.

3. Give the person choices: "I could meet after school today, or come in early tomorrow. What works for you?"

Model the social competencies and problem solving of a good apology.

In Chapter 6, pages 107–108, we offer tips for a good apology. Leaders build a learning community and a network of strong social connections through many modes, including making apologies, in private and public. In a workshop for principals, we taught the skills of apologizing. One participant was so enthused by the potential of apologizing in order to solidify relationships that he said, "Do you think I should make mistakes on purpose so I can do apologies?" There was a moment of silence, and then everyone laughed when he said, "Right, I suppose we are making enough mistakes without trying."

Recognize and praise.

We know one high school principal who left his office at the end of every class period. He did this to stretch his legs, get a feel for the mood of the school, and be seen outside of the formality of his office—but most importantly, he did it to say hello and praise as many people as he could every day. He'd stop a student in the hall and say, "Loved your effort in the play last night," or "Your math teacher told me you have really been trying hard lately." He'd poke his head into a classroom and say to the teacher, "Thanks for your suggestion at the staff meeting," or "I saw you at lunch, talking to a student who was escalating, and you really helped her calm down. That was great to see." Sometimes he'd just say, "Good morning, Ms. Jones." To students he'd give a quick, "Hello, Jared," or "How are you doing today, Sasha?" or, "Malik, glad you came to school today!" This ritual was his favorite part of the day, always lifting his spirits. Teachers learned to send him information about students who would feel better if the principal knew they were doing well. His ritual raised the expectation that recognizing every person in the building, and what they were striving to do, made a difference, and it did. And it felt so good to do it.

Praise can come in notes in mailboxes, in e-mails, on a small card slipped into a student's hand, as shout-outs in staff meetings, written as feedback in the margins of a handout, and in one-to-one conversations. We know a principal who realized that for most students in most schools "being sent to the principal's office" was synonymous with being disciplined. He turned that practice on its head by asking students to come to his office in order to tell them the ways he had seen and heard that they were making progress. Sometimes he called them in to simply express his concern during a stressful time in their lives. Part of his enjoyment with this practice was using the power of his office to enjoy more time with students. It wasn't long after he began this practice with students that the principal realized he could expand the meaning of "being called to the office" for the adults in the building too.

Schools are overflowing every day with good works: academic, interpersonal, athletic, artistic, community building. By establishing rituals of recognition for these efforts, leaders not only build a strengths-based environment, they develop innumerable social connections that make their own efforts more sustainable.

Be part of school rituals.

The old saying that it is lonely at the top is more a warning than destiny. Find a role for yourself in school rituals so you are not standing on the sideline while everyone else is developing social and professional connections. Our survival as a species is wired into our capacity to join in communities. That evolutionary imperative should not be sacrificed when you sign on to be an administrator. Ask for a cameo role in the school play. Roll up your sleeves with a team of students on service day. Sit in with the school band on a song.

Share leadership.

Nurture your team and a positive vision of the school's future by letting others chair or cochair meetings and committees, make announcements, and represent the school. Offer staff training and coaching in facilitation, speaking, and planning. You will show that leadership is collaborative and an opportunity to learn, and that you are aware that staff could feel vulnerable in leadership roles. In the process, they will experience their own sense of autonomy and purpose, and you will have communicated trust, an important aspect of all relationships.

You will learn much by observing the staff in action, and you might even be able to catch your breath as they move the school forward. In the story above about the principal who shared his interests, one big benefit of his approach was that he could hand the reins off to others. By being clear about his interests, the staff were scaffolded to be successful as leaders of the initiative. He then could turn his attention to other matters. Preparing the school culture to allow for distributed leadership helped to minimize his worries of giving up control, and created a stronger school community.

Your office location matters.

There's no absolute right place to have an office as a school leader, and sometimes you have no choice but to use the space assigned to you. Either by the space you choose, or by managing the entrance and waiting areas to your office, consider

- Will the community see me as part of their support system?

- Will I be able to work without distractions when I really need to get something done?

- Will I be able to talk casually with people when I need a break?
- Will I easily be able to assess the tone of the school?

We know of one principal who had an extremely large office, and convinced the assistant principal to share it. This allowed them to quickly compare notes, brainstorm, laugh, vent, and split up responsibilities. They kept the assistant principal's former office available as a meeting room, or for when either of them needed privacy. Those moments turned out to be far fewer than the times their shared experience in the office was a bonus. The message to the rest of the community was also very clear: having someone to share the work, and the ongoing experiences of the work, were critical to problem solving, support, and sustaining one's effort.

Another principal keeps a small table and chair in the hallway by her office. She uses it when she has routine paperwork to finish. The location allows her many opportunities to say hello to members of the school community, building her own sustaining network of social connections. She is also well positioned to increase the frequency with which she can recognize and praise students and staff, a critical practice described earlier in this chapter.

Share with your staff how you work best.

Students develop autonomy by coming to understand their strengths and work styles, knowing when to rely on their strengths and when it is a good time to take a risk expanding other skills. Administrators also have a profile of strengths and weaknesses, and ways they know they are most effective. Don't expect the staff to guess how you'd like them to interact with you—let them know: "If you tell me an idea in the hall when I am heading to a meeting I won't remember what you said. Better to jot a note on a small piece of paper and hand it to me; I will read it later and get back to you. That's how I keep track of new ideas." "I'm glad that you took initiative to reach out to parents. I'd like to know ahead of time any meetings you've set up so I am not taken by surprise if I see a parent whose name I should remember." When leaders articulate their preferences, they establish more effective social connections, and staff problem solving improves.

Research has established that everyone, including school leaders, work best when they are focused on a single task—multitasking is a myth. The administrator above, who warns a staff person that he cannot listen carefully while walking in the hall to a meeting, is modeling how to be focused. Schools need to become better environments for concentrating, making good use of available resources, and completing tasks with a high degree of pride in personal mastery. When leaders sacrifice too much mastery in the rush of work, and reinforce the myth of multitasking to get it all done, they erode their own best efforts.

School leaders play an important role for the community in undermining the myth of multitasking. If school leaders do not want students to be on their cell phones during classes, leaders need to close their own laptops during professional development, and refrain from sending text messages during meetings. In the words of a sage, "You are not indispensable unless you are immortal." Take a breath, do one thing at a time, and model for staff and students what good work habits look like.

Develop your own professional supports.

Leaders can nurture their own strength and cultivate wisdom by building a support network for themselves. Just as teachers do not need to be isolated as professionals within the walls of their classrooms, leaders also need to break the archetype that they work best independent of feedback and nurturance. Learning on the job is not a sign of weakness that must be hidden, for fear of loss of authority. Atul Guwande (2011), a highly regarded surgeon, wrote about obtaining a coach for himself in his article, "Personal Best: Top athletes and singers have coaches. Should you?" He finds that his fellow doctors, and even his patients, wonder what his having a coach means about his practice. It turns out to mean that he becomes a better surgeon. But he has to fight even his own beliefs that someone like him should be able to go it alone.

Find yourself a coach, or a team of peers, and have regularly scheduled meetings. There are many retired school administrators who delight in coaching. You can also meet with other school administrators in your district, or in nearby districts. To do so you have to make the time, and realize that getting support is important for you doing your job well over a long period of time.

When a teacher, or student, or fellow administrator asks you who that was going into your office, say, "That's my coach," or "That's my support team." In that moment, you are modeling so much of what the rest of this book is about.

Take your time.

Many leaders have it as a source of pride to be the first ones in the building in the morning, and the last ones out the door at night. Doing so models that passion and commitment to students demand that we go beyond the minimal requirements of our job descriptions. These leaders are often seen moving quickly through the halls, heading to yet another critical meeting.

It is a true that leaders cannot expect more of their staff than they are willing to do themselves. Therefore, leaders must also model slowing down, appreciating the little moments in the day, and finding and expressing joy in their daily efforts. Consider the following:

- Leave work on time occasionally.

- Eat lunch away from your desk.

- Find a regular activity to do slowly. We know of a school leader who had a staircase by his office, and always walked the steps one at a time in a very mindful manner. He said the extra few seconds this ritual took, versus bounding up the stairs, slowed his pace and allowed him to think more clearly.

- Spend time with students. Watch the community at its best, when students are engaged and joyful. Poke your head in an art class, or watch the students rehearsing the school play. Ask teachers to give you a heads-up when their class will appreciate your visit. Even the busiest school leaders can put ten minutes into the weekly schedule to leave the office to be with students. It may be the ten minutes you look forward to most. This ritual can remind you that your seemingly endless management tasks allow all these other beautiful activities to take place.

- Structure into the work week time for reflection. The stimulation of experiences within a single day as a school leader is extraordinary. Throughout this book are activities for students to reflect upon their experiences so that their understanding can crystallize, helping them to be more autonomous learners, and developing their sense of a positive future. Leaders need and deserve parallel practices. Such reflection can be done with a coach, mentor, or peer group. You can also keep a journal, and schedule a few minutes each week to answer the following:

  o What am I learning about the school?

  o What am I learning about my style of leadership?

  o What can I do this week to be the leader I want to be?

Principal Roland Barth (1990) wished his office door labeled him as "head learner." Time for reflection makes such a lofty expectation far more likely to be achieved.

For further reading, we recommend the book, *The Mindful School Leader: Practices to Transform Your Leadership and School,* by Valerie Brown and Kersten Olson (2015).

12

Schoolwide Structures, Practices, and Policies That Support the Whole Teen

As this entire book reveals, approaches for teaching and supporting whole teens are not accomplished with one specific curriculum or program. The presence or absence of an array of predictable schoolwide structures will determine how you answer many questions: Is every student in your school known well by at least one adult? Do all of the students effectively use the school community to thrive as whole teens? Structures predict the *probability* that students feel known, capable, and motivated—or not. A meaningful class or club can outweigh a few negative experiences, but the structures of the whole school should support whole teens.

Some of the structures explained in this chapter would require fairly modest changes in many schools. Others would be significant changes and we don't offer them lightly. We know some changes would take a lot of work over several years; we've worked with schools during these changes. However, the traditional high school structure, designed in the late 1800s, in which students pass from room to room, adult to adult, subject to subject, is an obstacle to building community, effective support systems, and coherent meaningful learning. You can compensate for fragmented structures with lots of practices found earlier in this book that foster community and participation in classrooms. We would be remiss, however, if we don't at least mention that changing structures is an option. Short of expanding this book by several more volumes, we review several practices and structures below to help you identify those that can be a good next step for your school or district.

Schoolwide Vision and Organization for the Whole Teen

Articulate a focus on the whole teen.

We've worked with districts that have crafted a multiyear goal to foster resiliency, or social and emotional skills, or similar outcomes. Their districtwide goal keeps the focus on the agenda for administrators and school boards, making that goal a priority for professional development and purchases.

In one district, as part of a process of updating the goals, leaders convened focus groups—groups specifically for parents with children currently enrolled, groups for local business people and civic leaders, and groups for residents without children in the schools. Everyone was asked about the competencies they believed were priorities for the district's students. The answers across all groups were notably consistent. They prioritized intrapersonal and interpersonal competencies—problem solving, communication, decision making, collaboration, respect for others, and self-awareness—and metacognitive skills—learning how to learn, think critically, study effectively, and produce high quality work. Academic proficiency came in third behind the other competencies. The focus group interviews led to crafting a districtwide goal for social-emotional learning (Johnson & Bonaiuto, 2009).

The goal of focusing on the whole teen is the first step. Making an actionable plan must follow. We hope you are finding many ideas for that plan within this book and in the discussions that your teachers, students, and all constituents have on its topics.

Report on the whole teen.

Report cards don't report on the whole teen. Neither do standardized tests. But those structures don't prevent a school, grade, team, or individual teacher from sharing more observations and measures of how teens are learning and growing. Some teachers report to families the data on homework completion rates, participation in class discussions, utilization of extra help, and peer support activities.

Some schools and districts report to their communities about student involvement in extracurricular activities, number of students in internships, attendance rates, visits to the counselors' offices, the numbers of students serving as mentors or participating in service projects. Many schools and districts use school climate survey data (see more about climate surveys further in this chapter), risky-behavior survey data, and mental health data to assess and report students' sense of physical safety, emotional safety, engagement in the curriculum, use of alcohol and substances, and levels of anxiety. These measures can show if LGBTQ students feel safe, if low-income students are participating fully in after-school programming, if ELL students feel welcome, and if student stress is going up or down.

When districts report these kinds of data to stakeholders, they engage the community in understanding the status of their teenagers. The whole teen becomes the responsibility of the whole community. This effort can lead to partnerships, interventions, sharing resources, and increased family involvement.

The middle school model helps a lot! Advisory groups and other structures help too. ☐

Structures that create more consistent connections are more likely to foster a sense of belonging, more likely to provide needed supports, and more likely to offer meaningful participation for the whole teen.

If you lead, teach, or counsel in a middle school—a real middle school, where a few teachers jointly share a group of students, and have regular meetings to monitor their progress—you've got a big head start. Some high schools are divided into "houses," in which students have house-based community building and learning activities, and one administrator and counselor who are consistent throughout their four years. Other schools are intentionally small or are organized around a theme (for example, arts, science, social justice, or career-technical schools), fostering more coherence in relationships or curriculum.

Increasingly, middle schools and high schools are implementing advisory programs. Advisories are small groups, smaller than classes because the students are divided among all (or almost all) adults in the school. Whenever possible, the group and advisor stay together multiple years, meeting frequently enough to build a sense of community. Advisees make decisions together, decide on and run rituals, celebrate and support each other, shaping an environment that is neither as teacher-directed as a class nor as informal or individual as homeroom or study hall. Most often advisories are not part of report card evaluation; the whole student is the focus—not a curriculum. Knowing his advisees well, the advisor coaches them on ways to manage school, build interpersonal skills, and envision and access a positive future.

With advisories, teachers who teach only one grade often come to appreciate adolescence as a long developmental pathway, not just a single grade-level experience, and feel a larger commitment for successfully shepherding students to graduation. For advisories to serve their purposes, they should not be overwhelmed with announcements and bureaucracy, nor serve as health and wellness classes, which should be taught by people specifically trained in that content. Like all other specific practices or structures, advisories by themselves do not solve a school's climate or support challenges—they are one piece of the fractal. (For more information, see *The Advisory Guide*, Poliner & Miller Lieber, 2004.)

Have longer relationships with your students. ☐

When adult-student relationships last ten months, or in the case of half-year schedules, five months, relationships are short and fragmented. Community building and in-depth support are especially meaningful when adults have the opportunity to work with a group of students over multiple years. Teachers who loop with their students can take enormous advantage of the continuity and familiarity. To create more longevity and cohesion in relationships with students, schools can

- **Implement advisory groups** that stay together and with the same advisor for multiple years.

- **Have teachers loop** with their academic classes. For example, a math teacher might teach ninth- and tenth-grade math classes each year, keeping her students for two years. We know one school in which the humanities teachers loop all four years of high school with their students! (Note that in that school, students take humanities, rather than separate English and social studies, so the students are juggling fewer adults, which also builds more familiarity.)

Restructure senior year to provide meaning and support.

For varied reasons, senior year is not serving enough seniors well. Some have met the requirements to graduate and have been accepted into college or other postsecondary training programs. They have months of high school left, without the same pressures and without obvious meaning. Other students are still working to complete graduation requirements, but are struggling to focus. Low-income and first-generation college-goers often find the transition from high school to college challenging, and their senior year is not designed to make that transition successful. Senior year—all of it or the second half—can be structured to engage all students.

- **Develop in-depth internships or extended service-learning projects**. Hold a support seminar at school dealing with the self-management and organizing skills needed for the internship or project, and skills for relating with coworkers and supervisors.

- **Take college classes within the high school.** Some schools have college classes taught at the high school or taken online, allowing students to experience increased academic standards and meet a college professor. These courses expand the high school's options for advanced studies and allow students to start progress toward a college degree, within a known and supportive environment.

- **Take college classes at the college.** Taking a class at the college offers a different level of excitement and opportunity to build more skills for independence, including dealing with greater freedom and possibly greater anxiety. Some schools support those students by having them sign up for classes with another high school student as a partner, having a high school teacher check with them regularly, having a college student "buddy," or having a support seminar at the college or at the high school.

- **Hold seminars or a class on specific skills that students find worthy of their attention.** These seminars can cover financial literacy, résumé writing, and skills and habits needed for college or jobs.

There are many resources for more ideas, information, and insights. A few we recommend are

- "Why 12th Grade Must Be Redesigned Now—And How" (Vargas, 2015)

- *Crossing the Stage: Redesigning Senior Year* (Sizer, 2002)

- "Facing the Culture Shock of College," an article about first-generation college-goers for educators and for students themselves (Cushman, 2007)

Practices and Structures That Foster Student Voice and Identity

Use school climate surveys; have students help interpret the results.

When students fill out school climate surveys seriously, you will gather a lot of important data. Imagine how your students—including disaggregated groups of your students, as emphasized in Chapter 2—might respond (on a scale of "strongly agree" through "strongly disagree") to statements such as these:

- An adult at school would notice if I were in a slump or having a problem.
- Most students in my school don't really care about each other.
- My teachers really care about me, not just my grades.
- It's easy to be myself at school.
- Most students in my school think it's okay to cheat.
- Most students in my school treat others respectfully.
- Most students in our school do their best to learn in classes.
- In my grade, students encourage each other about the postsecondary steps we're taking.
- Our school's rules make sense to me.
- I feel safe in the hallways and bathrooms.
- Our school has clubs and teams that I like participating in.
- My family feels comfortable coming to events at this school.

There are many tools asking these and other questions. But, as Michael Fullan (2001) has written, information becomes knowledge only when people decide what it means within their social context. Otherwise, it's just "information glut" (p. 6). Students can help enormously to give meaning to the data. They can explain what a certain question means to them, which issues are pressing from their perspective, or what important aspects of school culture were omitted from the survey.

We have also encouraged schools to use focus group interviews of students, especially in schools where students feel over-surveyed or where they deliberately distort their answers. Students have been quite surprised that adults wanted their insights, were really listening and writing their responses, and did so over pizza.

Identify and celebrate a wide range of positive student activities.

Does your school have a display case for sports teams' photographs and trophies? How about a display case for the debate team, anime club, chess club, and drama club? Consider what events honor which student activities, and which are highlighted in the school news and announcements. To support identity development, it's important to appreciate the diverse interests and skills of your diverse array of students.

- Set up one or more bulletin boards or showcases in the hallway for clubs and activities.

- Set up displays for photos and interviews with students who hold jobs, volunteer, take care of an elderly relative, study a musical instrument, build models, or design clothing.

- If Spirit Day has celebrated only the football team, think about revamping it so that it's a chance to celebrate musicians, actors, chess players, and service club members too.

Most schools are filled with students who are making strong commitments that build positive identities and demonstrate the diversity of the community. Treat them with as much pride and give them as much attention as the best athletes in the school.

Involve students in school decisions and projects.

Adolescents can rise to the occasion in impressive ways when they are given the opportunity and are treated seriously. They can learn that participating in community can take many forms, a lesson to take with them into their adults lives—being a good citizen isn't just about voting during elections. Encourage students to fill the following roles:

- Serving on the interview committee for a new principal, teacher, counselor, or coach

- Serving on restorative justice review teams

- Initiating schoolwide changes via a known "pathway to change" roadmap—identify their allies, and engage adults in serious dialogue about school improvement

- Crafting sayings promoting growth mindset posted in hallways or staircases

- Speaking at faculty meetings about their experiences; for example, religious minority students or LGBTQ students can describe what they experience as supportive or as obstacles to their learning

- Contributing designs for the logo of a new school program, and select the winning logo

- Taking care of display cases or gardens

- Discussing and voting on themes for English classes

- Serving on peer mediation programs

- Serving as liaisons to local organizations (police, motor vehicle bureau)

- Serving as greeters in the main lobby/office

- Having a role on stage in schoolwide assemblies

- Serving in student government that is designed to be truly representative—when representatives are elected from, and remain in, homerooms or advisories, more students volunteer to run for election, and all students can talk regularly with their representative

Encourage students who may not have thought about participating in any of the above roles. There are lot more potential leaders than might be noticed at first. You can help students rise to the occasion through individual or small-group coaching, or through a student leadership training.

Hold town meetings for the whole school, or by cluster, house, or grade level. □

Town meetings serve many interests and perhaps the most significant one is the power of community in the lives of whole teens. In one high school where we worked, alumni reported that of all the predictable parts of the schedule, the town meeting was what they remembered most. As one said, "It's where we were all together, heard everything together, discussed real issues, and had a say in what was going on." Older students can model responsible leadership by working on agenda committees and chairing the meeting. Town meetings can and should be structured to provide more than an outlet for disseminating information efficiently—although hearing the school leaders tell you in person about an issue conveys a lot of respect to the students in that room. Town meetings can employ many of the structures for small group discussions found in the culture of conversation practice in Chapter 4, pages 62–64. Consider following those discussions with focus groups, votes, and surveys. The follow-up actions will be better received because of the spirit of public conversation and the student participation that town meetings generate.

Use the school walls, publications, and events to welcome all cultures. □

In Chapter 2, we explained why it's so important for students to see their identities represented in school. In Chapter 9, we emphasized including diverse cultures in the academic curriculum. There are many ways to reflect students' identities schoolwide, showing students and their families that they are welcome. By being robustly included, they will need less mental energy to be vigilant as an outsider, and have more mental energy for learning.

- Have welcome signs in the lobby in all the languages spoken in the school. Students can make them. Have signs everywhere in multiple languages.

- Serve food at open houses that comes from students' cultures.

- Have images and posters that reflect students' varied backgrounds. Students can participate in selecting them.

- Develop relationships with local translators to support families in school meetings.

- Offer translations of all school policy and procedure materials.

Involve students in internships. □

Internships can be valuable experiences to foster social competence, problem solving, autonomy, and sense of purpose and future. They are not small endeavors. Similar to starting advisories or a basketball team, a solid internship program takes a lot of preparation and structure. Many students need significant support to have a positive experience: what to wear, how to be punctual, what behavior is expected, how to talk to supervisors, how to learn about the work at hand.

Leaders have to develop the infrastructure to manage transportation issues, insurance, student evaluation on site, communication systems between the school and the internship site, and tracking attendance and performance. Though internships require significant effort and resources to establish, they can have enormous benefits.

Schoolwide Support Systems and Practices for the Whole Teen

Examine and adjust the level of stress in the system. ☐

We recently worked with all the administrators in a school district who were concerned by the increasing reports of stress-related illnesses in their schools. "There's one piece of advice we want to start with," we said as we looked at them rushing into the room from their last meeting, squeezing out one last text message and one last side conversation. "Slow down!" The laughter evoked was appreciative and rueful.

There are many reasons to attend to the whole teen. Those reasons are as grand as harnessing all the potential in the next generation to foster democracy, innovation, and human kindness. In the short run, we have to teach them many skills, and we can't do that when everyone is stressed out. The *New York Times* ran a front-page article titled "Is the Drive for Success Making Our Children Sick?" The evidence, both statistical and anecdotal, is yes. No one individual is to blame—as we saw with the adults in our workshop trying to do one more task before our presentation began, most everyone wants to complete their responsibilities. There is simply too much to do and not enough time to give each task the full attention it demands.

Students can and should learn stress management skills. They'll face challenges throughout their lives—illnesses, changes in jobs, too many needs, too little time. However, students do not have all those skills yet, and even if they did, all those skills cannot compensate for the level of unnecessary stress that schooling has introduced into their lives. One principal at the workshop above suddenly looked up and said, "It's not fair for us to expect students to deal with all that stress without reducing some of the things we do that cause them stress!"

The combined practices in Part II of this book would relieve much student stress, and the entire school would be improved. Along the path toward that comprehensive vision, leaders can apply structural and procedural adjustments as well. We offer here a few of the more common options for immediate action:

- **Limit homework.** Use the standard ratio of 10 minutes per grade: a seventh grader faces no more than 70 minutes of homework a day, and a twelfth grader no more than 120 minutes—and those are the top limit, not the average. Have homework-free vacations and regularly scheduled weekends without homework.

- **Emphasize quality rather than quantity in homework assignments and make explicit homework guidelines.** Administrators and faculty can discuss the purpose of homework, review how they prepare students for doing homework tasks, and reconsider the length of readings or the number of problems. Leaders must dispel claims that the *amount* of homework is a sign of rigor. (See the homework story in Chapter 4 on pages 57–58.)

- **Have teachers and administrators stand by their doors and say hello** to the students as they pass from one class period to the next.

- **Let students keep trying.** Allow them to retake tests. Allow students to negotiate deadline extensions, with structures such as a daily work schedule, to demonstrate their effort and progress.

- **Invest in the arts** (visual, performance, industrial) **and a range of physical education options** (dance, yoga, fitness training) beyond typical team sports. The whole teen usually flourishes when given the opportunity. If the system cannot provide enough opportunities, allow students to complete the requirements in the community and don't replace it with another class in their schedule.

- **Slow down.** See the recommendations in Chapter 11 for school leaders to develop their own daily practices of appreciating the moment. Everyone will benefit.

Have a structure to talk about the whole student.

One of the great things about the middle school structure is that teams of teachers share the same students and meet to discuss their progress. In high schools, however, teachers typically meet by department. In that grouping, it's rare that teachers share the same students, and therefore can't problem solve about any individual.

All secondary schools can have a meeting structure to monitor progress and expand opportunities for students. If there are four students identified for each meeting, teachers can attend if they have those students in their classes. To best support students, groups will benefit from a small number of practices that focus on the whole teen. In particular,

1. Dedicate as much time talking about the student's strengths and aspirations as you do his weaknesses and needs. Use a timer. Because teachers have emotional reactions and connections with students, their expressions of frustration and worry can consume the bulk of meeting time. However, believing in the student and supporting him depends upon articulating his strengths and making plans to leverage those strengths. Structure meeting time for those priorities.

2. Include art teachers, vocational teachers, physical education teachers, and other members of the school community who know this student. These adults often have vital information about areas where the student is demonstrating motivation and persistence.

3. In addition to discrete academic skills and test scores, focus on the four areas of resilience: social competence; problem solving; autonomy; positive sense of the future. When making plans for interventions, the team will benefit from the opportunities that framework provides to identify emerging skills in struggling students. Those skills often point toward practices found in Part II of this book, practices that multiple teachers can employ. Academic achievement is linked to those areas of resilience.

Make the most of your guidance counseling and student support system.

The American School Counselor Association recommends a counselor-to-student ratio of 1 to 250. Researchers focused specifically on urban, low-income students have found a ratio of 1 to 100 to be effective (Miller Lieber, 2009). The national average, however, was 1 to 470 in 2011–2012 (U.S. Department of Education, 2014). Having more counselors can certainly help, but shifting the numbers alone isn't sufficient. We know of schools with 1 to 250 ratios, where counselors are still meeting students for the first time in eleventh or twelfth grade.

In contrast, some schools have reorganized the counseling roles and structures.

- Some schools have implemented "**guidance seminars.**" Counselors in these schools have learned that not all guidance tasks need to be done individually; some are actually better done with a group using interactive exercises or discussions. In these groups, they shape the peer culture. An example: a high school has a 1:200 ratio of counselors to students. Each guidance counselor has fifty students per grade, divided into two groups of twenty-five. Guidance seminars are built into the schedule, with one regular length period per schedule cycle. The counselor meets in the first half of the year with her ninth-grade groups, working on adjusting to high school, and with her twelfth-grade groups on applying to colleges. She meets with the same regularity in the second half of the year with her tenth-grade groups exploring careers and pathways, and starts the postsecondary process with the eleventh graders.

  A student in that structure has the same counselor throughout high school and is in that counselor's guidance seminar group fifteen to twenty times every year. The structure assures that each student feels known, has an adult to go to with a problem, gets access to needed tutoring and support systems, and makes personalized future plans.

- **Some schools restructure counselor roles so the adults juggle more hats, rather than the students juggling more adults.** In many schools, a student sees a registrar to sign up for classes, a guidance counselor to talk about her future, a social worker for support on personal issues, and a community partnership coordinator for internships and summer opportunities. We've worked with schools that have shifted from these specialists who each know a portion of the teen, to a broader role that supports the whole teen: "student development counselors." The same number of adults, each playing more roles, allows fewer students per counselor.

  Though the transition in roles prompted some anxiety and required training, the counselors consistently reported that they were certain they were providing more effective and efficient service to students. They could help students connect the dots between their courses, progress, challenges, and future dreams. They also reported having more job satisfaction themselves. Several described now knowing the happy aspirational side of the students, not just their array of challenges. One counselor told us about an interaction with a pregnant teen: "In my old district, I would have been expected to send that student to another adult. Some of the students would have gotten to the next adult, some wouldn't. Many would have used up their self-advocacy courage on that first knock. Referring the student on down the line is not the same thing as giving them help."

Use discipline to teach responsibility to others and accountability for oneself.

Zero tolerance policies and "no excuses" behavioral standards are contrary to growth mindset, resiliency, and social-emotional learning. All learning involves making mistakes, sometimes big mistakes. To foster healthy development, adults have to engage with students when they make mistakes, teach them better skills, and help them build better habits. That practice does not mean there are no consequences for behaving badly; it means that the consequences fit the transgression and have a learning component.

There are now two decades of experience and research showing that overly harsh school discipline practices do not change behavior. Instead, they've often fostered the school-to-prison pipeline. Students who are repeatedly suspended fall farther behind academically, are less connected to support systems that might help them, and don't learn to behave differently by being out of school. The biggest effects of such policies are on students of color and students with disabilities (Ashley & Burke, 2009). In short, "There is no evidence that zero tolerance policies improve student behavior, the school climate, or overall school safety" (p. 9).

Restorative justice is introduced in Chapter 4 as an approach for classroom discipline practices. Schoolwide implementation can include teen courts, peer mediation, restorative justice circles, and mentoring, providing a much greater impact. Whether your school can implement any of those specific structures, the philosophy and approach relate to all schools.

Implement orientation programs that build community and culture.

Students who are new to your town or city, and the rising class entering your school, might have gone to schools with positive cultures, or they might not have been so fortunate. They might be coming from a few different schools with different cultures, possibly even rivalries. Shaping a welcoming culture for your new students is an important step to make the learning environment most beneficial, and for preventing potential challenges. Sitting in a large auditorium, listening passively to the rules, and being given a handbook and a locker assignment does not build a community and does not let a teenager know how to be successful. Consider conducting an annual orientation program that includes the following:

- Interactive experiences, for example, a treasure hunt to find their way around the school
- Meeting adults whom the students will need to rely on in small groups and asking them two questions (possibly part of the treasure hunt)
- Older students facilitating name games or short activities that relate to the spaces found on the treasure hunt
- Older students explaining the rules they think are most important
- Team-building exercises, especially for students who will be in the same advisory group, cluster, or house

- Visions-for-the-future activities

- Discussions about what learning experiences work best for them, and what makes it hard to learn; these conversations can lead to a group agreements process (see Chapter 4, pages 59–61, for tips on crafting group agreements)

Continue to build community throughout the year.

Organize cluster, house, grade-level, or schoolwide rituals that involve everyone, such as picnics, field trips, service days, hikes, pajama day, or Halloween costume day. Choosing a book that everyone will read over the summer, or a shorter reading during the year, creates a common intellectual experience, one that can be expanded upon in classes.

Make support information part of the school culture.

In one school we know—and this can be done even in a class—a student group developed and disseminated a list of resources to help all students manage their many responsibilities. The students made presentations at school assemblies to advertise lesser known resources. The listing was posted in the school's lobby, distributed in packets of information at the beginning of each year, and posted on the school's website. The students were representing to each other that difficulties and frustrations were inevitable, that students don't have to go it alone, and that learning to access support is a step toward developing autonomy to take care of themselves. The sign in the lobby looked like this:

If you think your class is not the right fit for you—Guidance Staff in Room 217

If you want to find a peer tutor—Ms. Harper, Room 312

If you want to take a learning styles inventory—Mr. Vasquez, Room 18

If you can't find an online resource—the Student Tech Team, Room 111

If you want to talk privately to a counselor—Ms. Chen, Room 40

If you have health concerns—Ms. Donovan, Health Center, Room 12

Establish a tutoring program, including peer tutoring.

Provide simple procedures for students to get academic help. Advertise the option for tutoring in signs around the school and on the school website. Ask peer tutors to speak at assemblies to ease the anxiety of those who may need a tutor. Partner with higher-education institutions to expand your array of tutors.

Provide mentors to students.

Students can gain much from mentors—a perception that school is relevant to success, encouragement to persevere, practice talking with an adult, the beginnings of a network, and ideas about jobs and what a day-in-the-life looks like. Mentors often serve as role models for how to be an adult woman or man, different from the images in the media or students' neighborhoods.

Many civic associations and colleges have community partnerships with schools to provide mentors. Whenever possible, establish relationships with long commitments. Launch the program with training for the mentors and a get-to-know-you workshop for mentors and mentees to break the ice. Activities and conversation prompts can surface that they have much in common; for example, when they were both new to a school or workplace, felt frustration learning something new, or had challenges with collaboration partners.

In whatever ways relationships with mentors are structured, they should be safe and nonevaluative, a chance to connect, explore options, hear perspectives, reconsider values, get feedback—all part of developing social competence, problem solving, autonomy, and sense of future.

13

Faculty Culture That Supports the Whole Teen

It is critical that the faculty culture reflects, on the adult level, all of the goals for the whole teen: social competence and coherence, engaged and supportive problem solving, creative use of autonomy, and sense of mission and longevity. Roland Barth (2006) described the impact of faculty culture on all student experience:

> One incontrovertible finding emerges from my career spent working in and around schools: The nature of relationships among the adults within a school has a greater influence on the character and quality of that school and on student accomplishment than anything else. If the relationships between administrators and teachers are trusting, generous, helpful, and cooperative, then the relationships between teachers and students, between students and students, and between teachers and parents are likely to be trusting, generous, helpful, and cooperative. If, on the other hand, relationships between administrators and teachers are fearful, competitive, suspicious, and corrosive, then *these* qualities will disseminate throughout the school community.
>
> In short, the relationships among the educators in a school define all relationships within that school's culture. (p. 9)

The fractal of faculty culture supports the whole teen or it undermines that mission. Faculty culture is an invisible web connecting aspects of the fractal school—including how the adults learn together, problem solve, and support each other.

How would you assess the adult culture of your school? Consider a few characteristics.

Our whole adult community is friendly; we chat; we have some fun rituals.		Lots of us don't know each other; familiarity is limited to just a few colleagues.

We support each other's professional improvement.	← • • ○ • • →	We don't get or give support; we sink or swim on our own.
When issues arise, we meet, problem solve together, and jointly uphold our decisions and plans.	← • • ○ • • →	When problems arise, we complain in the parking lot or via texting, blame someone, or keep our heads down.
With new initiatives, we deliberate, discuss, decide, implement, monitor, tweak, and implement some more.	← • • ○ • • →	We're skeptical of new ideas. When launched, they'd better work quickly. If they don't, it was clearly a bad idea.
We respect and support colleagues who try new ideas to serve our students.	← • • ○ • • →	We are focused on compliance, with no energy or encouragement for creativity.
We have future-oriented and optimistic images of our students.	← • • ○ • • →	We are focused only as far into the future as the next big test.

Obviously, if your assessment on these few characteristics is closer to the left column, the adults in your school are part of a constructive community, engaged in working out issues together, striving toward high standards, open to learning and new ideas, all practices that support their own resilience as educators. If your assessment is closer to the right column, you've got isolated and uninspired adults spending time on unproductive and defensive actions. These are conditions for getting stuck in problems, not overcoming them.

In a school we worked with, we explained that students would more readily develop skills for autonomy if they had regular opportunities to help make decisions for the class and for themselves. A teacher responded, "Why should they have any autonomy? We don't have any!" Providing students with opportunities for decision making was an affront to him. He was a teacher who truly cared for his students, and it is unlikely that any administrator knew how deeply restricted he felt as a professional.

If the teachers in your school don't experience connectedness, problem solving, autonomy, and sense of purpose, they are unlikely to encourage parallel skills and attitudes in students. If teachers are isolated in their own roles, disconnected from the sense of mission that drew them to teaching, pessimistic about the impact they're able to make, and going through rote motions about which they had no say, they will have a hard time offering students experiences they haven't had.

Public pressure and criticism, testing, and frenzied days are challenges. Even within those challenges, faculty can find ways to be creative, offer each other support and optimism, and solve challenges together. Victor Frankl (1946/1984), neurologist, psychiatrist, and Holocaust concentration camp survivor, said, "Everything can be taken from a man but one thing: the last of the human freedoms—to choose one's attitude in any given set of circumstances, to choose one's own way" (p. 75). A school leader supports staff to choose their best attitudes. A school leader intentionally builds a culture to support the whole teen. The faculty must be part of that intentional building.

This chapter offers practices for the adult community beyond or adapted from those offered elsewhere in the book. From earlier chapters, we especially encourage you to apply these practices within the adult community:

- Talking lists and interactive formats in discussions (Chapters 4, 6, Appendix)

- Appreciative inquiry (Chapters 4 and 6)

- Learning about each other's working styles (Chapter 5)

- Self-reflecting and debriefing after meetings (Chapter 5)

- Listening patiently, giving effective feedback, speaking from one's own perspective (Chapter 6)

- Setting goals (Chapter 7)

Practices for a Faculty Culture That Supports the Whole Teen

Get to know each other, even if you're in a big school.

People need to feel part of a community, welcomed, recognized for their contributions, and supported through their challenges. In many of the large schools we've worked with, not only do the adults not know even each other's names, they feel awkward about asking. As with students in Chapter 3, we encourage you to use name games in the opening meetings with faculty, not just introducing the few recently hired people. Learning everyone's names, or meeting just five people you haven't met before, can change the atmosphere.

If the principal facilitates the exercise, she sends a message that community building is important. It's also valuable if the principal participates while another administrator, teacher, or counselor facilitates, modeling that she values community and shared leadership. One principal described get-to-know-you exercises as far from his comfort zone, and almost backed off his plan to use one, but plunged in and led one anyway. (The exercise went smoothly.) Importantly, in a later faculty meeting, he mentioned to the whole faculty that he'd been nervous about it, and this was a growth area for him. In that moment, he also modeled having a growth mindset.

Since it's unrealistic to expect everyone to remember everyone's name after one meeting, create a website for faculty showing the names, photos, and roles of all staff members. Or, put up bulletin boards for the same purpose, perhaps showing new babies, pets, a musical instrument, a piece of sports equipment, a telescope, or other meaningful experience or object. One high school has a hallway bulletin board on which faculty members voluntarily displayed their own high school pictures—it was the most talked about display in the school, and it created a surprising number of fruitful conversations with students.

In the same way that saying hello to students at the beginning of class is important, make a regular practice of beginning meetings and workshops with a short greeting, even if it's just saying hello within table groups.

The purpose for knowing peers is the same for adults as it is for whole teens—developing a support network to do a difficult job well through the year. In a high functioning school, adults ask each other for advice, console one another, praise effort, and even occasionally initiate a difficult conversation about a critical incident. Knowing names is not just about being polite; it is the foundation of doing great work.

Names are only the beginning. It matters if people eat lunch separated by department or cluster, or together in a central space, which fosters more cohesion. Either way, community rituals make a big difference in bringing people together. Sharing cooking interests that showcase diverse cultures fosters a sociable atmosphere. Hold an annual fall pot-luck soup and bread lunch (imagine a long table of slow cookers) before an early release workshop. Make a schedule for different departments or clusters to supply bagels. Share holiday cookies representing diverse cultures, or pies on March 14 (pie day on Pi Day!).

Reconnect with your mission, both personal and the school's.

People who enter the field of education are generally driven by a desire to make a difference in some way. Staying connected to that personal mission is inspiring; being disconnected from it is deflating. The school's mission statement might be a tool to inspire, but not if it's just a sentence or paragraph on the wall and the website. Those locations are the usual burial places for mission statements, assuring that they won't engage or energize anybody.

Set aside time (occasionally) to share stories in faculty meetings about

- what drew everyone to choose teaching, school counseling, or other role;

- classroom experiences that demonstrate a lofty phrase in your mission statement;

- ways the whole teen is being supported;

- a club, team, or performance group that is demonstrating part of the mission.

Emphasize growth mindset.

If you believe in growth mindset for students, believe in it for adults too! We've worked with high-achieving, affluent schools implementing advisory groups in which teachers were very skilled in their content areas and held themselves to high standards. As advisory was launched, they demonstrated some of the same angst and perfectionistic standards as their students. They were risk averse and quick to blame, whether it was blaming the program or the committee or the kids themselves for needing such a program. In contrast, we also worked with a school in a similar community when they implemented advisory, while learning about growth mindset. The principal opened the first workshop stating that all advisors, the committee, and the program as a whole wouldn't be perfect at first, that they were launching something new and significant. He repeated this theme throughout the year and the program was implemented accordingly—the committee collected input, tweaked the program, and communicated that they were listening to the input and implementing improvements.

Harvard Business School professor Rosabeth Moss Kanter has observed, "Everything can look like failure in the middle" of an implementation process (Heath & Heath, 2010,

p. 168). While the above examples had to with advisory program implementation, a growth mindset will help to implement any new curriculum, instructional approach, or assessment practice. Don't let glitches along the way undermine the bigger vision.

Set group agreements—yes, with the adults.

In workshops, we've been asked by teachers, "Make agreements? Us? But we're adults." In case anyone on your faculty is puzzled, you can offer this passage from Robert Kegan and Lisa Laskow Lahey's (2001) *How the Way We Talk Can Change the Way We Work*:

> *[W]ithout agreements, there can be no violations.* There can be private objection certainly. People can feel personal outrage at the acts of others in organizational life. ('I can't believe you went over my head and took that to him without talking to me about it! How could you do such a thing?') "How could you do such a thing?" is the voice of personal outrage. But in the absence of publicly shared agreements, an honest reply (though seldom given) could be, "I never agreed I wouldn't."
>
> The outrage continues: "Well, I just assumed I could count on you. I'd never do a thing like that to you, or anyone else. This isn't the way I understood we were working together." The outrage continues, but it is private, personal outrage. A personal bond is damaged. The organization as a whole is damaged. But nothing owned by the organization—nothing of the public life of the organization—has been violated. There is certainly a cost to the quality and future effectiveness of the organization, but there is no public violation because there has never been a public agreement with respect to the principle that the offended party holds dear. (pp. 112–113)

Faculty interaction can be enhanced by group agreements for faculty meetings, leadership councils, professional learning communities, departments, clusters, or committees. Please see Chapter 4, page 59, for tips on crafting group agreements. To launch the process, here are some options we've used with adults:

- **Use a working styles exercise** (as in Chapter 5, page 76), having like-styled groups identify what makes meetings work well for them, then share, meld, and agree on a set.

- **Use the reading above,** discuss the excerpt, and have pairs or trios brainstorm proposals for agreements. Pose a question for the brainstorm that fits the purpose of the group. For example, for a professional learning community, the question might be "What agreements will help us learn together?" or for a decision-making group, it could be "What agreements will help us be effective decision makers?"

- **Pose an appreciative question** if you're making agreements after you've been together for a couple of meetings: "In our meetings, when we've been at our best—engaged, constructive, efficient—how have we been interacting and operating? What agreements do we need to foster such engagement in our meetings?" Brainstorm in small groups, then share, meld, and agree on a set.

Faculty agreements also provide a chance for staff to see how a similar procedure can be implemented in their classrooms. Just as with students, adults learn by experiencing, debriefing, and adapting ideas to their needs.

Make your current culture visible.

Culture includes everything—from whether the entranceway feels welcoming to the quality of instruction. A school culture that strives to work with the whole teen permeates the environment. Culture can be hard to discern, the unnoticed wallpaper. There are varied tools and exercises you can use to make the culture visible and therefore discussible. We offer a few below. No matter what tool you use, frame the discussion in neutral, constructive terms. "We concentrate on classroom practice so often, and rightly so, and we need to have a healthy professional culture to do our best and to overcome inevitable challenges. We have a survey (or exercise) to take stock and see what we can improve."

- **What are faculty and staff talking about?** One aspect of culture worth exploring is what the adults are talking about, and where those conversations are happening. Having productive and constructive discussions is surely a cornerstone of any school improvement. Are faculty members complaining or troubleshooting? Is there a consistent reference to the whole teen and the potential of all students? Are the conversations taking place in meetings where proposals can be discussed and launched, or in private conversations? We've used Tool 13-1 in many schools to prompt this conversation. One caveat—as with any discussion of faculty culture, don't open the topic and then treat it lightly. Improving faculty culture is serious and subtle. Be ready to implement community-building rituals to foster familiarity, text-based discussions to develop common understandings, and slower and more deliberate practices in meetings to surface issues.

- **Use an interactive exercise** if the faculty already has a congenial culture. We are not suggesting an interactive exercise with many of the topics generally covered in an anonymous climate survey. But topics dealing with teachers' mindsets about their own practice can work in an opinion continuum. (See the Appendix for details on the format.) Choose sentences that are within a reasonable comfort zone, asking everyone to line up from "strongly agree" to "strongly disagree." For each sentence, ask a few people from different parts of the line to give a reason for choosing their spot, and be sure to have time to debrief, discuss, and troubleshoot.

  - I usually have enough time to reflect on my work.
  - I have enough time to talk with students.
  - I am learning how to expand my practices for whole teens.
  - I like giving feedback to colleagues.
  - I get sufficient feedback from colleagues.
  - My lessons don't have to be perfect to be good.
  - I've had good experiences of taking risks trying something new.
  - I have enough opportunities to be a teacher leader.

- **Use faculty climate surveys.** Schools use data regarding students all the time; data can be very useful among adults as well, with the benefits of anonymity and aggregate responses. Responses to such questions as "Teachers talk about our school in proud, positive terms," "Faculty members have effective mechanisms for problem solving and proposing new ideas," "Adults in our school demonstrate trust and confidence in each other," "Teachers' accomplishments and efforts are recognized and applauded," and "Teachers talk about students with a sense of investment and pride," can be very telling, and can lead to productive reshaping of faculty rituals, discussions, and support mechanisms. Disaggregating the data for novice, midcareer, and veteran teachers, or different grade levels or departments can offer important insights, but only if responses will still be anonymous. Asking one identifying question might be safe; asking two on the same survey usually isn't—the one novice science teacher is identifiable. In some school communities, staff will need to know that the collective responses will not be made public, at least in the first year.

Apply the "tell-to-collaborate continuum" to decisions and communicating.

When everyone knows how a decision is going to be made, they can adjust their expectations and participation accordingly. If they don't know what decision-making mode is being used, they won't know how to contribute. People can assume they'll be involved when, in fact, the decision has already been made. Or, people can assume that decision making is up to the leaders, and miss the chance to give input. "'How we do things around here shouldn't be a mystery" (Benson, 2015, p. 35).

The "tell-to-collaborate continuum" is a tool that greatly helps to clarify decision making and input roles. See Chapter 4, pages 55–56, for an explanation of the continuum and its uses in classrooms. Here are some examples when each mode is an effective choice within the adult school community:

- **Tell:** Tell all adults what online behavior will and won't get them into legal trouble.

- **Sell:** Extol the positives about a new community partnership—Faculty may or may not be optimistic that a partnership that includes more visitors and changes to the schedule will really help the school. If the partnership has already been confirmed, the leader needs to sell the staff on how the advantages will outweigh the drawbacks.

- **Test:** Implement a new system for supporting substitutes—The administrator considers past routines and glitches, then crafts a new system. She tells the staff she will collect their input for the first two months of the new system, allowing her to adjust it based on their feedback.

- **Consult:** Develop a mentoring program for newly hired teachers—School leaders gather input from many people as they craft a new staff orientation plan, knowing the new program will be more effective with the benefit of wider input. The leaders then design the final draft of the program for implementation.

- **Collaborate:** Change the discipline practices—Everyone will have to implement the new practices autonomously and creatively in every room and hallway in the school. People will be more prepared to do so when they all thoroughly understand the reason for the change, and when they have helped to shape the practices to fit their area.

Read and discuss together.

When faculties develop the norm of sharing articles and books—and discussing them in effective ways—they have an endless and inexpensive source of inspiration and ideas. Importantly, they build common understandings and habits for mutual learning. Most school staffs will need a number of ongoing efforts to develop a whole teen culture—an adult culture of shared reading is an important tool toward that end.

However, if the experience of reading together includes the same three people arguing every time, polarizing every topic, or dismissing every new idea, the opportunity will do the opposite—it will confirm camps of thought and limited relationships. The key is the effective discussion—making sure that everyone participates, the atmosphere is psychologically safe, and that lots of ideas are surfaced. We suggest discussing a group agreement: "Read to learn and understand, not to dismiss and rebut" or "We're reading for wisdom, not cleverness."

There are many protocols, often used in small groups to maximize participation. Find one that works well for the given reading. Some of the protocols below utilize a note-taking page, which can be done individually, or within a group using easel paper.

- **Golden Nuggets:** Read the article or passage, starring two or three nuggets that are especially meaningful for your students, community, or instructional challenges. In groups of three, have one person offer one nugget they chose, explain what was meaningful about it, and then let others share their thoughts on the same nugget. Make sure each person gets a chance to share at least one nugget.

- **Notes to Self:** As you read, keep track of important insights (!!!), questions (???), affirmations of things you already do (✓✓✓), and steps to take (→→→) using Tool 13-2. Focusing on one thought bubble at a time, have each person in your small group share something they noted, then listen to others' comments. Continue to the next bubble, making sure different people are first to speak.

- **Text-to-Practice Connections:** Tool 13-3 is a note-taking page that leads to action-oriented discussions.

- **Jigsaw:** Divide everyone into trios or quads with a reading that splits smoothly into three or four sections. Each person takes a section. After time for reading, people who read the same text sit together to discuss its key points. Then everyone goes to a mixed-segment group to explain their portions. Also see "Quotes Café" in the Appendix for a version that involves movement and works with very short readings or quotes.

- **Idea Web:** Have everyone read an article or passage. Put a central question or phrase in the middle of the board, for example, "connections to our practice" or "ideas for our implementation process." Have people silently write thoughts that web off of the central phrase, and that web further off of comments written. People can draw arrows to connecting thoughts, check ideas they agree with, or write question marks next to comments they don't understand. Follow the webbing by discussing connections, strong patterns, and clarifications in small groups and the whole group. (This protocol is sometimes called a *chalk talk*.)

There is an important fractal at work in the above activities. Teenagers need to be part of a community of peers while also being able to have their own opinions and values—an important component of autonomy, purpose, and social connection. Adults have the same needs. School staff members hold a range of beliefs, and come to work with a depth and breadth of experiences that can help fulfill the school's mission. Their sense of belonging, autonomy, and purpose are honored by exploring their understanding of essential texts. The activities below can help school leaders minimize the times that staff diversity slips into unhealthy discord.

Recognize and leverage "bright spots" in the school.   □

"To pursue bright spots is to ask the question 'What's working, and how can we do more of it?' In the real world, this obvious question is almost never asked. Instead, the question we ask is more problem focused: 'What's broken, and how do we fix it?' This problem-seeking mindset is a . . . predilection for the negative . . . [We have] a problem focus when [we need] a *solution focus*" (Heath & Heath, 2010, pp. 45, 48). Starting with the problem, what's wrong, is often deflating—the opposite of motivating. To support a resilient environment for the adults that will support their problem solving and positive sense of future, build from bright spots.

Examples of "bright spots" questions or inquiries are

- "Romi's been very withdrawn since coming out as gay. Whose class rituals are helping her stay connected?"

- "What parts of the school day are working well for our immigrant students? What are the key qualities that we could weave in elsewhere?"

- "What clusters/departments have found ways to ratchet down the stress level?"

Remember that making change requires emotional engagement, not just intellectual awareness. "Most of the big problems we encounter in organizations or society are ambiguous and evolving . . . To solve [these] bigger, more ambiguous problems, we need to encourage open minds, creativity, and hope" (Heath & Heath, 2010, p. 123).

Use language and formats
that raise issues in a neutral way.   □

In some faculty cultures, disagreeing with a colleague in front of others, especially administrators, is not the norm. In other faculties, any issue raised becomes a polarized debate. In yet others, the norm is for a small number of teachers, the same ones repeatedly, to offer strong opinions on many topics. Some colleagues agree; others disagree and are too intimidated to speak. None of those cultures lead to all teachers having their own experiences of building the courage and habits to speak up, solve problems effectively, or participate actively and constructively in community. A few ways to build new habits follow.

- **"Take a stance."** With any given proposal, split the faculty in half randomly. Ask half the group to identify the pros, and the other half to identify the cons. For people whose individual belief favored the other view, the exercise stretches their perspective. For everyone, it's a safe process for discussing a stance, since it's not necessarily their stance. (D'Auria, 2010)

- **Introduce the language and concepts of "positions" and "interests"** (see Chapter 4, pages 56–58, for an explanation; also see examples for school leaders in Chapter 11, page 206) to the whole faculty, and use it regularly. Arguing over positions—initial ideas or demands—rarely leads to good decisions or good relationships. By focusing on the interests, many discussions can be more creative and generate better and longer lasting solutions, while deepening respect for others.

- **Frame issues with neutral language.** It's very easy for people to experience someone else's idea as being in competition with their idea, rather than in addition to, or a slight variation of their idea. Leaders, including unofficial leaders, can change the atmosphere: "Okay, there are different opinions in the room. Of course there are; we're different people. We're bound to have different perspectives. Let's explore and see what we've got."

- **"Let's have a dialogue rather than a debate."** Preview Tool 13-4 before the discussion. Talk about the group agreements that will engender a dialogue.

Manage the emotional climate, stress, and pressure.

Adults' brains handle emotions and stress with more experience than adolescents' brains; otherwise, the process is not so different. Adult stress has multiple impacts on students. "First, research with both teachers and parents suggests that when adults are stressed and/or depressed, their interactions with children become less warm, more harsh, and more conflictual. Second, teachers who have limited emotional regulation skills may have trouble coping with stress and struggle to model effective stress management for students. Third, neuroscience research shows that stress also disrupts cognitive regulation processes, including attention, memory, and problem solving" (Jones, Bouffard, & Weissbourd, 2013, pp. 63–64).

All of the practices in this chapter contribute to a more supportive faculty climate. In addition, faculty benefit from emotional outlets, exercise, and calming rituals. Try any of the following, or others that your faculty propose.

- Organize a walking club or yoga class.

- Start meetings with greetings or positive stories.

- Establish a gratitude ritual, mindfulness practice, or humor ritual at the beginning or end of meetings. (See Chapter 8, page 157, for specific ideas.)

TOOL 13-1 Collegial Culture Reality Check

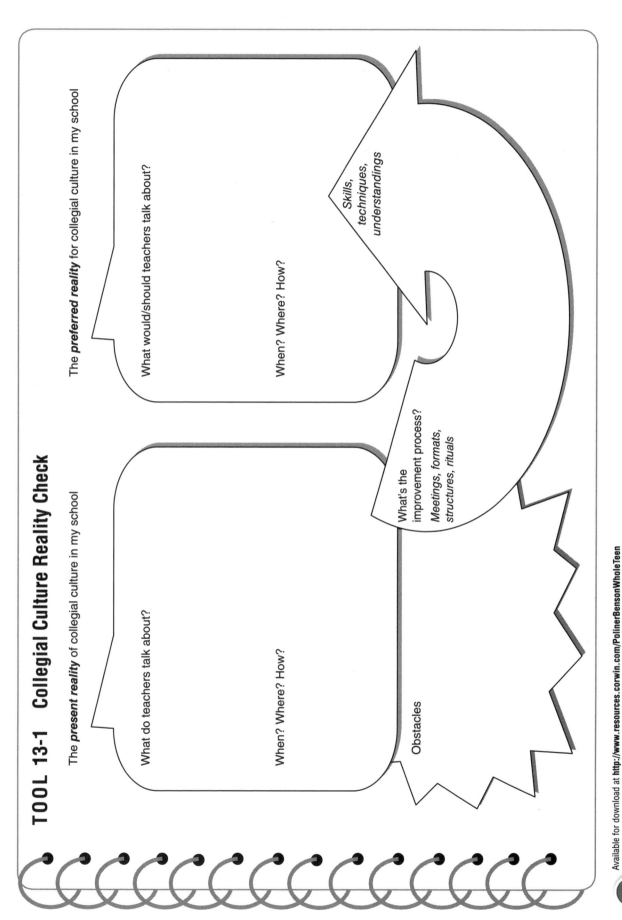

The **present reality** of collegial culture in my school

What do teachers talk about?

When? Where? How?

Obstacles

The **preferred reality** for collegial culture in my school

What would/should teachers talk about?

When? Where? How?

Skills, techniques, understandings

What's the improvement process? *Meetings, formats, structures, rituals*

TOOL 13-2   Notes to Self: Aha! Huh? Yup. Do.

? ? ?

! ! !

↑
↑
↑

✓ ✓
✓

238

TOOL 13-3   Text-to-Practice Connections

✳ Star your biggest surprises and most impactful changes.

Information and ideas that stand out:	Connecting this information to teaching and learning . . . what would change?
	⇒
	⇒
	⇒
	⇒
	⇒
	⇒
	⇒
	⇒
	⇒

TOOL 13-4   Dialogue versus Debate

Dialogue	Debate
Dialogue is collaborative: the sides work together.	Debate is a type of fight: two sides oppose each other to prove each other wrong.
Dialogue builds a learning relationship between people.	Debate builds a competitive relationship between people.
Dialogue encourages the participants to identify questions and goals they could share.	Debate encourages each side to articulate its own questions and goals.
In a dialogue, the goals are finding common ideas and new ideas.	In a debate, the goal is winning with your own ideas.
In a dialogue, everyone contributes to solving a problem.	In a debate, one person and viewpoint wins; the other is dismissed.
In a dialogue, you believe that many solutions might exist, and that different people have parts of the best solutions.	In a debate, you believe that there is one solution, that you have it, and other solutions are not considered.
In a dialogue, you are sensitive to each other's feelings, hopes, and ideas.	In a debate, you do not care about the feelings, hopes and ideas of others.
In a dialogue, you contribute your best ideas to be improved upon.	In a debate, you contribute your ideas and defend them against challenges.
In a dialogue, you listen to each other to understand and build agreement.	In a debate, you listen to each other to find flaws and disagree.
In a dialogue, you search for the good parts of other people's ideas.	In a debate, you search for weaknesses in others people's ideas.
In a dialogue, you may consider new ideas and even change your mind completely.	In a debate, you do not admit you are considering new ideas and you must not change your mind, or you lose.
Dialogue encourages you to evaluate yourself.	Debate encourages you to criticize others.
Dialogue promotes open-mindedness, including an openness to being wrong.	Debate creates a close-minded attitude, a determination to be right.
Dialogue encourages you to see all sides of an issue.	Debate encourages you to see only two different sides of an issue.
Dialogue invites keeping the topic open even after the discussion formally ends.	Debate, by creating a winner and a loser, discourages further discussion.

Source: Poliner & Benson (1997).

14

The Novice Teacher
Comes Into the School

We placed this chapter at the end of the book to allow the needs of novice teachers to have the final word. If our schools are incubators of the nations' future, then our fate is truly tied to the success or failure of our next generation of teachers. All the limitations and potentials of a school, at every layer, are magnified for novices; how we support them to persevere and thrive will mirror our success, or failure, to do the same for whole teens.

Teaching is an extremely complex task. To initially survive in the job, a new teacher must manage discipline, write lesson plans for every class every day, memorize the unique rules of the school, communicate with parents, work with peers, and complete the endless paperwork. Knowing how to do all those tasks is just the beginning.

To be an excellent teacher, one must develop mastery in all the above, and then much more. One must also develop a rich understanding of content area skills and knowledge, nurture a class culture that supports a diverse student body, understand child and adolescent development, assess student progress using multiple measures, and accommodate the variety of special needs that impact learning.

No one reaches mastery in one or two years, or simply by matriculating in a teacher preparation program. Most assuredly, no one is a fully competent teacher, much less a master teacher, after attending a six-week teacher induction program. Mastery takes time, and a setting that supports long-term professional growth. Just as it takes a whole school to provide the supports for whole teens, schools must invest in supports for the whole novice teacher.

Unfortunately, up to 50 percent of new teachers leave the profession before they have taught for five years. A study of those short-term teachers reports that the main factors in leaving the profession include a lack of administrative support and the absence of an induction and mentoring program (40 percent of new teachers who did not receive an induction program were gone after the first year, compared to just 18 percent who did participate in an induction program) (Ingersoll, 2003).

A robust support system is much greater than a day or two of orientation at the start of a new school year, in the midst of all the other preparations. Certainly new teachers need to hear on the first day of school the same welcoming speech from the superintendent that all teachers will hear. They will receive administrative updates and class lists that the veteran teachers also receive. That's not enough. The fractal nature of schools suggests that the attention paid to new teachers will reflect the level of attention paid to the most vulnerable students in the school.

What is the impact on schools of significant teacher turnover? Students are taught by a continuing succession of new teachers who are not as skilled as their veteran peers (Murnane & Phillips, 1981; Rockoff, 2004). Economically, schools are spending over $7 billion annually recruiting, hiring, and trying to train new staff (Koplowski, 2008). The sink-or-swim tradition of dropping teachers into the deep end of the work after a couple of days of summer orientation may be drowning us in mediocrity. The notion that only the most resilient and gritty new teachers will endure is a thorough misunderstanding of the complexity of resilience and grit, and of what we need to do to educate our children.

The good news is that a growing number of schools are beginning to provide a more robust support network for novice teachers, and some teacher induction programs at colleges and universities are offering multiyear support programs for their graduates. Online resources are expanding to fill the gap as well.

In this chapter we describe school-based practices that have good outcomes for retaining novice teachers. Most importantly, when school systems provide new teachers with a package of those best support practices, there is a 50 percent reduction in loss of first year teachers, and their students record higher levels of achievement (Ingersoll, 2012). Many school administrators say that hiring good staff is the most important task for creating a high-performing school—they should consider the process of hiring as continuing well beyond the signing of the initial employment contract.

We divide the chapter into two sections: practices new teachers can develop on their own to thrive and practices school leaders can put into place to support the growth and retention of their new staff.

 ## Practices for Novice Teachers to Foster Their Resilience

Take good care of your emotional health.

There are plenty of opportunities for both new and veteran educators to feel frustrated, disappointed, and confused—that comes with the territory of caring. So make sure you take care of yourself, including appreciating the sweet moments of your days.

- **Enjoy the kids you teach**. Say hello to every one of them every day. If you have a group that is difficult to manage, make extra sure you enjoy the students with whom you have established a connection. For instance, after an interaction that called for you to be a disciplinarian, wander over to a student who might easily smile back at you. Most students most of the time want to get along with their teachers; remembering that preference will allow you to enjoy every opportunity they offer you to connect—because they look to you to feel noticed and affirmed. The opportunity to enjoy kids is always just a moment away.

- **Keep a journal.** Your journey is a special one. Honor your efforts and the wisdom you are developing by reflecting back on your work.

- **Set goals for yourself.** The work is hard, possibly harder than you imagined, and the journey to sustained excellence will have many stages. Your school system will probably give you a set of competencies that will be used as the framework of your official evaluation. You can start from that list to prioritize your own goals—you can't do them all at once anyway! Most people feel empowered when identifying what they believe is important for their own growth. As part of your evaluation cycle, you may also be able to include your own assessment of your progress.

- **Listen closely to your self-talk**. There are no perfect educators. When you have been less than perfect, you have likely been modestly effective, a good place to start. Even your most beloved childhood teacher had bad days, spoke at times a little too brusquely, taught a lesson with a confusing segment, and missed opportunities. If you hear yourself being a harsh self-critic, you can reframe your inner conversation. Remind yourself of what did go well and build from that: "Okay, today my set-up of the groups worked; it's just the debriefing I have to improve. Next time, I'll prepare better questions." Or a simple, "Today was better than yesterday." The first time through any experience grants you wisdom to do better the next time, or even the next day. "I will learn and improve" is self-talk that lasts a lifetime.

Seek a mentor teacher.

The school may assign you a mentor. If not, in most schools, there are many veteran staff who could serve you well in that role. If you don't have a mentor, ask your supervisor for a recommendation of someone in the school who you can approach. Be clear about what you'd like for the relationship; for example, "I need someone to talk through my lesson plans," "I'd appreciate someone who won't mind my asking for a second or third time how to run a quotes café," "I'd appreciate someone who could help me pace myself so I make sure to eat lunch," "I want to sit once a week and just vent and share ideas." If you had a college instructor with whom you made a good connection, reach out to that instructor, either to seek her mentoring or for a recommendation for a mentor.

Build peer support.

Your system may convene a regularly scheduled meeting of new teachers. If that structure is not in place, reach out to other new teachers in the system. The personnel office can tell you where in the system new teachers are working. Even one peer can be a big help. If they are as new as you to the profession, they will likely be just as interested in meeting. If you are a recent graduate of a pre-service teaching program, reach out to your former classmates. Research online for the growing number of supports and networks for new teachers.

Observe other classes and advisories.

There are many ways to be a successful teacher or advisor. You are in a building filled with professionals who inevitably demonstrate a wide range of approaches. Just ask. Share anything specific you want to observe (how they begin a class, ways they deal with off-task students, bringing closure to a lesson), so the teachers can let you know if and when they can provide you what you are looking for. Ask your supervisor for recommendations of the teachers who have well-established best practices.

Take extra good physical care of yourself.

The physical stress of teaching accumulates slowly and steadily; good habits are important safeguards. Eat in as healthy a manner as you can. Go to the bathroom when the schedule allows it; don't wait until you're desperate. Start, maintain, or expand your exercise routines. When you have built a good relationship with the students, suggest they join you occasionally during class for a minute of stretching.

Practices and Structures for School Leaders to Support Novice Teachers

Orient to the mission.

Orientation is a chance to maintain the inspiration that likely brought this person into the profession. Talk about the importance of the work teachers do from day one: helping each adolescent become a better person, binding a community around common values, helping to secure democracy for another generation. Provide examples of how teachers in the school are fostering the highest ideals of the school's mission. Offer examples that are not complicated or intimidating—remind new teachers that in the day-to-day effort to respect each student they are pulling the mission forward.

Provide a mentor.

Let mentors know they can focus on all aspects of the job. Certainly mentors will provide guidance for the nuts-and-bolts details of the work, such as how to fill out forms. Choose mentors who are also able to share what makes them excited about being an educator. Encourage mentors to talk about how the mission of the school is fulfilled when meeting with parents, running an advisory, serving on committees, and caring for the neediest students. Encourage mentors to also share the ways they manage the stress of the work so novices don't feel that it is their own fault for feeling stressed.

Assign co-advisors.

Most novice teachers have had training in the basics of being an educator; few have had similar training to be an advisory group leader. Let novices learn to play this important role well by starting in a partnership. Given that advisories should be smaller than classes, have a more relaxed atmosphere than classes, and focus on culture building and personal support, they can be an ideal forum for novice teachers to observe a skilled veteran share decisions about group rituals, facilitate discussions, and offer individual coaching. The novices can step into those tasks as they gain confidence. All of these observations will help novice teachers become skilled advisors—and better teachers.

Schedule time to meet with novice teachers. ☐

Be in touch with novices well beyond the requirements of observations. Ask them to sit for ten minutes and fill you in. Drop by their class in the morning to say hello, and praise them for any ways they are displaying effort toward the school's mission. The boss's acknowledgement all by itself can buoy up struggling new teachers. Listen to their stories, honor their growth, and recognize and affirm incremental improvements in their work. Those improvements may be in delivering lessons, and they may also be in how they greet students, how they participate in staff meetings and trainings, and how they reach out to parents.

Support novice teachers observing your best staff. ☐

If you have an available in-house substitute, with a little coordination, the substitute can cover thirty minutes of the novice teacher's day so he can observe one of your strongest teachers. No in-house substitute? Wouldn't it be a great message about the value of new teachers if one of the administrators stepped in for thirty minutes to provide that coverage?

Give explicit guidance for nonteaching duties. ☐

As hard as teaching is, we have found many staff most stressed by lunch duty, dismissals, and other nonteaching responsibilities. Tell new teachers how it is done. Pair them up with a veteran teacher. Don't leave them to figure it out on their own—they have enough to make sense of already.

Organize a seminar for beginning teachers. ☐

This is an opportunity to build community. If it's not in the budget and you can't free up time within the contracted schedule, you can make participation voluntary. Veteran teachers can volunteer, or be paid, to be part of the seminar. Let the teachers know you will join them when they request your participation. Urge the group to share not only their struggles and efforts in the classroom, but their successes and the ways they are taking care of themselves.

Schedule common planning time with other teachers in the same subject. ☐

This recommendation may clash with the innumerable other priorities that go into any school's master schedule. We recommend that you put common planning times into the mix of possibilities, finding ways to do it as often as the schedule allows.

Reduce the course load or extra duties. ☐

If the contract doesn't allow for reducing a course or duty, use your position and influence to advocate for this schedule flexibility in the next contract. If you can provide even one extra planning period a week, it will be helpful. In the middle school model, and with explicit administrative support, teams of teachers may be able to arrange their duties to provide more planning time for their novice peers.

Offer assistance from a classroom aide.

Aides often are unencumbered by highly detailed job descriptions. Their schedule flexibility may allow you to assign them more time with the novice teachers. Administrators may need to provide coaching and direction for the new teacher, who likely was never instructed on how to work well with an aide.

Reduce novice teachers moving from room to room to teach.

Teaching is hard enough; teaching from a rolling cart and without the chance to shape a classroom atmosphere is even harder. Keep novice teachers working in one room as much as possible. Let them feel that they have moved in.

Appendix

Formats and Facilitation Tools

Fishbowl Conversations

Fishbowl conversations (used in Chapter 6) involve two to five people seated in a center circle, the fishbowl, while everyone else is seated around them. The fishbowl often has an empty chair. Fishbowl conversations are a way for a few people to discuss something, while others listen and observe. The format can be useful for a controversial topic that would be overwhelmed with many voices, or a demonstration topic, allowing the listeners to learn.

The fishbowl participants start talking about the topic at hand. As the conversation continues, an outer circle listener might think of an idea to contribute. She can walk to and sit in the empty chair. At that point, someone else in the fishbowl chooses to step out, and sits among the listeners. The process continues with people choosing to participate in the fishbowl or the listening group.

In another version, there is no empty chair. When someone from the listening group wants to enter the fishbowl, she taps the shoulder of someone in the inner circle and they trade seats.

Importantly, the listeners are not passive. When the fishbowl discussion ends, and the group debriefs, the listeners should have observations about key turning points in the conversation, ideas that seemed misunderstood, or other insights.

Go-Rounds

Go-rounds (used in Chapters 3 and 6) are a simple format to make sure each person has a chance to speak. You can use a go-round for a quick Monday check-in or for more serious discussions. Perhaps your group has been discussing ideas for a decision and you're not sure all ideas have been aired. Start by giving the participants quiet think time so they are prepared to speak when it is their turn. Asking everyone to say a few words about their thinking, in order around the group, will surface areas of agreement and points still to be worked out. Go-rounds work best in a circle.

Allow passing for participants who don't want to speak, and come back to them after the rest of the circle has spoken in case they'd like to speak at that point. If given students pass frequently, chat with them. Perhaps they need more think time ahead, or don't like being among the first few to speak, or have another reason.

Be sure to start with different people around the circle for different go-rounds.

Also, to make sure everyone feels as comfortable as possible to speak, protect go-rounds from questions, responses, or rebuttals.

Idea Webs

Idea webs (used in Chapter 13, work well with students too) are a way for an entire group to react to a reading and see everyone's reactions, rather than listen to a person-by-person discussion.

Have everyone read an article or passage. Put a central question or phrase in the middle of the board, for example, "connections to our theme of justice" or "ideas for our community's future," any prompt that relates to the reading and your reason for choosing it. Have people silently write thoughts that web off of the central phrase, and that web further off of comments written. People can draw arrows to connecting thoughts, check ideas they agree with, or write question marks next to comments they don't understand. Follow the webbing with time to read everyone's comments. Then discuss connections, strong patterns, and clarifications in small groups and the whole group. (This protocol is sometimes called a *chalk talk*.)

Listening Labs

Listening labs (used in Chapters 4 and 6) assure that students get a chance to speak and listen to a variety of perspectives from their peers. Listening labs are done in groups of three to five students, who sit around a table together or in a small circle. There is a very specific set of procedures, which will assure that each student has a chance to speak and listen. The steps are

1. Give the class a prompt and allow quiet think time for students to develop their responses. The prompts can be in any subject area: What was your favorite scene in the story and what made it your favorite? What was your method for solving the math problem we have for homework? What can we do about the mess in the room at the end of the class? Which country would you most like to visit, and for what reasons?

2. Ask one person in each group to volunteer to be first speaker.

3. Say, "start," and the first speaker has the floor for one minute (or any predetermined amount of time), *uninterrupted.*

4. After a minute, call, "switch," the current speaker can finish his or her sentence and then the person to right of first speaker has the floor for one minute.

5. Continue to call "switch" until all have had their chance to share their thinking.

6. After all have spoken, give the group a few minutes to finish any thoughts, ask clarifying questions, and make comments.

Note that the first few times that you use a listening lab, it will be well worth debriefing.

(?) Think of when it was your turn to talk. Could you tell that your listeners were listening? How did they show they were listening?

(?) How did it feel to talk to silent, attentive listeners?

(?) What about when it was your turn to listen—Show on a fist-to-five how it felt to be silent and attentive. Showing a fist means "It was awful, I kept wanting to jump in!" Showing five fingers means "It was easy; I was really interested; I didn't have to restrain myself."

(?) What techniques helped you listen carefully and silently?

We find that many people are not accustomed to either role—listening patiently or being listened to patiently. Don't be surprised if students do not like the format at first, saying it felt stiff or unnatural. Imagine a world in which being listened to patiently does feel natural—isn't that worth working toward?

Lists

Lists, such as the ones in *Life Lists for Teens* (referred to in Chapter 6), are a way to offer or identify several tips for studying, talking with teachers, or any other purpose. Here are a few options for using them:

- Find a list with useful tips. Hand it out, circling and discussing the best ideas, adding other ideas, rewording ideas to be in students' language or to add examples.

- Read the title of a good list, encouraging students to write the tips they think should be on it. Mention the most important tips from the list if students don't think of them. Or, hand out your list, compare, and combine.

- Role-play any ideas that might take practice or that might have helped with a recent situation (in conjunction with the ideas above).

Opinion Continuum

An opinion continuum (used in Chapters 3 and 9) is very easy to set up, and can be used in every subject or in advisory groups. The format gives students a chance to take a stand, literally, and see that opinions among their peers vary, which is often both comforting and celebrates autonomy. All you need are a few statements (connected to a lesson or theme) and a space that works for standing along a continuum.

You can use one long wall of a classroom, cafeteria, gym, or hallway, or space for a curving continuum so people can see each other. Identify the ends of the continuum verbally or with signs, such as

- a scale of 1 to 10

- "strongly disagree" through "strongly agree"

- "really dangerous" through "totally safe"

- "nothing like me" through "completely like me"

Explain that you've got a few statements, and that you'll read them one at a time. You'll give students a few seconds to consider their opinion on the topic before they move to the part of the continuum representing their opinion. Tell the students they'll talk about the different views. Then you'll read another statement; everyone will have a chance to think, move, and talk, as you read successive statements.

1. Read the first statement. Give think time.

2. Have everyone move to the spot of the continuum representing their view.

3. After they have found their spot, briefly interview a few of them: "Marcus, you're in the 'strongly disagree' area. What ideas got you to that spot?" "Sara, you're near 'strongly agree.' What makes you feel so strongly?" "Lila, you're more in the middle. What led you to be in the middle?"

   Tell students they can shift up or down the continuum as they listen to their peers, if they find their opinion changing as they listen. By recognizing students who stand in clusters, and students who stand in a spot on their own, and by asking them to talk briefly about themselves, you are underscoring that having ideas and beliefs is worthwhile, wherever you stand.

4. Continue with the next statement, giving think time, moving, and talking.

Here are a few examples of opinion continuum options from a number of subject areas. Each statement would be one of several on a theme: "The United States should not have dropped an atomic weapon on Japan." "Defense is harder work than offense in basketball." "Reading the novel was not as interesting as watching the movie." "Working quickly in math is more important than thinking slowly."

Variation

- Rather than asking individual students to speak, once they've chosen where to stand, have them chat with others who are near them. Then ask one person to explain her own and others' reasons for choosing that area. Ask students at other spots as well.

Pair-Shares and Turn-and-Talks

Pair-shares and **turn-and-talks** (used in many chapters) are ways to set up partner conversation pairs. In either format, be clear about the task or question. Pair-shares can be with anyone in the group, for which you might have a tool to determine pairs (deck of cards, colored index cards or craft sticks in a basket). Pair-shares are useful to get people moving and talking with someone they didn't sit next to. Turn-and-talk formats are very efficient, since the conversation partner is the immediate neighbor. Turn-and-talk formats can be a recurring structure, for example, after every two major concepts are presented, use the turn-and-talk with a focus question to come up with examples, connections, or insights.

To support the higher-order thinking that the teenage brain is developing, provide listening directions as much as speaking prompts.

- What did your partner say that confirmed what you already believed?

- What did your partner say that sparked your thinking? In what ways?

- Compare and contrast what your partner said with what you said.

- Create a synthesis of your two statements.

Quotes Café

Quotes café (used in Chapters 7, 8, and 13) is an interactive way to have students reading several quotes or short texts, in rounds with a different partner each round.

1. Have each student read a quote or short text, and then chat with a student who has the same quote or text. Their goal is to identifying key information they want to share about their text. Students will keep the same text throughout all rounds. When the pairs have had enough time to identify their key points, ring a bell or flick the lights to denote a shift to the next step.

2. Ask students to find a partner who read a different passage. The students in these new pairings share with each other what they thought was important or interesting from their own readings.

3. Ask students to find a third partner, and again they share their key points from their readings.

4. Continue with the same process until everyone has had a chance to hear about each quote or text. If there are many quotes or texts, you may choose to stop the process after each student has spoken with a few partners.

5. Debrief by asking, "What information or insights were new? Interesting? Important?"

By numbering each quote or text, or using different colored paper for each quote or text, students will be able to quickly find a partner who has information they have not yet heard.

Determine the amount of time per round based on the length of your quotes or texts, usually ranging from two to five minutes for each round.

Variations

- Exchange passages before switching partners.

- Split the passages to use on more than one day.

- As part of the debriefing, hand out a page with all the quotes so you can refer to them in the future.

- Follow the quotes café with a reflection as described below with you or a student choosing the quote.

Quotes Reflections

Quotes reflections (used in Chapters 7 and 8) allow the whole group to consider and discuss a quote or very short reading. Quotes about success, failure, perseverance, or teamwork can prompt meaningful reflections and discussions, as can the brain research paragraphs in Chapters 7 and 8.

The process is

1. Choose a quote or passage to project onto the board or hand out, possibly also reading it aloud.

2. Post one or more questions to consider and discuss: How does the quote connect to you? What does the quote say about ____? What surprised you? Interested you?

3. Discuss the quote or short reading in pairs and/or with the whole group.

Variations

- With an upcoming topic, ask students or advisees to find quotes to share.
- Ask readers to identify the one word, or one phrase, that they think represents the most important idea in the quote and explain their choice.

Role-Plays

Role-plays (used in Chapters 6 and 7) offer practice with conversations and situations so that students have tools ready when similar interactions take place. They are especially useful for when thinking on the spot might be challenging, such as making requests of teachers, asserting a need with friends, or responding well in an interview. Role-plays also help students to stretch perspectives when they play a role that's unfamiliar or one they would normally oppose.

1. Explain the situation and the role. Give think time to prepare: What is their goal? What could their opening line be? What tone should they take?

2. Students act the scene.

3. Reflect and debrief—with comments from the participants as well as observers.

   - ❓ How do you feel about your interaction—were you acting the way you'd wanted to?
   - ❓ What phrases or actions seemed to help?
   - ❓ What do you wish you had said or done differently?
   - ❓ What was surprising or uncomfortable about being in the role?
   - ❓ What additional observations or suggestions do the observers have?

4. Conduct another round of role-plays to immediately apply the new ideas.

5. If the role-play involved an emotionally charged situation, help students release it. Encourage them to take a few noisy deep breaths, shake their head and arms, or use a self-talk sentence, such as, "That was a role, not me. What I believe is . . . ."

Variations

- Call "freeze" midway for suggestions, then resume.
- Trade roles to stretch perspectives.

Talking Lists

Talking lists (used in Chapters 4, 6, and 13) are very helpful when several people want to contribute to a discussion. Typically, when lots of people are trying to participate in a discussion, instead of focusing on the current speaker's ideas, they listen to the speaker's breathing pattern, waiting for a chance to jump in. When a group uses a talking list, everyone knows when their turn is coming; they can relax and really listen.

People who want to talk need to raise a hand. You (or a student) write their names on the board, or chart paper, that everyone can see. When people raise their hand to speak, put their names at the bottom of the list. Once a name is on the list, that person no longer needs to keep up her hand. People speak in order of the names on the list. Each time someone speaks, cross out that person's name.

When the talking list is visible, you will notice patterns of participation—those who speak frequently and those who speak rarely. Participants often notice their own patterns and adjust their participation. You can also speak to them to encourage participation or restraint.

References

Ackerman, M. A. (2004). *Conversations on the go*. Minneapolis MN: Search Institute Press.

All Tech Considered. (2016, January 25). *Get a grip on your information overload with 'Infomagical'.* Retrieved from http://www.npr.org/sections/alltechconsidered/2016/01/25/463232382/get-a-grip-on-your-information-overload-with-infomagical

Ashley, J., & Burke, K. (2009, October). *Implementing restorative justice: A guide for schools.* Retrieved from http://www.icjia.state.il.us/assets/pdf/BARJ/SCHOOL%20BARJ%20GUIDEBOOOK.pdf

Barnwell, P. (2014, April 22). My students don't know how to have a conversation. *The Atlantic*. Retrieved from http://www.theatlantic.com/education/archive/2014/04/my-students-dont-know-how-to-have-a-conversation/360993/

Barth, R. (1990). *Improving schools from within: Teachers, parents and principals can make the difference.* San Francisco, CA: Jossey-Bass.

Barth, R. (2006, March). Improving relationships within the schoolhouse. *Educational Leadership, 63*(6), 8–13.

Bedsworth, W., Colby, S., & Doctor, J. (2006). *Reclaiming the American dream.* Retrieved from http://www.bridgespan.org/Publications-and-Tools/Education/Section1/Reclaiming-the-American-Dream.aspx#.V2hfaPkrJQI

Benard, B. (2004). *Resiliency: What we have learned.* San Francisco, CA: WestEd.

Benard, B., & Marshall, K. (2001). *Protective factors in individuals, families, and schools: National longitudinal study on adolescent health findings.* Minneapolis: National Resilience Resource Center, University of Minnesota/Minneapolis and the Center for the Application of Prevention Technologies.

Benson, J. (2014). *Hanging in.* Alexandria VA: ASCD.

Benson, J. (2015). *Ten steps to managing change in schools.* Alexandria, VA: ASCD.

Benson, J., & Poliner, R. (2012). *Dialogue: Skills for classroom and community.* Retrieved from http://192.185.167.72/~leaders/leadersandlearners.org/Home_files/Dialogue-Skills%20for%20Classrooms%26Community.pdf

Boston Public Radio. (2015, November 30). Interview of Michael Norton by Jim Braude and Margery Eagan.

Brooks, R., & Goldstein, S. (2001). *Raising resilient children.* Chicago, IL: Contemporary Books.

Brown, P. L. (2013, April 3). Opening up, students transform a vicious circle. *The New York Times*. Retrieved from http://www.nytimes.com/2013/04/04/education/restorative-justice-programs-take-root-in-schools.html?_r=0

Brown, V., & Olson, K. (2015). *The mindful school leader: Practices to transform your leadership and school.* Thousand Oaks, CA: Corwin.

Canfield, J., Hansen, M., & Kirberger, K. (1997). *Chicken soup for the teenage soul: 101 stories of life, love, and learning.* Deerfield Beach, FL: Health Communications.

CASAColumbia. (2012, September). *The importance of family dinners VIII.* Retrieved from http://www.centeronaddiction.org/addiction-research/reports/importance-of-family-dinners-2012

Centers for Disease Control and Prevention. (2014). Lesbian, gay, bisexual, and transgender health. Retrieved from http://www.cdc.gov/lgbthealth/youth.htm

Cervone, B., & Cushman, K. (2015). *Belonging and becoming: The power of social and emotional learning in high schools.* Cambridge, MA: Harvard Education Press.

Coates, T.-N. (2015). *Between the world and me.* New York, NY: Spiegel & Grau.

Cole, S., Greenwald O'Brien, J., Gadd, G., Ristuccia, J., Wallace, L., & Gregory, M. (2005). *Helping traumatized children learn: Supportive school environments for children traumatized by family violence.* Boston: Massachusetts Advocates for Children.

Cooperider, D., & Witney, D. (2005). *Appreciative inquiry: A positive revolution in change.* San Francisco, CA: Berrett-Koehler.

Cozolino, L. (2013, March 19). *Nine things educators need to know about the brain.* Retrieved from http://greatergood.berkeley.edu/article/item/nine_things_educators_need_to_know_about_the_brain

Cozolino, L. (2014). *Attachment-based teaching: Creating a tribal classroom.* New York, NY: W. W. Norton.

Cushman, K. (2005). *First in the family: Your college years: Advice about college from first generation students.* Providence, RI: Next Generation Press.

Cushman, K. (2007, April). Facing the culture shock of college. *Educational Leadership, 64*(7), 44–47.

Daniels, H., Bizar, M., & Zemelman, S. (2001). *Rethinking high school: Best practice in teaching, learning, and leadership.* Portsmouth, NH: Heinemann.

D'Auria, J. (2010). *Ten lessons in leadership and learning: An educator's journey.* Newton, MA: Teachers 21.

Delpit, L. D. (1998, August). The silenced dialogue: Power and pedagogy in educating other people's children. *Harvard Educational Review, 58*(3), 280.

Duckworth, A. L. (2016). *Grit: The power of passion and perseverance.* New York, NY: Simon & Schuster.

Dweck, C. (2007, October). The perils and promises of praise. *Educational Leadership, 65*(2), 34–39.

Espeland, P. (2003). *Life lists for teens.* Minneapolis, MN: Free Spirit.

Eredics, N. (2015). *Building inclusive schools for children of all abilities.* Retrieved from https://www.noodle.com/articles/building-inclusive-schools-for-children-of-all-abilities

Fergus, E., Noguera, P., & Martin, M. (2015). *Schooling for resilience: Improving the life trajectory of Black and Latino boys.* Cambridge, MA: Harvard University Press.

Fisher, R., Ury, W., & Patton, B. (1991). *Getting to yes: Negotiating agreement without giving in.* New York, NY: Penguin.

Frankl, V. (1984). *Man's search for meaning.* New York, NY: Simon & Schuster. (Original work published 1946)

Fullan, M. (2001). *Leading in a culture of change.* San Francisco, CA: Jossey-Bass.

Fuller, E. (2012). *Examining principal turnover.* National Education Policy Center. Retrieved from http://nepc.colorado.edu/blog/examining-principal-turnover

Going big. (2008). *This American Life.* Retrieved from http://www.thisamericanlife.org/radio-archives/episode/364/transcript

Groopman, J. E. (2007). *How doctors think.* Boston, MA: Houghton Mifflin.

Guwande, A. (2011, October 3). Personal Best: Top athletes and singers have coaches. Should you? *The New Yorker.* Retrieved from http://www.newyorker.com/magazine/2011/10/03/personal-best

Haberman, M. (1991, December). The pedagogy of poverty versus good teaching. *Phi Delta Kappan, 73*(4), 290–294. Retrieved from http://orthohosmag-lausd-ca.schoolloop.com/file/1278179292392/3729077694349233798.pdf

Hamedani, M.-Y. G., Darling-Hammond, L. (2015). *Social emotional learning in high school: How three urban high schools engage, educate, and empower youth.* Stanford, CA: Stanford Center for Opportunity Policy in Education.

Hammond, Z. (2014). *Culturally responsive teaching and the brain: Promoting authentic engagement and rigor among culturally and linguistically diverse students.* Thousand Oaks, CA: Corwin.

Hardiman, M. (2012). *The brain-targeted teaching model for 21st-century schools.* Thousand Oaks, CA: Corwin.

Hattie, J. (2009). *Visible learning: A synthesis of over 800 meta-analyses relating to achievement.* Thousand Oaks, CA: Corwin.

Hattie, J. (2012). *Visible learning for teachers: Maximizing impact on learning.* New York, NY: Routledge.

Heath, C., & Heath, D. (2010). *Switch: How to change things when change is hard.* New York, NY: Broadway Books/Random House.

Henderson, N. (2013, September). Havens of resilience. *Educational Leadership, 71*(1), 22–27.

Immordino-Yang, M. H. (2016). *Emotions, learning, and the brain: Exploring the educational implications of affective neuroscience.* New York NY: W. W. Norton.

Ingersoll, R. M. (2003). *Is there really a teacher shortage?* Seattle: University of Washington, Center for the Study of Teaching and Policy. Retrieved from http://depts.washington.edu/ctpmail/PDFs/Shortage-RI-09-2003.pdf

Ingersoll, R. M. (2012). *Beginning teacher induction: What the data tell us.* Retrieved from http://www.edweek.org/ew/articles/2012/05/16/kappan_ingersoll.h31.html

Jensen, E. (2005). *Teaching with the brain in mind* (Rev. 2nd ed.). Alexandria, VA: ASCD.

Jensen, E. (2009). *Teaching with poverty in mind: What being poor does to kids' brains and what schools can do about it.* Alexandria, VA: ASCD.

Jensen, E., & Snider, C. (2013). *Turnaround tools for the teenage brain: Helping underperforming students become lifelong learners.* San Francisco, CA: Jossey-Bass.

Johnson, G., & Bonaiuto, S. (2009). Accountability with roots. *Educational Leadership, 66*(4), 26–29.

Jones, S. M., Bouffard, S. M., & Weissbourd, R. (2013, May). Educators' social and emotional skills vital to learning. *Phi Delta Kappan, 94*(8), 62–65.

Kegan, R., & Laskow Lahey, L. (2001). *How the way we talk can change the way we work: Seven languages for transformation.* San Francisco, CA: Jossey-Bass.

King, L. (2016). Baby steps toward restorative justice. *Rethinking Schools, 24*(4). Retrieved from http://www.rethinkingschools.org/archive/29_04/29-4_king.shtml

Kirby, E., & McDonald, J. (2009). *Engage every student: Motivation tools for teachers and parents.* Minneapolis, MN: Search Institute Press.

Koplowski, C. (2008, April 5). *Why they leave.* Retrieved from http://www.nea.org/home/12630.htm

Krovetz, M. L. (2008). *Fostering resilience: Expecting all students to use their minds and hearts well.* Thousand Oaks CA: Corwin.

LeDoux, J. E. (1994). Emotion, memory and the brain. *Scientific American, 270*(6), 50–57.

Lenhart, A. (2012, March 19). *Teens, smartphones & texting.* Retrieved from http://www.pewinternet.org/2012/03/19/teens-smartphones-texting

Levine, M. (2006). *The price of privilege: How parental pressure and material advantage are creating a generation of disconnected and unhappy kids.* New York, NY: HarperCollins.

Lieberman, M. D., Eisenberger, N. I., Crockett, M. J., Tom, S. M., Pfeifer, J. H., & Way, B. M. (2006). Putting feelings into words: Affect labeling disrupts amygdala activity in response to affective stimuli. *Psychological Science, 18*(5), 421–428.

Lofthouse, G. (2015, December 17). *How language influences emotion* [Interview with Tiffany Watt Smith]. Retrieved from http://www.theatlantic.com/health/archive/2015/12/the-book-of-human-emotions-language-feelings/420978/

MacGregor, M. G. (2006). *Everyday leadership: Attitudes and actions for respect and success, a guidebook for teens.* Minneapolis, MN: Free Spirit.

Medina, J. J. (2014). *Brain rules: 12 principles for surviving and thriving at work, home, and school* (2nd ed.). Seattle, WA: Pear Press.

Mehta, J. (2015). *The allure of order: High hopes, dashed expectations, and the troubled quest to remake American schooling.* Oxford, England: Oxford University Press.

Miller Lieber, C. (2009). *Increasing college access.* Cambridge, MA: Engaging Schools.

Murnane, R., & Phillips, B. R. (1981). What do effective teachers of inner-city children have in common? *Social Science Research, 10*(1), 83–100.

Nakkula, M. (2008). Identity and possibility: Adolescent development and the potential of schools. In M. Sadowski (Ed.), *Adolescents at school: Perspectives on youth, identity, and education* (2nd ed., Chap. 1). Cambridge MA: Harvard Education Press.

Nakkula, M., & Toshalis, E. (2008) *Understanding youth.* Cambridge, MA: Harvard University Press.

National Center for Education Statistics. (2015). *Fast facts: Dropout rates.* Retrieved from https://nces.ed.gov/fastfacts/display.asp?id=16

Perkins-Gough, D. (2015, October). *Secrets of the teenage brain: A conversation with Frances E. Jensen. Educational Leadership, 73*(2), 16–20.

Perry, T., Steele, C., & Hilliard, A., III. (2003) *Young, gifted, and Black: Promoting high achievement among African-American students.* Boston MA: Beacon Press.

Phelan, P., Davidson, A. L., & Yu, H. C. (1996) *Adolescents' worlds: Negotiating family, peers and school.* New York NY: Teachers College Press.

Poliner, R. A., & Benson, J. (1997). *Dialogue: Turning controversy into community: A curriculum for secondary schools.* Cambridge, MA: Engaging Schools.

Poliner, R. A., & Miller Lieber, C. (2004). *The advisory guide: Designing and implementing effective advisory programs in secondary schools.* Cambridge, MA: Engaging Schools.

Pope, D. C. (2001). "Doing school": How we are creating a generation of stressed out, materialistic, and miseducated students. New Haven CT: Yale University Press.

Putnam, R. D. (2015). *Our kids: The American dream in crisis.* New York, NY: Simon & Schuster.

Quaglia, R. J., & Corso, M. J. (2014). *Student voice.* Thousand Oaks, CA: Corwin.

Ragsdale, S., & Saylor, A. (2007). *Great group games: 175 boredom-busting, zero-prep team builders for all ages.* Minneapolis, MN: Search Institute Press.

Rechtschaffen, D. (2014). *The way of mindful education: Cultivating well-being in teachers and students.* New York, NY: W. W. Norton.

Redding, S., & Walberg, H. (2012). *Promoting learning in rural schools.* Retrieved from http://www.adi.org/about/downloads/Promoting_Learning_in_Rural_Schools.pdf

Rees, N. (2014, February 10). 3 Things That Should Be Done to Help Rural Schools. *U.S. News and World Report.* Retrieved from http://www.usnews.com/opinion/blogs/nina-rees/2014/02/10/3-ways-to-help-rural-schools

Reeves, D. (2008). The learning leader/Leadership for student empowerment. *Educational Leadership, 66*(3), 84–85.

Richmond, E. (2015, December 29). When restorative justice in schools works. *The Atlantic.* Retrieved from http://www.theatlantic.com/education/archive/2015/12/when-restorative-justice-works/422088/

Rockoff, J. E. (2004). The impact of individual teachers on student achievement: Evidence from panel data. *American Economic Review, 94*(2), 247–252.

Rossen, E., & Hull, R. (2013). *Supporting and educating traumatized youth.* New York, NY: Oxford University Press.

Rothstein-Fisch, C., & Trumbull, E. (2008). *Managing diverse classrooms: How to build on students' cultural strengths.* Alexandria, VA: ASCD.

Sadowski, M. (Ed.). (2008). *Adolescents at school: Perspectives on youth, identity, and education.* Cambridge MA: Harvard Education Press.

Schenck, J. (2011). *Teaching and the Adolescent Brain: An Educator's Guide.* New York, NY: W. W. Norton.

School Leaders Network. (2014). *Churn: The high cost of principal turnover.* Retrieved from http://connectleadsucceed.org/sites/default/files/principal_turnover_cost.pdf

Senge, P. M. (1994). *The fifth discipline fieldbook: Strategies and tools for building a learning organization.* New York, NY: Currency, Doubleday.

Sheffer, S. (2014, February 18). Do ACT and SAT scores really matter? New study says they shouldn't. *PBS NewsHour.* Retrieved from http://www.pbs.org/newshour/rundown/nail-biting-standardized-testing-may-miss-mark-college-students/

Silverstein, O., & Rashbaum, B. (1994). *The courage to raise good men.* New York, NY: Viking Press.

Sizer, N. F. (2002). *Crossing the stage: Redesigning senior year.* Portsmouth, NH: Heinemann.

Sizer, T. R. (1997). *Horace's school: Redesigning the American high school.* New York, NY: Houghton Mifflin Harcourt.

Sizer, T. R., & Sizer, N. F. (1999). *The students are watching: Schools and the moral contract.* Boston MA: Beacon Press.

Sladkey, D. (2013). *Energizing brain breaks.* Thousand Oaks, CA: Corwin.

Smink, J., & Reimer, M. (2015). *Rural school dropout issues: Implications for dropout prevention strategies and programs.* Retrieved from http://dropoutprevention.org/wp-content/uploads/2015/05/13_Rural_School_Dropout_Issues_Report.pdf

Smith, J. (2003). *Education and public health*, Alexandria, VA: ASCD.

Stansbury, K., & Zimmerman, J. (2000). *Designing support for beginning teachers.* Retrieved from https://www.wested.org/online_pubs/tchrbrief.pdf

State high school graduation rates by race, ethnicity. (n.d.). Retrieved from http://www.governing.com/gov-data/education-data/state-high-school-graduation-rates-by-race-ethnicity.html

Steele, C. M. (2010). *Whistling Vivaldi: How stereotypes affect us and what we can do.* New York, NY: W. W. Norton.

Stone, D., Patton, B., & Heen, S. (1999). *Difficult conversations: How to discuss what matters most.* New York, NY: Viking Press.

Tatum, A. W. (2005) *Teaching reading to Black adolescent males: Closing the achievement gap.* Portland, ME: Stenhouse.

Tokuhama-Espinosa, T. (2014). *Making classrooms better: 50 practical applications of mind, brain, and education science.* New York, NY: Norton.

Turkle, S. (2012a, April 22). The flight from conversation. *The New York Times.* Retrieved from http://www.nytimes.com/2012/04/22/opinion/sunday/the-flight-from-conversation.html

Turkle, S. (2012b, October 17). In constant digital contact, we feel 'alone together' [Interview with Terry Gross]. *Fresh Air.* Retrieved from http://www.npr.org/2012/10/18/163098594/in-constant-digital-contact-we-feel-alone-together

Turkle, S. (2015). *Reclaiming conversation: The power of talk in a digital age.* London, England: Penguin.

U.S. Department of Education. (2014). *United States student-to-counselor ratios for elementary and secondary schools—2011–2012 data year.* Retrieved from https://www.counseling.org/docs/default-source/public-policy-faqs-and-documents/2013-counselor-to-student-ratio-chart.pdf?sfvrsn=2

Valenzuela, A. (1999). *Subtractive schooling: U.S.-Mexican youth and the politics of caring.* Albany: State University of New York Press.

van der Kolk, B. (2014). *The body keeps the score: Brain, mind, and body in the healing of trauma.* New York, NY: Viking Press.

Vargas, J. (2015). *Why 12th grade must be redesigned now—And how.* Retrieved http://www.jff.org/publications/why-12th-grade-must-be-redesigned-now—and-how

Vygotsky, L. S. (1978). *Mind in society.* Cambridge, MA: Harvard University Press.

Wang, A., & Linden, E. (1986). *Lessons: An autobiography.* Reading, MA: Addison-Wesley.

Watt Smith, T. (2015a). *The book of human emotions: An encyclopaedia of feeling from anger to wanderlust.* London, England: Profile Books.

Watt Smith, T. (2015b, September 11). *From Schadenfreude to ringxiety: An encyclopedia of emotions.* Retrieved from http://www.theguardian.com/books/2015/sep/11/schadenfreude-ringxiety-encyclopedia-of-emotions

Weir, B., & Marx, T. (2009). *Harlem agency hopes to end poverty cycle.* Retrieved from http://abcnews.go.com/GMA/Weekend/story?id=7134484&page=1

Wheatley, M. J. (1992). *Leadership and the new science: Learning about organization from an orderly universe.* San Francisco, CA: Berrett-Koehler.

Wheatley, M. J., & Kellner-Rogers, M. (1996). *A simpler way.* San Francisco, CA: Berrett-Koehler.

Wood, C. (2007). *Yardsticks.* Turner Falls, MA: Northeast Foundation for Children.

Woolley, A., Malone, T. W., & Chabris, C. F. (2015, January 18). Why some teams are smarter than others. *The New York Times.* Retrieved from http://www.nytimes.com/2015/01/18/opinion/sunday/why-some-teams-are-smarter-than-others.html

Wormeli, R. (2015, October). The seven habits of highly affective teachers. *Educational Leadership, 73*(2), 10–15.

Index

CORWIN

A SAGE Publishing Company

Helping educators make the greatest impact

CORWIN HAS ONE MISSION: to enhance education through intentional professional learning.

We build long-term relationships with our authors, educators, clients, and associations who partner with us to develop and continuously improve the best evidence-based practices that establish and support lifelong learning.

Solutions you want. Experts you trust. Results you need.